HISTORY OF
BANKING IN SCOTLAND

AGENTS

AMERICA . THE MACMILLAN COMPANY
64 & 66 FIFTH AVENUE, NEW YORK

AUSTRALASIA THE OXFORD UNIVERSITY PRESS
205 FLINDERS LANE, MELBOURNE

CANADA . . THE MACMILLAN COMPANY OF CANADA, LTD.
ST. MARTIN'S HOUSE, 70 BOND STREET, TORONTO

INDIA . . MACMILLAN & COMPANY, LTD.
MACMILLAN BUILDING, BOMBAY
309 BOW BAZAAR STREET, CALCUTTA

HISTORY OF
BANKING IN SCOTLAND

BY

ANDREW WILLIAM KERR
F.R.S. (Edin.)

THIRD EDITION

A. & C. BLACK, LTD.
4, 5 & 6 SOHO SQUARE, LONDON, W.1
1918

First Edition published 1884
Second Edition published 1902
Reprinted with slight corrections 1908
Third Edition, revised and entirely reset, published 1918

PREFACE TO THIRD EDITION

A NEW edition having been called for, the opportunity has been availed of to insert a considerable amount of new matter; and two chapters, Nos. XXIX. and XXX., bringing down the narrative to the present time, have been added. These embody a special study of the period by Mr. Frank H. Allan of the Bank of Scotland, the able editor of the *Scottish Bankers' Magazine*, to whom I tender my hearty thanks for his careful and felicitous treatment of the subject. I am also indebted to Mr. J. S. Cockburn, General Manager of the National Bank of Scotland, Limited, for bringing to my notice several contemporary publications regarding the Darien Company and economic conditions of the period. An expression of thanks is also due to several gentlemen for courteous and helpful response to inquiries.

A. W. K.

4th July 1917.

PREFACE TO FIRST EDITION

THE substance of the following pages appeared as a series of articles in a financial magazine during the years 1880–83. These articles are now presented in a collected form, after revision and extension, in the hope that they may be of service to those who are interested in the progress of Scottish banking. The author cannot hope that he has escaped making errors, but he has taken all possible care, by collation of authorities and otherwise, to ascertain the correctness of his statements of facts. As to the opinions expressed from time to time, he is, of course, solely responsible.

No similar work having, so far as the writer is aware, been ever before published, allowance will, perhaps, be made for incompleteness and other faults arising from the difficulty of obtaining information. Scottish bankers, and financiers generally, have, with few exceptions, been slow to record their experiences and opinions. Consequently the data from which such a work as the present must be constructed exist only in a meagre and scattered form. A general idea of the sources of information will be obtained from the footnotes throughout the volume.

CONTENTS

CHAPTER I

CONTENTS

CHAPTER XVI

CHAPTER XVII

CHAPTER XVIII

CHAPTER XIX

CHAPTER XX

CHAPTER XXI

CHAPTER XXII

CHAPTER XXIII

CHAPTER XXIV

HISTORY OF BANKING
IN SCOTLAND

CHAPTER I

ORIGIN AND DEVELOPMENT OF SCOTTISH BANKING

THE state of Scotland at the close of the seventeenth
century—the period at which Scottish banking commenced—was not favourable to commercial enterprise.
Foreign and domestic wars and tumults had, from time
immemorial, drained the country of its hardiest man-
hood and of its scanty treasure. Commerce, except
in that minimum proportion which is indispensable to
the distribution of the necessaries of life, had never had
opportunity to establish itself. The nation was sunk
in poverty. Even the few large landowners could only
be called wealthy in comparison with the plain living
commonalty, who could with difficulty supply their
wants. Even the officers of the Crown were in the enjoyment of but petty incomes, which the evil fortunes
of the nation frequently interrupted the payment of.
The currency was debased in quality and scarce in
quantity. It would appear that payment in kind was
usual in the settlement of rents, and it is probable that
barter in some forms was not uncommon in the more
remote country districts.

The history of Scotland as an independent country
is one of almost constant misfortune; for even the
brilliant victories gained by the Scots over their great

enemies, the English, were but the barriers which averted
ruin. They did not, like the triumphs of the French or
of the Spaniards, add new territory to the State, or increase the wealth of the kingdom. They merely enabled
the unconsolidated community to continue its rude
existence in independence at the cost of chronic penury,
intensified by internecine feuds and periodic *coups d'État*.
Eventually the nation reaped a rich reward for the sufferings it had endured in the struggle to preserve its freedom,
for it gained access to boundless fields for the exercise of
its restless energy, achieved large profits for its untiring
activity, and became united into one of the most law-
abiding and industrious countries in the world. At the
time when our history begins, however, the clouds of
night were still overshadowing the country ; and the sun
of prosperity, destined to shine with undimmed splendour,
had not yet risen on the national horizon.

The Union of the Crowns of England and Scotland in
the year 1603, by the accession of James VI. of Scotland
to the throne of England, put an end to the hereditary
warfare waged for centuries between the kingdoms ; but
though the wounds were bound up they were not healed,
and international jealousy and dislike still prevented the
full advantage of community of interests. As being
the weaker power, Scotland suffered most in this new
phase of its struggle with its domineering associate, who
ever and anon checked its enterprise whenever it seemed
to trench on English prerogatives. It did, however,
snatch an uneasy rest during the forty years which
elapsed before the great civil war between the Commons
and the Crown broke out in 1642. In that six years'
struggle, as in all the succeeding troubles, the efforts of
Scotland were generally spent on the losing side. The
Scots, indeed, escaped the brunt of the conflict, but they
suffered terribly in the end by the iron hand of Cromwell,
whose power they had well-nigh crushed at Dunbar,
but for the infatuation of their clerical dictators prevailing

over the military skill of their sagacious general, Leslie. Through the Commonwealth and the restored Monarchy, the country's grievances continued ; and it was not until the peaceful revolution of 1688 placed the constitution on a firm basis, that there was even the possibility of prosperity for Scotland ; and not until the effects of the legislative union of the countries in 1707 had had time to develop themselves, that the nation's spirit was at rest.

With the revolution settlement of domestic affairs began a new and brighter era in the commercial and financial history of Britain, which the warlike foreign policy of successive administrations was not potent enough to neutralise. England drifted from one quarrel into another, and accumulated a national debt which at last reached an amount unequalled in the world's experience, until, in our days, German ambition sought to crush French aggression under the weight of financial difficulties, and later has striven to secure, by skilfully organised iniquity, the hegemony of the world. While the national exchequer was empty, and irregular methods were adopted to replenish it,—nay, even as the immediate consequence of a system of State lotteries and forced loans,—the foundation of the great fabric of British finance was laid. That it was laid in such unfavourable circumstances, established on the erroneous principle of monopoly, and fostered by exclusive privileges, granted as the price of pecuniary aid to the Crown, has been the source of woes unnumbered to the banking system of England. But, as far as Scotland was affected by it, the influence of the change of dynasty was only good. The Highland interest being strongly enlisted in favour of the Stuarts, did, it is true, assert itself by force of arms ; but this was no new experience, and it was soon overcome. The nation, as represented by the more consolidated portion of the community, was enabled to follow the lead in the organisation of a financial system, and, by reason of its independent constitution, to found it in a free and untrammelled condition.

It has been a fortunate circumstance for Scotland that, in borrowing the idea of establishing joint-stock companies for the advancement of industrial enterprise, the Parliament of Scotland avoided the temptations yielded to by the Parliament of England, and did not seek to fill the national coffers at the expense of the future interests of the nation. Banking in England has been crippled and enfeebled by the pernicious monopolies granted to, and the onerous responsibilities imposed upon, its first joint-stock bank ; while in Scotland the banking system has been developed and matured under natural and unfettered conditions. Thus, south of the Tweed, banking legislation, in a series of makeshift patches, has produced a multiplicity of conflicting interests which have to be subjected periodically to readjustment, in order to preserve even partial satisfaction among the unequally weighted competitors. In the history of banking in Scotland, on the other hand, there is comparatively little trace of unequal legislative treatment—all the banks competing in most essential points under similar conditions. What unfairness actually exists is due entirely to the introduction of English ideas, and is limited, for the most part, to the department of note-issuing, as regulated by the Act of 1845.

We are not at present discussing the merits of Sir Robert Peel's measures, but we desire to point out that they introduced, for the first time, the principles of restriction and exclusion in Scottish banking legislation. The Scots Parliament of 1695 did, indeed, recognise the principle of monopoly, when establishing the Bank of Scotland ; but it was understood (and the result justified the supposition) that the exclusive privileges granted to that corporation were designed merely to give it a fair chance as an entirely new experiment, and were not to be renewed at the end of the term of twenty-one years for which they were granted. That this special encouragement should have been granted was unquestionably wise. It would have been unfortunate, if, at that early stage, the development of banking had been checked, through competition in a field where the probability of success, on the part of even one establishment, was absolutely uncertain. Had a similar course been pursued in England—had the exclusive privileges of the Bank of England been withdrawn as soon as its probation was over, the roll of English bankers would have been a much less melancholy catalogue than it has proved to be, and the currency question need never have occasioned the trouble and vexation which have characterised it up to the present time.

But, unfortunately, the poverty and ambition of successive Governments made them the creatures of their powerful creditors, and tempted them into erroneous principles of legislation, which have produced the most artificial financial system existing in the world. Through struggles and crises, amendments have been made which enable the units of the system to hang together—the inevitable jarring which occurs every few years being temporarily overcome by some special arrangement, generally involving the creation of one or more new species of banks. Thus it happens that, at the present time, there are several distinct classes of banks in England, each subjected to peculiar legislative provisions. At the same time, owing to the operation of the enactments limiting the number of partners in private banks, and discouraging amalgamations, there has always been an unfortunately large number of small establishments whose fortunes depend on the prosperity of particular localities, and the resources of small coteries, instead of having the broader basis of the general experience of the nation, and the wealth of large proprietaries. This condition has, however, been greatly modified during recent years by the numerous amalgamations which now constitute such great corporations as Lloyds Bank, Barclay's Bank, Parr's Bank, and the London City and Midland Bank.

The Scottish banks, too, show some diversities in the legislative conditions under which they exist, for which they are indebted to English statesmanship. But the national spirit of Scotland has to a large extent prevailed over attempts to reduce the uniform and matured system, evolved by wholesome experience, unfettered by Governmental interference, to the hampered condition of the English banking system.   The inequalities existing—viz. the privilege of undesignated limitation of liability of stockholders in some of the banks, and the disproportion in the amounts of authorised issues of notes among the several establishments—are not such as to interfere with free competition between the members of Sir Robert Peel's charmed circle.   They are, indeed, recognised as grievances, but the banks are content to let them lie over.   To contrast with the multiplicity of classes of banks in England, there are three in Scotland —namely, chartered banks, presumed to be limited in virtue of the character of their incorporation ; chartered banks, formerly unlimited, now limited by registration under the Companies Act 1879 ; and banking companies incorporated and limited under the Companies Acts 1862–80.   As the two latter classes are practically the same, there are really only two classes of banks in Scotland. Under the provisions of the Companies Acts 1862 to 1879, all essential constitutional distinctions disappear as far as the Legislature is concerned, and there remains only the partly sentimental injustice of enforcing on all but the three oldest banks the addition of the invidious and inelegant word " limited " where, in point of fact, the distinction is altogether inappropriate.

The first-mentioned class of banks embraces the Bank of Scotland, the Royal Bank of Scotland, and the British Linen Company (now the British Linen Bank).

The second class includes the Commercial Bank of Scotland (Limited) and the National Bank of Scotland (Limited). The third class consists of the Union Bank of Scotland (Limited), the North of Scotland and Town and County Bank (Limited), and the Clydesdale Bank (Limited). Together these form the roll of the Scottish banks in the order of their formation. The Bank of Scotland is established under special Acts of Parliament ; the other two old chartered banks, and the two senior " limited " banks, are incorporated by Royal Charter ; and the three youngest banks are enrolled under the Companies Acts of 1862–80 and amending Acts. All of them exercise the power of issuing notes, and carry on business in all the departments usually included by British economists under the term banking.

These operations may be classified broadly into borrowing, lending, and investment. The companies obtain money from their own members to form the capital and other private funds of the corporation, and from the public under notes payable to bearer on demand, deposit receipts, current accounts, letters of credit (now generally called drafts), for the remittance of money between various localities in the United Kingdom and abroad, and circular notes for the use of travellers abroad. The money thus obtained is lent on the security of bills at a currency (usually three to six months after date), cash accounts, over-drafts, heritable and personal bonds and other securities, to mercantile firms and other customers. It is understood that advances by bankers should be on tangible and readily convertible security. In this connection it should, perhaps, be noted that advances are now largely made on what are termed fixed loans—that is loans, usually of round sums and for fixed periods, such as the bi-monthly stock exchange accounts, or one, two, or three months—on the assignation of approved marketable securities, with a margin of 20 or 30 per cent to be maintained between the amount of the loan and the value of the securities at the current market quotations. In all cases the banks retain, however, their right to call up advances when they consider it advisable to do so. The acceptance of bills on account of customers has become an important part of banking business. A large proportion of the funds is held in reserve as cash, investments in first-class Government and other stocks, short loans to financial houses, and bills of exchange of the most approved description.

To the efficient carrying on of their business, and establishing themselves on broad bases, the Scottish banks have spread their branches over Scotland so thoroughly that there is no district, with an appreciable nucleus of population, unprovided for. All the large banks have, moreover, opened offices in London, and the Clydesdale Bank has, in addition, a few branches in the north of England, while the British Linen Bank has also an office in Northumberland. Thus, although there are only eight distinct banking establishments having their headquarters in Scotland, there are 1255 bank offices. The amount of capital administered by the banks is more than £207,000,000, of which about £17,000,000 consist of the private funds of proprietors, £167,000,000 of deposits, and £15,000,000 of bank notes, the balance of £8,000,000 being represented by acceptances and drafts. There are 32,500 stock- and share-holders, and probably 550,000 depositors, of whom more than three-fourths appear to be deposit-receipt holders. While, as among themselves, the banks carry on a very active competition, their dealings with the public are regulated by tariffs drawn up in concert, and adjusted from time to time by mutual consent. Thus, as regards rates of interest, discount, and commission, there is practical uniformity throughout the country — the discretionary powers in these matters being of small extent. As far as terms are concerned, therefore, customers have no inducement to favour one establishment more than another. Of the eight existing banks, five have their head offices in Edinburgh, two in Glasgow, and one in Aberdeen. The Edinburgh banks were all established before any of the others, and transact about 69 per cent of the entire banking business in Scotland. The Glasgow banks conduct 24 per cent, and the one provincial bank conducts 7 per cent of the business.

This, then, is roughly the position of banking in Scotland at the present time. It is indeed a mighty edifice, built up (as the sequel will show) from a very small beginning by shrewdness, economy, and industry during the last two hundred and twenty-two years. The history of banking in Scotland is most intimately associated with the national progress from poverty to wealth ; and the characteristics of the system of banking which have been developed are in many points unique, and marked by the peculiar circumstances which have moulded the Scottish character. The result of the experiment so modestly attempted in 1695 has, despite many and grievous failures, and at least one deeper stain than the financial community of any other nation has cause to blush for, been a great success. In treating of English banking, if we have represented it historically in an inferior light, we do not mean to gloss over or extenuate the weaknesses displayed, especially during last century, by Scottish bankers, nor to deny the glory due to their southern brethren for the magnificent financial fabric they have reared under conditions which, if commercially superior, have been legislatively inferior. And in regard to scientific exposition and research, Scottish bankers cannot bear comparison with the financiers of England. English banking, following the commercial prosperity of the country, has become the most widely extended in its range, and the most voluminous in the amount of its transactions, of the banking systems of the world. But Scottish banking has this peculiar glory, that it has been in large measure the means of producing and securing the prosperity of the country, which has in turn expanded it to the proportions we have described.

In making such a comparison, it must, however, be borne in mind that the political and commercial positions of England and Scotland have always been widely different ; and that, of course, as a matter of cosmopolitan importance, the state of English banking is of much greater moment than that of Scottish banking. At the same time, the history and operations of the Scottish banks have not only great interest for the people of Scotland, but vitally affect the welfare of the empire and of the world. In the words of an able writer on Scottish banking : " The banking question, whether discussed in London or Paris, always reverts to the history of the Scotch banks as a fragment indispensable to the controversy." [1]   Their operations have been so admirably adapted to the requirements of the country, and have so effectively led its agriculture, manufactures, commerce, and every branch of industry to a high state of prosperity, without special devotion—as is usual in other countries—to particular departments of business, that they are universally looked to as efficient exponents of practical banking.

The existing banks are all public joint-stock corporations. For about seventy-five years there has been no private banking firm in Scotland, among the last being the famous house of Sir William Forbes, J. Hunter & Co., who amalgamated in 1838 with the Glasgow Union Bank, afterwards the Union Bank of Scotland, although their firm-name continued to be used for a few years in connection with the Edinburgh business of the bank. The less conspicuous house of Alexander Allan & Co. appeared in the Edinburgh directories as bankers for about twenty years later ; but it would seem that for some time previous they had practically ceased the active conduct of banking

[1] *The Scotch Banks and System of Issue*, Robert Somers, Edinburgh, 1873, p. 71.

business. With this exception, the last private banking firm extant in Scotland was Dunlop, Houston, Gemmell, & Co., who carried on business as the Greenock Banking Co. until 1843, when they amalgamated with the Western Bank of Scotland. Shortly before these events, a shock had been given to the system of private banking by the failure of several firms, and the withdrawal from business, on account of losses, of the important firm of Ramsays, Bonars, & Co.

Private banking has, however, been a very important element in the history of Scottish banking, at least one-half of the establishments formed in the country having been on that principle, while several others, although nominally joint-stock, may for most purposes be included in the category. Considerable, and in some cases large, fortunes were made by private bankers, but their ultimate success does not seem to have been great, as only about half-a-dozen reached the stage of amalgamation, the others being either sequestrated or wound up. In all, there appear to have been at least ninety-five distinct banking establishments formed in Scotland up to the year 1845. Since then no new bank has been formed.[1] Of that list, thirty-six failed and were wound up, ten passed out of existence from unexplained reasons—in all probability for the most part insolvency—six retired voluntarily, thirty-five amalgamated with other banks, and eight remain in business.[2]

It will thus be seen that the narration on which we are about to enter is by no means unchequered by sad vicissitudes. Indeed, the operations of the Scottish banks have been attended by a large amount of mis-

---

[1] The Scottish Banking Company (Limited) was formed at Dundee about thirty-five years ago, but as its affairs were not made public, it cannot with certainty be included among the banks in Scotland. It was wound up a few years later, after an inglorious career.

[2] The North British Bank, an exchange company, and not a bank was sometimes included in the published lists of the banks in Scotland. See *post*, Chap. XX.

management and recklessness, and have produced a full proportion of bankruptcies, entailing ruin on partners, and sometimes loss to creditors. It is but justice, however, to add, that the cases where creditors have suffered severely are comparatively few in number, and are confined entirely to the smaller class of offices. The total amount of the deficits is in but trifling ratio to the aggregate liabilities of the banks.

CHAPTER II

THE DARIEN COMPANY

It is a curious fact in the history of Scotland, that the first considerable effort at joint-stock enterprise made there was at once the most ambitious and the most unfortunate, was accompanied by the largest amount of patriotic enthusiasm, and was the most unsuited to the national circumstances, of any in which the nation has been engaged. The fortunes of the Company of Scotland Trading to Africa and the Indies were for long, and to some extent are yet, a sadly-remembered episode in the annals of the kingdom. But, grievous as was the blow inflicted on the nation by the ruin of their darling Darien scheme, and culpable as the English authorities, from their Sovereign downwards, were in their conduct towards the company, it may be doubted if the enterprise possessed in itself the elements necessary to success, and if the national enthusiasm did not get diverted into an entirely wrong channel. Now that the lapse of time permits an unbiassed judgment, it appears almost an absurdity that a nation who had never been able to secure the blessings of peace and prosperity within their own borders should, while so much remained to be done at home, have tried to imitate their wealthy neighbours in the creation of a colonial empire. The amount of capital sunk, and the number of human lives lost in that deplorable attempt might, if saved and utilised at home, have greatly antedated the advent of national prosperity.

In fairness, however, to our courageous ancestors, it must be admitted that the means of utilising the national energies were then in a very deficient state. The accessories necessary to the production of commodities on such a scale, and of such quality, as successfully to compete with foreign markets, were not possessed by the people ; the motive power of industry—capital— was not within their reach. What they could do with the limited powers at their command they did, toiling at their linen and other manufactures, protected by their Parliament's prohibitions against the use of the superior fabrics of foreign nations. But, from the time when they got the aid of a banking system and a sufficient currency, they made great strides, not without stumbles, it is true, yet more rapidly and more surely than any other nation before them.

When the Scottish leaders got personal experience of the power of English commerce, and of the influence of trading associations in promoting wealth, they were not slow to evince a desire to procure the same advantages for their native country. The troublous times appear, however, to have interfered with practical action ; and it was not until late in the seventeenth century that the Legislature began systematically to make special provision for the encouragement of trade. One of the most important of the measures passed was the Act, William and Mary, 1693, chapter 32, " for the encouraging of Foreign Trade," in which " our Sovereign Lord and Lady, the King and Queen's Majesties, Considering how much the Improvement of Trade concerns the Wealth and Welfare of the Kingdom, and that nothing hath been found more effectual for the improving and enlarging thereof than the Erecting and Encouraging of Companies, whereby the same may be carried on by Undertakings to the remotest Parts, which it is not possible for single Persons to undergo," proceeded to authorise the association of merchants and others for commercial enterprises in all parts of the world " where Trade is in Use to be followed," with promise of protection and encouragement.

It would not seem, however, that much practical result immediately followed this measure ; but it paved the way for two important Acts of the session 1695, incorporating the commonly-called Darien Company, and the Bank of Scotland. The former was the product of the fertile genius of William Paterson, whose character and abilities have been variously estimated. It is evident that he was a man of great energy and perseverance, and had powers of perception and organisation of a high order. Driven, at an early age, from his native Dumfriesshire by adverse circumstances, he passed into England and engaged in trade, apparently with much success. There he took an active and influential part in financial and commercial discussions, in which he shows that, although not entirely free from the erroneous views prevalent at that time on such subjects, he was very far in advance of his contemporaries. He projected the Bank of England, and succeeded, in spite of considerable opposition, in getting it established in 1694, and was one of its original directors. But, owing to disagreements with his colleagues, he did not retain his seat at the board many months, and he does not seem subsequently to have taken any part in the management of the bank.

After directing his energies to the establishment of an " Orphan Bank " and other schemes, Paterson conceived his great project of establishing a colony on the Isthmus of Darien for trading purposes. It was expected that this colony would become the *entrepôt* of the trade of Europe with Asia, as well as with the West Indies. In one of his letters to the Darien Company, Paterson says : " The time and expense of navigation to China, Japan, the spice islands, and the far greater parte of the East Indies, will be lessened more than half, and the consumption of European commodityes and manufactories will soon be more than doubled. . . . Thus the door of the ·

seas, and the key of the universe, with anything of a reasonable management, will enable its proprietors to give laws to both oceans, and to become arbitrators of the commercial world." [1]

At first Paterson endeavoured to launch his project in England ; but it was treated with indifference or disfavour by those he consulted. He then went to Holland, in the hope that Dutch and Hamburg merchants would favour the idea ; but no more success attended him there. Returning to England, it is said that Fletcher of Saltoun " persuaded him to trust the fate of his project to his own countrymen alone, and to let them have the sole benefit, glory, and danger of it." It would seem, however, that although the scheme was to be a Scotch one, English and Dutch support was still sought, and it was obtained when Scotch enthusiasm seemed to promise success. In his scheme he appears to have had influential associates both in Scotland and London. An Act authorising and incorporating a company for carrying out the proposal was obtained from the Scots Parliament on 26th June 1695. In the words of Paterson's biographer, " the original plan was to share the hazards of the design, in reasonable proportion, between the Scots and the English ; and foreigners were to be invited to join them both. . . . The original leaders of it, whose names are inserted in the Act, were nine [ten] residents in Scotland, with Lord Belhaven and the Lord Provost of Edinburgh, Sir Robert Chiesley, at their head ; and eleven residents in London, merchants, with William Paterson and Thomas Coutts at their head. . . . Mr. Paterson is found to be a subscriber for £3000, and his servant for £100." [2]

The floating of the Indian and African Company of Scotland met with great opposition from interested parties in London ; its promoters were threatened with

[1] *Memoirs of Great Britain and Ireland*, Dalrymple, London, 1771–88, vol. iii. p. 93.
[2] *William Paterson : His Life and Trials*, S. Bannister, Edinburgh, 1858, p. 129.

impeachment, and the English, Dutch, and Hamburg subscriptions, which had been obtained to the extent of £500,000, were withdrawn at the command of the king, who was pressed to such action by the English Parliament. After in vain seeking renewed countenance in Holland, the promoters appealed to Scotland alone. The appeal was strikingly successful. " The frenzy of the Scots nation to sign the Solemn League and Covenant never exceeded the rapidity with which they ran to subscribe to the Darien Company. The nobility, the gentry, the merchants, the people, the royal burghs, and most of the other public bodies, subscribed." The national spirit was raised to a high pitch of enthusiasm by the jealous opposition of the English, and by the hope of great profit from the adventure. Although at that time the country was so poor that its total currency did not exceed £800,000 (according to authoritative estimates), a capital of £400,000, of which more than half was paid up, was eagerly subscribed.

Much time was occupied in preparation for the departure of the expedition, in the course of which Paterson was unfortunate enough to get involved in the loss of several thousand pounds of the company's money. An investigation at the time cleared his personal character, but from that time his influence in the enterprise was greatly diminished. From being the prospective leader he became a mere supernumerary. At last all was ready, and, " on the 26th day of July, of the year 1698," says Sir John Dalrymple, " the whole city of Edinburgh poured down upon Leith to see the colony depart, amidst the tears and prayers and praises of relations and friends, and of their countrymen. Many seamen and soldiers, whose services had been refused, because more had offered themselves than were needed, were found hid in the ships, and, when ordered ashore, clung to the ropes and timbers, imploring [to be allowed] to go, without reward, with their countrymen."

The expedition consisted of five well-armed ships, laden with merchandise, and having twelve hundred men on board. They arrived at their destination on 27th October 1698,[1] with but small loss, and the colony was formally established as New Caledonia, with New Edinburgh as its chief town. But difficulties and hardships were soon encountered, and severely tried the colonists. English opposition was carried to so great an extent, that the West Indian and American colonies were forbidden to sell food to the Scottish expedition, or to give them any assistance. Relying on obtaining from the neighbouring colonies such supplies as they might need, the Scots had brought with them little more than they required for the voyage. They were therefore reduced to depend for sustenance on the produce of the country, and that was both scanty and bad. Disease broke out, and many of the colonists died. Divided command among the leaders led to serious dissensions, and, encouraged by the openly manifested opposition of the English authorities, the Spaniards became menacing. Denied any assistance from the neighbouring colonies, the adventurers endured great miseries, under which their spirit was broken. At last, to avoid starvation, they abandoned the colony.

Eight weeks afterwards a second expedition arrived. These suffered as severely as their predecessors, and in one respect were even worse circumstanced. Four Presbyterian clergymen, who had been entrusted with the spiritual oversight, began to lecture and denounce them for their sins, continuing their services for hours without intermission, relieving each other by turns, while their heart-broken and wearied flock sat dumb before them. When they had been three months in the colony, they were joined by another party. Though apparently small in numbers, they brought a great

---

[1] *A Defence of the Scots Settlement at Darien*, [Edinburgh] 1699, p. 52.

accession of strength in the person of the able soldier, Colonel Campbell of Finab. The Spaniards soon advanced a strong force against the colony both by sea and land. Campbell gallantly defeated the land force, and maintained a brave defence against the ships. After enduring great privations, to which many of the colonists succumbed, they were obliged to submit. A third expedition, consisting of about thirteen hundred men, did not fare better than their predecessors, and were forced to abandon the enterprise. After having capitulated to a large Spanish force, on honourable terms, the Scots finally evacuated the colony in April 1700. Of the original expedition, only thirty persons are reported to have returned to Scotland ; and, according to an account published in 1787, " from first to last, two thousand Scotsmen lost their lives in this unfortunate adventure." [1]

The effects of this catastrophe on the Scottish nation were very marked. The great loss of life and property which had been sustained was felt throughout the land and among all classes, for the movement had been a national, not a party one. The people might, however, have mourned their dead, and borne their pecuniary losses, with that equanimity which they had so often displayed on other trying occasions, had it not been for the knowledge that their griefs were due to the neglect of their Sovereign and the jealousy of his English subjects. As it was, their vexation broke out in wrath. " Nothing," says Sir Walter Scott, " could be heard throughout Scotland but the language of grief and of resentment. Indemnification, redress, revenge, were demanded by every mouth, and each hand seemed ready to vouch for the justice of the claim. For many years no such universal feeling had occupied the Scottish people."

While, as we have indicated, the Darien enterprise was probably an over-ambitious one for poor Scotland

[1] *History of Edinburgh*, Alex. Kincaid, Edinburgh, 1787, p. 284.

to undertake, a dispassionate examination of the circumstances leaves no room for doubt that the nation
was very badly treated by King William, his Government,
and the English Parliament. These also showed a
shortsighted policy, dictated largely by jealousy, as the
Scottish attempt at colonising, if accorded such a measure
of support as relationships demanded, might, whether
eventually successful or not, have been of material
benefit to the British interests in the West Indies. The
tardy recompense which, as we shall see, was eventually
accorded for the financial losses incurred, was no real
compensation for the injury done. The lost and wrecked
lives constituted a sore wrong which was almost wholly
avoidable, and fully warranted the wrath of the Scots.

CHAPTER III

THE BANK OF SCOTLAND

It was in the midst of the experiences described in the last chapter that the earliest of Scottish banks came into existence, and passed the first few years of its career. On the 17th July 1695, three weeks after the incorporation of the African and Indian Company, the Scots Parliament passed an " Act for erecting a Publick Bank," [1] which, together with six other Acts subsequently obtained, forms the constitution of the Bank of Scotland. The preamble recites how " Our Soveraign Lord, considering how useful a Publick Bank may be in this Kingdom, according to the custom of other Kingdoms and States ; and that the same can only be best set forth and managed by Persons in Company with a Joynt Stock, sufficiently indued with these Powers, and Authorities, and Liberties, necessary and usual in such Cases ; Hath therefore Allowed, and, with the Advice and Consent of the Estates of Parliament, Allows a Joynt Stock, amounting to the Sum of Twelve Hundred Thousand Pounds [Scots] Money, to be raised by the Company hereby Established for the Carrying and Managing of a Publick Bank. And further Statutes and Ordains, with Advice foresaid, That " certain persons named should have power to receive subscriptions from the 1st November to the 1st January succeeding, and that the subscribers " are hereby Declared to be One

[1] The quotations are from a print dated 1695.

Body Corporat and Politick, by the Name of the Governour and Company of the Bank of Scotland."

After sundry provisions regarding the election of office-bearers, and the general management of the bank, and other matters, it is enacted that during the space of twenty-one years " the Joynt Stock of the said Bank continuing in Money, shall be free from all Publick Burden to be imposed upon Money," and " it shall not be Leasom to any other Persons to enter into and set up an distinct Company of Bank within this Kingdom, besides these Persons allenarly in whose Favours this Act is granted." That the bank would issue notes was recognised, without specification of powers, by the provision " And sicklike, it is hereby Declared, that summar Execution by Horning, shall proceed upon Bills or Tickets drawn upon, or granted by, or to, and in Favours of this Bank."

They were debarred from any " other Commerce, Traffick, or Trade with the Joynt Stock , . . or Profits arising therefrae, excepting the Trade of Lending and Borrowing Money upon Interest, and Negotiating Bills of Exchange allenarly and no other," and from lending to or otherwise financially assisting the Crown, except where " a Credit of Loan shall happen to be granted by Act of Parliament allenarly." The Act concludes with the provision " that all Forraigners, who shall joyn as Partners of this Bank, shall thereby be and become Naturalised Scots-men, to all Intents and Purposes whatsoever."

Among the names mentioned in the Act are several which also appear in the African and Indian Company's Act ; but there is one notable exception. Seven London merchants are included in the list, of whom the names of John Holland and Thomas Coutts are specially interesting. But William Paterson, the founder of the Bank of England, the foremost Scotsman of the time in the domain of finance, he who, according to a contemporary poet, could " persuade a nation bred to war to think of trade," is too busy leading his countrymen on a will-o'-the-wisp chase to interest himself in a matter which far more concerned his country's good than all his dreams of foreign wealth. He even appears to have viewed the banking project with disfavour, but for what reason is not apparent.

To whom the credit for the original idea of a bank in Scotland is due seems unascertainable ; but it is understood that Mr. John Holland, whose name is inserted in the Act, a merchant in London, drew up its constitution at the request of several Scotsmen resident in London. At the outset, the governor and one-half of the directors were elected from among the proprietors resident in London, the deputy-governor and the other half of the board being chosen from among the Scottish proprietors. Mr. Holland was the first governor. Subsequently, from want of interest in the bank leading to a gradual decrease in the number of English proprietors, the practice of electing London directors was abandoned. Mr. Wenley says : " It would appear that Mr. Holland's Scotch bank had not found much favour with his English friends ; but there can be no doubt that, under his care, it had been judiciously planted, and had fairly taken root." [1]

Although, as we have seen, the Bank of Scotland got its credentials on 17th July 1695, it was not until the new year that the share-subscriptions were completed, and the bank actually commenced business. The capital was subscribed for in the proportions of two-thirds in Scotland and one-third in London. The payments on application for stock, amounting to £10,000 sterling, or 10 per cent of the subscribed capital, sufficed for the bank's requirements. They began at once to issue notes of £100, £50, £20, £10, and £5 sterling ; and in 1704 they adopted a £12 Scots (value £1 sterling) denomination.

---

[1] *Journal of Institute of Bankers*, vol. iii. p. 121.

It is somewhat extraordinary that, at the outset, the notes should not only have been in English currency, but of such high denominations. The number of people who could have had use for the larger of these amounts must have been very small ; and even £5 would be an unattainable sum for most of the population. The explanation is, doubtless, as suggested in the letter referred to below,[1] that the bank was dominated by the views of people accustomed to the conditions of business in London. Hence also the hesitation of the bank, until 1704, to issue small notes, which were essential to the efficiency of the circulation.

At first the lending of their capital and the issue of notes constituted the whole of their business, but very soon they attempted to engage in exchange business, for we find that in this first year of their active existence (1696) they established branches at Glasgow, Aberdeen, Dundee, and Montrose. It is possible that the immediate cause of this movement was an attempt made by the African and Indian Company to engage in the business of banking, as a set-off to their failure in Darien, and the unremunerative nature of their other commercial ventures. This action was, of course, a direct infringement of the legal monopoly of the bank, justifiable only by a literal interpretation of the prohibitory clause of the bank's Act, which forbade the setting up of " a distinct company of bank." Not feeling themselves strong enough, however, to contest the point, the bank allowed their opponents to carry on their competition undisturbed ; and very soon it was found that the latter were as unable to command success in banking as in their legitimate business, and they retired from the field.

[1] It is stated in the *Historical Account* that, in January 1699, they adopted a 20s. issue. The author subsequently, however, enumerates only the first five denominations as current in 1700 ; and his statement is otherwise unconfirmed. That it is probably an error is apparent from an interesting official letter printed in Appendix A. The notes, we are told, were then " engraven in one and the same character. only the amounts being different."

" They resolved," says our author, " not to quarrel with that (then) Mighty Company, nor plead the Bank's seclusive Privilege ; but rather to ly by for a little, and only so to manage their Affairs, as not to suffer an Affront in their Infancy, by a Demand on the Bank greater than the Amount of their Cash : And this they did effectually, but with some Loss to the Company ; for it obliged the Proprietors to advance two Tenths of their Stock, besides the Tenth paid in at subscribing, and put a stop to all Negotiations for a Time " (p. 4). In the year succeeding the establishment of the bank's branches, the directors, finding [1] that the expense of conducting them greatly exceeded the profit obtained, withdrew them, and the attempt was not renewed during the currency of their monopoly.   To meet their extended operations they had increased the paid-up capital to £30,000 ; but when they again confined their business to Edinburgh, it was reduced (May 1698) to the former amount by repayment of £20,000 to the proprietors.

In February of the year 1700, the Bank had the misfortune to be burned out of their office, which was situated in Parliament Close, during a considerable conflagration which occurred in the city, and removed to a close off the south side of the Lawnmarket. But, while the event occasioned alarm and inconvenience at the time, they do not seem to have sustained much injury therefrom. It was not long, however, before their affairs assumed a grave aspect.   The issue of notes had doubtless proved a great boon to the public, as well as a source of profit to the bank, but the use of them was not at this time so general as it afterwards became. As an addition to the currency they were acceptable ; but coin was still the recognised medium.

In 1704 a scarcity of coin, occasioned by a persistent drain of bullion (probably to meet the foreign payments of England in connection with the wars under Marl-

[1] Parliamentary Report, 1841.

borough, who gained his great victory over the French at Blenheim in August of this year), began to be severely felt.[1] A rumour " that the Privy Council was to cry up the value of species," as it was quaintly termed, brought matters to a crisis with the bank. In the words of an official print, dated 28th December 1704, and styled a " Memorial and Intimation from the Governour and Coy. of the Bank of Scotland," these circumstances " occasioned a very great, unexpected, and unaccustomed demand upon the bank, which at last had such effect, that on Munday the 18th of this instant December the money in the Bank was wholly exhausted, and thereby payments stopt." Thus, in language contrasting strangely with the euphonious circulars in which firms now announce their inability to meet the demands of creditors, did the directors of the Bank of Scotland intimate that they had suspended payment.

Confident, however, in the perfect solvency of the

[1] The economic state of Scotland at this time (and for long after) was very unfavourable, and occasioned an extensive pamphlet literature discussing the conditions and suggesting remedies. The anonymous author of *The Circumstances of Scotland Considered with respect to the present Scarcity of Money* (Edinburgh, printed by James Watson in the year 1705), ascribes " the decay of species " (Scots) to several causes : (1) to the Caledonia project (Darien scheme), (2) to the results of inferior linen and other exports, (3) Bank of Scotland notes (to which, however, he does not object), (4) to English and foreign coins being preferred to Scots, (5) to increasing use of silver plate. He states that the general ratio of gold to silver was $1 : 15\frac{1}{2}$, while in Scotland it was $1 : 16$. He refers to proposals for debasing the coinage or alternatively " crying up " its value, for the latter of which schemes a " Mr. H." appears to have been an advocate. He seems to have had considerable knowledge of economic conditions, and to have been fairly sound in his ideas for his day and generation, which is more than can be said for some of his contemporaries. The root of the evil appears, however, to have been a drain of silver from Scotland. The minted pieces alluded to are " 3, 2 and 1 lib.," 10 and 5 shillings— no doubt Scots. The 3 lib. piece = 1 crown of " 14 drop, 18 grains." The English crown is given as of 15 drop, 18 grains. The " drop " weight of silver was worth somewhat less than a groat or four pence.

Another nameless writer of the period paints a black picture of the state of the nation. He describes the deep poverty of the people, and reflects on the extravagance, want of enterprise, and idleness prevailing. He says that the balance of trade with France alone ran £50,000 sterling against Scotland annually.

corporation, they proceeded to state that application had been made to the Marquis of Tweeddale, the Lord High Chancellor, craving an inspection of the books. Thereupon the Earl of Loudoun, Lord Belhaven, the Lord President of the Court of Session, and others, met at the bank, and after examination they " find that the Bank hath sufficient Provisions to satisfie and pay all their outstanding Bills and Debts ; and that with a considerable Overplus, exceeding (by a fourth part at least) the whole foresaid Bills and Debts." A general meeting of the adventurers was called, who sanctioned the allowing of " annual rent " on the notes " from the stop," to procure their continued currency, and made a call of 10 per cent on the nominal capital, amounting to £10,000. This sum was repaid two years later. With these arrangements the difficulty was overcome, and the bank learnt its first lesson in the absolute necessity of maintaining an efficient bullion reserve. It had prob-ably been loth to supplement its falling stock, owing to the great expense attending such an operation. This will be readily understood, when it is remembered that the cost of bringing gold from London amounted then to 8 per cent or 9 per cent on the remittance. The year 1704 is further noticeable, from the first step in the establishment of the small-note currency, which subse-quently proved such an important factor, having been taken, by the bank then commencing the issue of notes of the value of £1 sterling. Their circulation was, how-ever, very limited until after the union of the countries.[1]

[1] The celebrated John Law of Lauriston was very active at this time in pressing on the Government and Parliament his favourite ideas of a forced paper currency ; but, largely owing to William Paterson's representations, without success. Others also carried on similar propaganda. One scheme proposed, of which Dr. Chamberlen, a supporter of Law, was the chief engineer, was to establish what was termed a land-bank, but would really have been a mortgage and note-issuing office. The idea seems to have been that land-owners should mortgage their properties against advances in Government notes. The mortgage was to run for twenty-five years only, with interest at 5 per cent per annum. Payments of interest were only

Three years after the incident we have just narrated
(1st May 1707), the legislative union of England and
Scotland was accomplished, after protracted and acri-
monious negotiation. That event is now regarded as a
mutual blessing to both nations ; but it was not generally
so considered at the time. Haughty and contemptuous,
the English looked on it as a means of staving off the
troublesome incursions of the northern wolves. The
Scotch, on the other hand, detested the proposition, and
but for intrigue and bribery among the members of
Parliament, the Act of Union would not have passed.
The people were not, however, long in finding out the
material benefits accruing to them from federal union
with their wealthy neighbours, and from that time
Scotland rapidly advanced in civilisation and commerce.
The national coinage being then in a very unsatisfactory
condition, the Bank of Scotland was entrusted with the
duty of superintending its improvement. " The Directors
undertook to receive in all the Species that were to be
recoined, . . . and to issue Bank-notes or current Money
for the same, in the Option of the Ingiver of the old
Species, and the Privy Council allowed a Half *per Cent*.
to the Bank for defraying Charges." The bank were
promised a reward after finishing the work ; but,
although they preferred their claim, they do not seem
to have secured its recognition.[1] The total metallic

to be accepted in the notes issued under the scheme. The loan was
not to be repayable, being met by the twenty-five yearly payments
of interest. Expenses were to be met by a supplementary issue of
notes. (*A Present Remedie for the want of Money*—no date.)

Another scheme was to issue exchequer bills against the public
revenue, estimated at £130,000 sterling, which would be receivable at
10 per cent discount in payment of taxes. All taxes were at the
same time to be increased in the same proportion. The African
Company's credit was also proposed as a basis for a similar issue.
*Considerations and Proposals for Supplying the present Scarcity of
Money and Advancing Trade.* (Edinburgh, no date, but in this period.)

Anonymity was a marked feature of the controversy, and was
doubtless due to intensity of feeling in the public mind occasioned
by the prevailing anxieties.

[1] *Historical Account of the Bank of Scotland*, 1728.

currency of Scotland at that time has been estimated at
£800,000, or, according to one authority, £900,000. Of
this, £411,117 : 10 : 9 was brought in, in exchange for
new coin. It is interesting to note that only
£239,636 : 13 : 9 was native coin, the rest consisting of
£132,080 : 17s. of foreign and about £40,000 English coin.
This operation took place in 1707.

While this reform was in progress, the bank got a
great fright : " For in *March* 1708 the *French* Fleet
appeared at the mouth of the Firth of *Forth*, in the (then)
intended Invasion. At which time the Bank had a very
great Sum lying in the Mint in Ingots, and a considerable
Sum in the Bank, brought in to be recoined, besides a
large Sum in current Species ; all which could not well
have been carried off and concealed." [1] In 1707 the
bank first assumed the *rôle* of a bank of deposit, but did
not then allow interest on the money paid in. During
the Jacobite troubles of 1715 the bank, being suspected
of favouring the Pretender's cause, fell into disfavour
with the Crown. To this is ascribed the favourable
reception, some years afterwards, of the request by the
Equivalent Company to have banking powers conferred
on them, and the special recognition and support accorded
to them for long afterwards as the great rival of the
Bank of Scotland.

It does not concern us to trace the course of the
rebellion, which, indeed, does not seem materially to
have affected the country in general. But it is interesting
to observe its effects on the bank. That establishment,
despite the insignificance of its financial position from
a modern point of view, appears to have been a considerable power in the land. It would appear that its influence
was (doubtless secretly) enlisted more in the cause of
popular patriotism (according to the light of those days)
than in the interest of public order and loyalty, as these
were regarded by the dominant party. For this dis-

[1] *Historical Account of the Bank of Scotland*, 1728.

affection to King George the bank was severely punished twelve years later ; and even at the time it suffered from the results of the rebels' action. The Town Council of Edinburgh made successful endeavours to provide for the security of the city ; but the approach of a detach-ment of the Pretender's party produced so much alarm among the citizens, that a severe run on the bank took place. It is recorded that " the enterprise began on the part of the rebels with an unsuccessful attempt to seize the Castle by surprise ; and the run on the Bank of Scotland was so great, that they stopped payment on the 19th September [having apparently sustained it for eleven days], and ordered their notes to bear interest from that date." Elsewhere, however, we are informed that " the Directors privately encouraged the Demand, lest the Money should fall into the Hands of Enemies. But the Directors took Care to retain the whole Cash belonging to the Government ; and after all the rest of the Money in the Bank was issued, they delivered the publick Money ; which was lodged in the Castle of *Edinburgh*, being about £30,000 Sterl." Tranquillity was restored by the arrival of troops from Holland in December following. The interest-bearing notes were withdrawn from circulation during May, June, and July 1716, " and the Directors proceeded again in Business and Negotiations." [1]

In that year, as the result in all probability of the interruption of its business, it does not appear to have paid any dividend. As this was quite an unusual circum-stance, even in those early days of the bank's history (as far as we are aware it occurred only once before and never after), and as, when dividends were resumed, they were at lower rates than those immediately preceding the cessation, it would seem that the bank had suffered considerably from the untoward train of events. The proprietors could, nevertheless, afford to dispense with a year's dividend, seeing their profits had been of a very

---

[1] *Historical Account of the Bank of Scotland*, 1728.

substantial character. From an apparently authentic record we find that, for the twenty-nine years ending with 1727 (the date of the incorporation of the Royal Bank), the allocated profits averaged 17 per cent on the capital. After the first stoppage (1704) the rate of dividend fell to 6 per cent, but it was rapidly raised again until it reached 30 per cent, at which it stood for three years prior to the second suspension (1715–16). In the succeeding eleven years the rate varied from 10 per cent to 22½ per cent, and the bank enjoyed an undisturbed and lucrative monopoly. Its exclusive privileges had lapsed in 1716, but no competitor had arisen to contest its sway in the domain of finance. Indeed, there are indications that in those days an opinion prevailed pretty generally that, while one bank was necessary, a plurality of banks was unadvisable and even dangerous. The great South Sea Bubble and the other speculative manias which in 1719–20 grievously afflicted the English nation, appear to have had little effect on Scotland.

The prosperity of the Bank of Scotland did not pass unobserved. Although up to 1726 no actual competition, other than the ineffectual attempt made by the Darien Company, seems to have been threatened, endeavours were made by other corporations to share their gains. One of the most curious of these was a scheme submitted by a Mr. James Armour, writer in Edinburgh, acting on behalf of the Royal Exchange Assurance Corporation of London. In advancing his scheme, Mr. Armour lays great stress on the benefit to be derived by the country from its acceptance ; but it is evident from his tone that he had some strong personal interest in the success of his proposals. Seemingly the bank directors had turned a deaf ear to his charming, for he issued a print of 25 pages, with the object of forcing the scheme upon their attention, and enlisting the support of the proprietors. This pamphlet is entitled, " Proposals for making the Bank of Scotland more Useful and Profitable, and for raising the Value of the Land-Interest of North Britain ; Edinburgh, 1722." It is dedicated to the Earl of Leven, Governor of the Bank, " to whom," says the author, " I'm perswaded, what is offered with a View to serve your COUNTRY and the BANK-COMPANY, will not be unacceptable." He then addresses the reader in the following words :—" Being commissioned by some very Honourable Gentlemen, as a COMMITTEE of the DIRECTORS of the ROYAL EXCHANGE ASSURANCE COMPANY at LONDON, to offer the following PROPOSALS to the GOVERNOR and COMPANY of the BANK of SCOTLAND, which, in my humble Opinion, are for the Interest, not only of the BANK-COMPANY, but also of the whole NATION, I think myself obliged to submit THEM to the consideration of every one who will take the Trouble to examine 'EM, and has Resolution enough to judge for himself. 'Tis in vain to write for him, who, for Want of this Resolution, submits himself and his Concerns to another's Conduct, without enquiring into the Reasons of Things, such a one may save himself the Trouble of examining these Proposals, and leave it for a Task to his DIRECTOR." He then devotes sixteen pages (in which a peculiar taste in printing is gratified to the full by the liberal use of large and small capitals, italics, and old English characters) to the statement and advocacy of his proposals. He opens with a reference to " The bad Effects of the *Scarcity of Money*, and a *sunk Credit* " then existing ; and continues, " 'Twill be needless for me to offer to set forth the Advantages of a 𝕻𝖑𝖊𝖓𝖙𝖞 of 𝕸𝖔𝖓𝖊𝖞, and an 𝖊𝖝𝖙𝖊𝖓𝖘𝖎𝖇𝖊 𝕮𝖗𝖊𝖉𝖎𝖙, establish'd on a solid Foundation, 𝖙𝖍𝖊𝖘𝖊 being obvious to every Man of common Understanding.

" Nor need I endeavour to prove what every one will readily admit, that 𝕷𝖆𝖓𝖉 is by much the surest 𝕱𝖚𝖓𝖉 of 𝕮𝖗𝖊𝖉𝖎𝖙, by reason that it is not only capable of being so Ascertain'd, as that it mayn't be alienated, to the Disappointment of those who trust to it ; but also that it is more like to retain its *Value*, than any other *Fund*." This is the basis of his argument; and he goes on to show that " The Fluctuation that lately happen'd of the Value of Land, . . . reckoning it after the Rate of *Twenty Years' Purchase*," had produced no real depreciation; " so that the 𝕷𝖆𝖓𝖉-𝕮𝖗𝖊𝖉𝖎𝖙 did not suffer so much as a *Damp* even under that *Fluctuation*."

The author then proceeds to state his case, and it may be most pleasing to the reader to have it in his own language in full. " Perhaps no Country in the World affords a better Opportunity for a *Land Credit*, than THIS of NORTH BRITAIN does, in Proportion to our Extent, not only by Reason that our 𝕽𝖊𝖌𝖎𝖘𝖙𝖊𝖗𝖘 are sufficient to ascertain the *Property of Land*, but also that we have already the Privilege of a BANK, empower'd expressly to lend upon it.

" 'Tis true, That, for a long Time past, this Bank hath been but very scanty in her 𝕷𝖔𝖆𝖓𝖘 upon *Land*, or upon any other *Security*; but whatever may have been the Motives of this Conduct for Time past, it is reasonable to think, That was the BANK strengthened with a greater Quantity of *Cash*, than she hath hitherto been provided with, and for which no immediate *Demand* could be made upon her, she might safely issue *Notes* in *Loans* upon *Land* and other *proper Securities*, to a much greater *Amount* than she hath done at any Time heretofore; and that not only for the Advantage of the *Bank Proprietors*, but also of the whole *Nation*.

" To enable our BANK to this, a *Committee* of the *Directors* of the *Royal Exchange Assurance Company*, authoriz'd to that Effect, have empower'd me to PROPOSE, That this *Company* will furnish the BANK of *Scotland* with £20,000 *st. in specie*; upon this *Condition*, That after allowing the *Bank Proprietors* a *Dividend* of £2500 *Sterling per Annum* of free Profits, upon the £20,000 *Sterling* already paid in by them of their CAPITAL, the **Superplus Profits** arising from the Interest of the **Loans,** shall be equally divided betwixt the Two Companies.

.　　.　　.　　.　　.　　.　　.

" The Committee of *Directors* of the aforsaid *Assurance Company*, being also perswaded that the **Settling** of an **Intercourse of Exchange** betwixt the Two Companies would not only conduce to the Good of the *Companies*, but of the whole *Nation* ; and considering that it will be for the Interest of that *Company* upon the Footing propos'd, that the Credit of our Bank be establish'd beyond Exception, they have also *instructed* me to offer it as their Opinion, That the *Assurance Company* shall honour and pay from Time to Time, **Bills of Exchange,** to be drawn by the Bank upon that Company to the *Amount* of £5000 *Sterling*, our Bank being only to answer that *Company's Draughts* to the Amount of what they shall have advanced and paid on the *Bank's* Bills for the Time. . . .

" Tho' 'tis evedint that *thus* the Business of *Exchange* is to be carried on with the *Assurance Company's Money*, yet 'tis propos'd, That the Bank shall have **Half the Profits** of what Exchange shall be got by these *Bills* to be drawn by both *Companies*, without risquing or advancing **One Farthing**."

The deposit of £20,000 was to lie for a period of nineteen years, with option to the Assurance Company to demand repayment on twelve months' notice, but with no option to the bank to repay of their own accord. As the bank had been paying dividends of 20 per cent on the first instalment of £10,000 of their capital, and of 5 per cent on the second instalment of the same amount, the sum of free profits specified was to preserve that position. Further profits, including those to be derived from the use of the Assurance Company's money, were to be divided equally between the bank and the company. The exchange business was to be kept separate, 1 per cent commission to be charged, drafts to be payable at sight, each party to pay their own expenses, and the profit to be divided equally.

Our author seems to have had doubts as to the acceptance of his scheme, for, towards the end of his pamphlet, he expresses himself thus gloomily and sarcastically : " I know that very often the most useful *Proposals* " [he has long before this exhausted his stock of special types] " have been treated with the greatest Contempt ; but a Man that has any Share of good Sense, must perceive how absurd this conduct is. If the World had been always averse to new Discoveries, we had been still as Barbarous as the most ignorant of our Ancestors " [a most profound depth surely], " and sure, one can't read the *Proposals* now offer'd with any Degree of Attention, but he must be ready to think, they will be *Accepted* with Pleasure, unless " [here comes the sting] " this is sufficient to *Reject* them that they are made *feasible*, and for the *publick Good*."

The Bank of Scotland had early experience of both forgeries and embezzlement. What was probably the first bank-note forgery in Scotland occurred in 1700, shortly after they were burned out of their office. It was discovered that a man named Thomas Macghie had taken to altering the £5 notes into £50 ones. This was facilitated by the practice of engraving all the notes in a similar form ; only the amounts being different. Distinct forms were subsequently used for each denomination. On discovery, Macghie fled abroad without having achieved much success in his villainy. Two other forgeries are said to have occurred before 1727. A case of embezzlement is thus reported in the *Edinburgh Courant*[1] (seemingly the first issue), February 1705. " This day [presumably 14th inst.] Robert Pringle, one of the tellers of the Bank, who lately went off with about 425 lib.

---

[1] As quoted in *Caledonian Jottings*, Edinburgh, 1st July 1908, p. 310.

sterling of the Bank's money, is to be try'd for life
before the lords of justiciary, upon a lybel rais'd at the
instance of the Treasurer of the Bank, and the said
Pringle's cautioners, with concourse of her majesty's
Advocat."

CHAPTER IV

THE EQUIVALENT COMPANY—THE ROYAL BANK OF SCOTLAND

WE now come to the period when the history of banking in Scotland begins to assume a general character. Hitherto the progress of one establishment has been all we have had to chronicle ; but, from the time when, in 1727, the monopoly of the Bank of Scotland ceased, the number of banking houses rapidly increased. The record of dividends paid by the Bank of Scotland, to which we have already referred, bears patent evidence to the effects of the change. The first blow to the exclusive reign of the Old Bank (as it came to be called) was the incorporation of the Royal Bank of Scotland. The competition thus brought into play must have been of a very serious kind. The Bank of Scotland had the prestige of thirty-two years of remarkable prosperity ; but its rival had the power of superior resources, and was backed by the special favour of the Crown. This latter circumstance was no direct loss to the Old Bank, as it had never experienced benefits of that description ; but the disfavour which its Jacobite proclivities had entailed on it, was calculated to handicap it severely in the contest which now commenced.

In 1727 the Bank of Scotland paid a dividend of 22½ per cent ; in the succeeding year—during which the Royal Bank carried on business—it paid 13⅓ per cent ; in 1729 the rate was only 3¾ per cent ; and during the succeeding fourteen years, ending with 1743, the average rate of dividend hardly exceeded 5 per cent. The contrast thus afforded with its previous experience speaks as graphically as any detailed account could (even were that to be had) of the seriously changed position of the Bank of Scotland, when it had to encounter the rivalry of other establishments. It did, indeed, in after years pay occasional exceptionally large dividends, and its increases of capital are understood to have been made largely from accumulated profits ; but there is reason to believe that these arose mainly, if not entirely, from special gains on what would now be considered speculative transactions, but which in the olden days of banking were deemed an important and legitimate department of the banker's business. Its ordinary banking profits must have been very largely encroached upon by the operation of competition, and this effect was much aggravated by the violent and expensive efforts it made to maintain its right to monopolise banking business.

In order to describe the origin of the Royal Bank of Scotland, it is necessary to go back to the time of the union of the countries. By the fifteenth article of the Treaty of Union it was stipulated that, as the customs and excises to be levied in Scotland would be proportionately applicable to the debts of England, a sum of £398,085 : 10s., together with a proportion of the prospective increase of Scotch revenue to be realised in after years, should be paid by England,[1] and devoted to the following purposes, viz.—1st, To reimburse private

---

[1] Sir Walter Scott says (*Tales of a Grandfather*, vol. ii. p. 301, *Edition*, Black, Edinburgh, 1857), that the Equivalent was to be repaid within fifteen years out of the revenues of Scotland ; but this does not appear to have been stated in the Treaty of Union, and was, indeed, inconsistent with the occasion of the compensation. Of course, under the new conditions, Scotland, as an integral part of the United Kingdom, would be liable for a proportion of debt incurred in this connection, but not for the whole sum. The interesting question arises if, with full powers in the easygoing ways of those days, the Government in London appropriated the Scottish revenues to such a purpose. Sir Walter was no random writer, and might have had access to knowledge of such action.

persons for losses incurred in connection with the re-coinage of the Scots currency ; 2nd, to repay the capital of the African and Indian Company (which was then to be dissolved) with 5 per cent interest per annum ; 3rd, to pay the public debts of Scotland (which seem to have consisted entirely of arrears of salaries, pay, etc., and not of borrowed money) ; 4th, the payment of £2000 per annum for seven years towards the encourage-ment of woollen manufactures ; and 5th, the payment of a like sum in after years for the encouragement of the fisheries and other industries. A Board of Commissioners of the Equivalent, of whom the Board of Trustees for Manufactures appear to have been the modern repre-sentatives,[1] was appointed to superintend these arrange-ments. The lion's share went to the Darien Company, whose capital amounted to £232,884 : 5 : 0⅔. It does not appear in what way the money was raised ; but, as it is improbable that the English Exchequer had free funds in hand to meet the charge, it may be presumed either that loans were obtained from private parties, or that a part of the sum due (perhaps the Darien Company's capital) was allowed to lie as debt owing. The latter supposition seems the more probable one.

It is stated that great delay occurred in the settlement of claims, the Government issuing debentures of £50 each to the creditors, but making no provision for their redemption or for payment of interest on them. How-ever, an Act was passed in 1719, being the fifth year of the reign of George I., settling the Equivalent as matters then stood, by which the proprietors of the debts were incorporated into a company called the Equivalent Company, with a capital of £248,550 : 0 : 9½. This sum consisted of £230,308 : 9 : 10⅝, due to general creditors, and of £18,241 : 10 : 10⅔, allowed to William Paterson as indemnification for his losses and services in connection

[1] Since 1907, The Board of Trustees for the National Galleries of Scotland.

with the Darien scheme. Whether or not Paterson lived to realise his good fortune is uncertain, as he died in the same year, but it would undoubtedly form part of his estate. The Equivalent Company was allowed an annuity of £10,000, until redemption of the principal, as interest, and £600 a year for salaries and expenses.

The company seems very early to have entertained the temptation to make further profits. The great prosperity of the Bank of Scotland dazzled them and others. Mr. Fleming states [1] " that in December, 1719, an overture of union was made to the Bank of Scotland by the Equivalent Proprietors ; another in the following year by the Edinburgh Society ; [2] and a third in 1721 by the Royal Exchange Assurance Corporation of London. But the directors resisted all their wiles. They said in substance, we have a very profitable concern, we have as much money as we require to sustain our credit, and when more is wanted, our own proprietors will find it." Although the Equivalent Company failed in this attempt, they did not give up thought of gratifying their desire to share in the profits of banking. When they commenced to agitate for an extension of their powers, so as to enable them to do banking business on their own account, we cannot say ; but, on 31st May 1727, a charter was granted to such of their number as chose to subscribe their stock into a new company, whereby they were incorporated as The Royal Bank of Scotland. Nine days after the date of the charter, and before it had passed the Great Seal of Scotland, the King, George I., died. The grant was thus in danger of lapsing ; and the Old Bank made vigorous efforts to secure this result. Under sign manual of the new King, however, the seal was duly appended on 8th July. That, and seven charters granted in after years,

---

[1] *Scottish Banking : A Historical Sketch*, James Simpson Fleming, Edinburgh, 1877, p. 12.

[2] For insuring houses against loss by fire. Its business was ruined by the establishment of the Friendly Society, a mutual office ; and, soon afterwards, it was dissolved under the Bubble Act.

and an Act of Parliament passed in 1873, form the constitution of the Bank.

The original charter of the Royal Bank of Scotland states that " Our Sovereign Lord, considering, That by an Act of Parliament made and passed in the fifth year of His Majesty's reign, entitled, An Act for settling certain yearly funds, payable out of the Revenues of Scotland, to satisfy public debts in Scotland, and other uses mentioned in the Treaty of Union ; and to discharge the Equivalents claimed on behalf of Scotland, in terms of the same Treaty ; and for obviating all future disputes, charges, and expences concerning these Equivalents," certain enactments had been made regarding the incorporation of the Equivalent Company, and " His Majesty did thereby for himself, his heirs, and successors, covenant, grant, and agree to and with the said Corporation or Body Politic, and their successors, that he, his heirs, and successors, should, from time to time, and at all times thereafter, upon the humble suit and request of the said Corporation or Body Politic, and their successors, give and grant unto them all such further and other powers, privileges, and authorities, matters, and things, for rendering more effectual their said grant, [of revenues and privileges], according to the true intent and meaning of the said Act, and of the said grant, which he could or might lawfully grant. . . . And considering that the said Corporation have, by their most humble application to His Majesty, requested, That he would be graciously pleased, by letters patent under the Great Seal of Scotland, to enable such of the Proprietors of the said Corporation as should subscribe their stock for that purpose, to have the power of Banking in Scotland only, with liberty to borrow and lend upon security there, . . . and that such power of Banking so established, would materially tend to the great benefit and advantage of that part of his kingdom ; . . . . therefore His Majesty, in compliance with the said request, and by virtue of his prerogative royal, and of his especial grace, certain knowledge, and mere motion, and for the benefit of his subjects in that part of his United Kingdoms, ordains a Charter to be made and passed under the Seal appointed by the Treaty of Union, in place of the great seal thereof, nominating " thirteen persons named, to receive subscriptions of stock, on or before 29th September 1727, and constituting the subscribers " one Body Politic and Corporate of themselves, in deed and name, by the name of The Royal Bank of Scotland," and to have perpetual succession, etc.

Among the specified powers granted are the " lending of money as they shall see fit, at any interest not exceeding lawful interest, on real or personal security, and particularly on pledges of any kind whatsoever, of any goods, wares, merchandises, or other effects whatsoever, and that the said company may keep the money or cash of any person or persons, and may borrow, owe, or take up in Scotland, on their bills or notes payable on demand, any sum or sums of money whatsoever." The Company was prohibited from trading in buying or selling wares of any sort, allowance being made to deal in bills of exchange, bullion, etc., and to dispose of goods lodged in security for advances, unredeemed lands purchased, etc. Voluminous regulations follow, which it is unnecessary to specify. Power is given to the General Courts of Proprietors to make calls, not exceeding 50 per cent in all, over and above the subscribed stock, " as to the majority of the Members in their General Courts shall seem proper, and so as not above ten pounds upon every hundred pounds of stock be called at one time."

This point is specially interesting from the fact that it has, in a subsequent able treatise on Scottish Banking,[1] been construed to imply direct liability of the proprietors for a further sum than the now fully paid-up capital. The question is one which might afford good opportunity

[1] *Our Scotch Banks*, Wm. Mitchell, S.S.C., 3rd edition, 1879, page 81.

for legal fencing in a Court of Law ; but there are two weighty objections to the theory which Mr. Mitchell has put forward. The first is that the enactment appears to have been a purely optional one, at the discretion of the bank itself, being inserted in the charter because, the capital consisting entirely of stock of the Equivalent Company, the bank would, without such power, have been destitute of ready money other than what might be supplied by customers. The second objection is, that as the provision was not renewed in any charter subsequent to the first—most of the charters being complete in themselves, and not mere additions, but absolute renewals of privileges on slightly different bases—it may be held to have been abrogated. But, even if it be held that it was not abrogated, it could only apply to that portion of the capital stock which was created by the charter in which the provision was inserted. As that original capital has, in all probability, changed hands, been sub-divided, and intermixed with later created portions of the capital, the attachment of liability would now be practically impossible. In any case, the total extent of the liability would only be about £55,000, subject to deduction of certain sums which had been called in exercise of the privilege.

We have treated thus fully of the charter of the Royal Bank, because of its unique character. There are three other chartered banks (excepting the Bank of Scotland, which, although popularly called " chartered," is strictly a Parliamentary Corporation), but none of their charters has the same historical value or antiquarian interest, although they may be more readable, on account of the smaller amount of verbosity and pedantic iteration they display. As a specimen of contemporaneous legal composition, it is somewhat of a curiosity, both from its redundant modes of expression and the simple clearness of its language. And above all, it is a most important element in the history of Scottish banking.

CHAPTER V

It was not without a severe struggle that the Bank of Scotland submitted to the encroachment on its hitherto undisturbed monopoly by the Royal Bank. Most strenuous efforts were made to prevent the grant of a charter, influence being made with persons of position in London, and, according to one authority, even bribery being resorted to. It is much to be regretted that the early history of Scottish banking should not have found efficient contemporaneous chroniclers. As it is, we have the merest glimpses into the progress of the banks even up to comparatively recent times. Were it not for Sir William Forbes' most interesting and valuable memoir, which the well-known firm of W. & R. Chambers brought to light fifty-eight years ago, we would have only a skeleton to study; and as it is, that record is mainly confined to the development of one bank—and that a private establishment—and only reaches back to within a few years of the period we are dealing with. There are two small works, however, of which a few copies are still extant, one of which is in the library of the Writers to the Signet, and from which Mr. Fleming gives some interesting extracts and details of this period. They were both published in 1728. The first is *An Historical Account of the Establishment, Progress, and State of the Bank of Scotland, and of the several attempts that have been made against it, and the several interruptions and incon-*

veniences which the Company has encountered. The second is a *Letter containing Remarks on the Historical Account of the Old Bank.* These are, so far as we know, the only publications by contemporary writers which treat specifically of this all-important crisis in our banking history, and they deserve to be better known than they are at present.

All the efforts of the Old Bank to frustrate the advent of its rival were of no avail. On the 31st May 1727, an incorporating charter was granted to the petitioning Equivalent Proprietors, and within the prescribed time stock to the amount of £111,347 : 19 : 10$\frac{5}{12}$ sterling was transferred as the capital of the new bank. As we saw in our last chapter, the charter gave power to the proprietors to assess the fully-paid stock to an extent not exceeding 50 per cent. Without this power the company would have been placed in an awkward predicament, as, although they had a paid-up capital greatly in excess of that of the Bank of Scotland, it was unavailable for banking purposes, being entirely in the form of Government debt. In order to enable them to proceed to business, they made calls in December 1727 and February 1728, amounting together to 20 per cent on the capital. At the former of these dates they appear to have opened their office, their first notes being dated 8th December 1727. A remittance of £20,000 in connection with the provisions of the Treaty of Union anent the encouragement of manufactures, to which we have already referred, seems to have been the occasion of special strife between the banks. As descriptive of the struggle, we cannot do better than quote Mr. Fleming's words :—

" Then came the tug of war. The Old Bank and the New are now face to face, each with its hot partisans eager for the fray. I fear not a few hard blows were struck in those early months of 1728. And yet, what monopolist ever patiently submitted to the surrender of

his privilege, or saw either reason or public advantage
in its sacrifice ?   And do we ever see, even in our en-
lightened days, the new institution welcomed into cordial
brotherhood with the old, until it has not merely deserved
but commanded respect ?   So it was with our two banks.
The Old was jealous and resentful ; the New was
aggressive and defiant.   Peace was hopeless until they
had tried each other's strength.   The struggle was short
and sharp.   The New Bank established its footing, and
the Old had for a time to succumb under the pressure
of its rival's demands.   The warfare culminated in the
use by the New Bank of the legal engines of horning,
inhibition, and arrestment, in the course of which Andrew
Cochran, the Lord Provost of Glasgow, of whom we
shall hear more, appeared on the stage.   The Court of
Session evidently thought that legal diligence was being
run rather hard, and stretched a point.   The Royal
Bank, writhing under a supposed denial of justice, was
more forcible than polite ;   for we find that the Lords,
' taking notice that the terms of a petition were indecent
and disrespectful to the Court, would not allow it to be
entered on the record.'   Then followed an appeal to the
House of Lords, who, on 9th May 1729, reversed all the
decisions of the Court of Session, and awarded to the
Royal Bank and Cochran the costs, which then formed
the only question between the litigants, the sums sued
for having been previously paid."

It was long before harmonious relations were established between the rivals, almost the first thing to cause
them to coalesce being the prospect of a third competitor
entering the field nineteen years later.   But gradually
a more creditable style of rivalry took the place of the
deadly quarrel described.   It was through the medium
of their note-issues that the banks harassed each other ;
and as the Old Bank's issue was greater than that of the
Royal Bank, the latter was enabled to operate with
more effect than the former.   Arnot, in his *History of*

Edinburgh (1816, p. 411), says : " Agreeably to the envious policy so frequent among commercial companies and states, when the Royal Bank was created, that company purchased up all the notes of the Bank of Scotland that they could lay hands on, and made such a run upon this bank as reduced them to considerable difficulties. To avoid such distresses for the future, the Bank of Scotland, on the 9th of November 1730, began to issue £5 notes payable on demand, or £5 : 2 : 6 six months after their being presented for payment, in the option of the bank. On the 12th December 1732, they began to issue £1 notes with a similar clause." [1]

Thus was initiated the pernicious practice of inserting an optional clause in bank notes ; but, as we have already shown, the system of deferring payment and allowing interest to accrue had been commenced long before. This proceeding must have been effectual for the purpose in view ; but, the example being generally followed in after years by other banking companies, it led to great abuses, which seriously reflect on the character of Scottish banking, until the year 1765, when a legislative prohibition was enacted against such optional clauses, as well as against notes for a smaller sum than £1. The custom greatly facilitated those excessive note-issues by persons of insufficient means which, in the middle of the eighteenth century, weakened public confidence in banks, and endangered the continuance of the right of issue. A writer in 1787, after describing the erection of the two oldest banks, says : " Other banking companies quickly followed, both in Edinburgh and other towns in Scotland, until at last they became a public nuisance, by issuing notes for the most trifling sums, at the same time that they were almost entirely destitute of capital for carrying on the business of banking, or any other." [2] One can sympathise with the harassed directors of the Bank of

[1] See also Logan, pp. 77-78.
[2] *History of Edinburgh*, Alexander Kincaid, Edinburgh, 1787, p. 82.

Scotland seeking to avert suspension of payments, but it must be regretted that they and their successors should have so grievously misapprehended the essential principles of note-issuing. Even later, when the development of financial economy has to a large extent lessened the utility of private note-issues, these are of great public service, notwithstanding the fox-and-the-grapes style of argument of non-issuing bankers. But it is essential to their character as efficient substitutes for money, that they should be convertible into specie on demand. Whatever tends to counteract that condition is unsound in principle.

We may here appropriately notice the origin of the now well-known and distinctive feature of Scottish banking called cash-credits. The name of the author of the system is unknown, but the Royal Bank has the merit of inaugurating it. The directors' minute is dated, we are informed, 12th March 1728, and on 31st May following the first cash-credit was granted to William Hog, Jun., merchant in Edinburgh, who afterwards became a private banker on his own account. The principle of the cash-credit was simply as follows. A trader or other person, not possessed himself of sufficient capital for the conduct of his business, but who could command the good opinion of two or three other persons of known position and repute, applied to a bank to have a current account opened in his name on which he could draw, on balance, to a fixed amount—say £500 or £1000—over and above what he might pay in to his credit. Thus the account might at any time show that he was due to the bank (say) £500 or £1000, or any less sum ; or, on the other hand, it might show any amount due to him by the bank. To secure the probable and fluctuating debt, the applicant and the other persons (he being called the drawer and they the co-obligants), signed a formal bond by which they, jointly and severally, guaranteed to repay to the bank, when called on, the amount of the debt and accrued interest. The bond also covered all other transactions of the principal debtor with the bank, such as liability on bills discounted ; but of course not exceeding in all, as regarded the sureties, the maximum sum agreed on, together with accrued interest. Interest ran only on the balance shown by the account at the close of business each day, not on the principal sum mentioned in the bond.

The universal adoption of the system in after years was accompanied by material benefits to the nation. In a poor but energetic country, such as Scotland was in those days, there are always many industrious and intelligent people who, from want of capital, are unable to exercise their powers beyond the limits of everyday requirements. If they are enabled, by the operation of credit, to increase their business, their profits are proportionally increased, and they are supplied with the means of repaying their creditors, and eventually accumulating private wealth. At the same time, the wealth of the nation is increased by the greater productiveness of the national industry. Thus it was that Scotland advanced through the instrumentality of its banking system, and in that system the practice of lending money without tangible security, in reliance on the respectability of the applicant, guaranteed by two or three responsible persons, has been, perhaps, the most potent element. The superior affluence of the general public nowadays renders the cash-credit system of less importance in comparison with other departments of banking than formerly ; but even yet, especially in small centres of population, its beneficial effects are largely operative.

Following the good example shown by the Royal Bank, the Bank of Scotland soon began to show the advantages of competition, by courting the favour of the public by increased banking facilities. In 1729 they adopted the cash-credit system, and in the same

year they commenced to allow interest at 5 per cent
per annum on deposits " on the Treasurer's bond."
These were presumably the precursors of the more
modern " deposit receipts." In 1730, as we have seen,
they took a decidedly retrograde movement ; but in
1731 they, with praiseworthy boldness, attempted, in
repetition of the essay of 1696, to establish a branch
system. The places selected were Glasgow, Aberdeen,
and Dundee, being the same as formerly, except that
Montrose was not again honoured with notice. The
times, however, were not yet ripe. Two years later the
branches were discontinued. In 1731 another change
was made in the deposit arrangements, by the introduction of the system of fixed periods, interest being
allowed at 4 per cent for twelve months' notice, and
at 3 per cent per annum for six months' notice.

At this point it is proper to allude to the origin of
the system of private banking, which forms a prominent
feature in Scottish financial history during the latter
half of the eighteenth and the first quarter of last
century. It is probable that the first private banking
firm in Scotland was the house of John Coutts & Co.,
Edinburgh. Sir William Forbes [1] tells us that the
founder was Patrick Coutts, a native of Montrose, who
was in business as a merchant in Edinburgh in 1696,
and who died in 1704. It is evident, however, from
subsequent statements in Sir William's narrative, that
John Coutts, the eldest son of Patrick Coutts, must be
regarded as the actual founder of the house. John
Coutts was born 28th July 1699, and was therefore only
five years old when his father died. The latter's business
is presumed to have " been in a great degree discontinued
by himself before his death, and wound up by the tutors
he left to his children."

---

[1] *Memoirs of a Banking-House*, Edinburgh, 1859. See also *Coutts
& Co., Bankers, Edinburgh and London*, Ralph Richardson, London,
1900.

Of the early years of John Coutts' life but few particulars have been preserved. In 1723 he was engaged in mercantile business in Edinburgh, but whether of a continuous or intermittent nature is not recorded. It is evident, however, that previous to 1730 he must have been a man of considerable importance, as in that year " he entered the Town Council of Edinburgh [a much more exclusive body then than now] as first merchant councillor." During two partnerships previous to 1744, the firm was John Coutts & Co., and subsequently it became Coutts & Trotter. Again, in 1749, it was changed to Coutts, Son & Trotter, when, we are informed, the capital was £4000, a much more considerable sum in those days than it would be deemed now. John Coutts died at Mola, near Naples, on 23rd March 1750 ; and when, a few years later, Mr. Trotter retired from the business, the firm became Coutts Brothers & Co.

There is no reason to suppose that during their earlier years the firm were carrying on banking business proper ; but, in addition to their ordinary business of " dealing in corn, buying and selling goods on commission," they were also engaged—as was usual with mercantile firms of credit in those days when the domains of commerce and finance were not distinguished so definitely as now— in " the negotiation of bills of exchange on London, Holland, France, Italy, Spain, and Portugal." Sir William Forbes continues : " The negotiation of bills of exchange formed at that period a considerable part of the business of Edinburgh ; for there were then no country banks, and consequently the bills for the exports and imports of Perth, Dundee, Montrose, Aberdeen, and other trading towns in Scotland, with Holland, France, and other countries, were negotiated in Edinburgh."

The firm's exchange business gradually developed into banking, and instead of being an adjunct of the mercantile department, that became subordinate to it. Corn and other speculations continued, however, to be indulged in until 1761, when Sir William Forbes—then the senior partner—abolished the practice. The original designation of John Coutts & Co. was renewed in 1763. After the death of John Coutts (at Bath on 4th August 1761) his sons opened a mercantile house in London, which developed into the banking firm of Coutts & Co. The house of Herries, Farquhar & Co. was also founded by members of the family. To the senior partner of the latter firm belongs the credit of the invention of circular notes (a species of letter of credit generally considered of more recent origin), for which he successfully established a regular system of correspondence with the principal cities of the continent of Europe. The outbreak of war seems to have interrupted the further prosecution of a scheme which, in later times, has been resumed on an extensive scale. Its present success, however, is more conspicuous than its profitableness.

Although, like other private bankers of their day, John Coutts & Co. for long engaged in operations dangerously inconsistent with legitimate banking, the business appears always to have been managed with considerable prudence, so that times of trouble were met with sufficient resources, and experience gained was always carefully profited by. In consequence of a quarrel with Messrs. Coutts & Co., of London, it was deemed advisable to drop the designation of John Coutts & Co. On 1st January 1773, therefore, it was changed to Sir William Forbes, James Hunter & Co., and by that name the house continued to be carried on during, and for some years subsequent to the termination of, its independent career. Under the direction of Sir William Forbes the firm rose steadily to a high position of credit and influence. Among Scotch private banking firms Sir William Forbes, James Hunter & Co. occupied undoubtedly the highest place. The others were in too many cases habitually addicted to those speculative transactions, the renunciation of which secured the permanence of Sir William's business.

The firm is gone, having been merged in the Union Bank of Scotland in 1843, after five years of practical amalgamation with the Glasgow Union Bank, but the business still exists ; and in virtue of this connection, the Union Bank can claim to rank as the third oldest bank in Scotland, while its business succession probably reaches back to the pre-banking era.

CHAPTER VI

RAMSAYS, BONARS AND CO.—REBELLION OF 1745—THE
BRITISH LINEN COMPANY

CONTINUING our reference to private bankers, the next
firm which falls to be treated of is that so well known
in the early years of the eighteenth century as Ramsays,
Bonars & Co. The business dates from the year 1738,
and the founder was James Mansfield, who is designated
as a "little draper"; but whether the adjective had a
personal or a business signification is not stated.[1] One
of the partners, John Mansfield, died in September 1760,
and, presumably in consequence of that event, in 1761
the firm appears as Mansfield, Hunter & Co. It was
subsequently changed to Mansfield, Ramsay & Co., and
so remained until in 1807 it became Ramsays, Bonars
& Co. This continued as the style until the dissolution
of the firm in 1837—an event brought about partly by
losses in speculations, and partly by the growing public
disfavour with which private banks were regarded.
The partners, however, continued in the enjoyment of
considerable wealth.

In the twelve years from 1826 to 1838 the number of
private firms was largely reduced, seven having merged
in joint-stock companies, six having failed, and two
having voluntarily given up business. Only six private
banks survived this period; and all of them, except

---

[1] From Sir William Forbes' references it would appear that his
drapery business was of a humble character.

Alex. Allan & Co. (who were extant in 1855) disappeared within a few years thereafter—two through failure, and three by amalgamation. Joint-stock banks were springing up all over the land, and the older banks were pushing out their branches. Private banks were looked on—not without reason—with increasing suspicion; and their joint-stock rivals—many of whom were hardly more deserving of confidence—enjoyed in inverse ratio the esteem of the public.

From 1825 to 1840 a fever, or rather mania, raged in Scotland regarding the profitableness of joint-stock banking; and during that time eighteen new establishments were formed, of which number only five now exist. This was, of course, only a manifestation of the general joint-stock epidemic rampant in the United Kingdom at the time. Much reckless competition and general mismanagement characterised the direction of these new companies; and although only two—the Western and the City—reached the point of stopping payment, several of those which were absorbed by stronger offices have been generally considered as in an insolvent condition when they transferred their businesses.

It does not appear whether or not the two firms who stand out as the pioneers of private banking in Scotland had any rivals during their early years. It is possible that one or two houses, such as the Fairholmes and the Cumings, were not much if at all behind them; but on this point there is no certainty. A dozen or more firms were in business fifteen years later, who all disappeared ere the close of the century, for the most part in the memorable year 1772. With very few exceptions these firms were merchants and commission agents as well as bankers—a combination of business which characterised Scottish private banking more or less throughout its career, and which proved very destructive to it. They were, moreover, not exactly in the position of competing with the joint-stock banks. While transacting all the operations of bankers, they acted as a sort of medium between the latter and the public. On the one hand, they were always customers of one or other of the public banks, whose notes they issued (it was not until a later period that some firms issued their own notes), and whose funds they borrowed to lend out on their own responsibility. We shall find that this system resulted in a very grave danger ; but it continued uninterruptedly for the greater part of a century.

Notwithstanding the efforts of the two banking corporations and their private coadjutors and rivals, the trade and manufactures of Scotland do not seem to have thriven to any considerable extent during the first half of the eighteenth century. It is probable that the people were generally more comfortable than they had been previously, as the comparative serenity of political affairs permitted them to work to more advantage than they had been able to do at any former time. But they were still very poor, and far behind their English neighbours in the arts of civilisation. Even the Irish appear to have been ahead of them in some branches of manufacture. A contemporary writer even goes the length of stating, in what it may be hoped is somewhat exaggerated language, that " luxury, corruption, avarice, and ambition are as rampant as ever. Our taxes are as high, and our debts, I am afraid, not much diminished. Our trade and manufactures continue in the same languishing condition. . . . These causes have spread a face of poverty over the whole nation, especially the distant manufacturing ones, which hath excited multitudes of poor wretches to several acts of violence, notwithstanding our army, as well as the Riot and Black Acts." [1]

The linen trade, however, received much attention, and seemed only to require the application of capital to develop into a national industry of a remunerative nature. An Englishman, writing in 1739, and sub-

[1] *Scots Magazine*, 1739, p. 9.

scribing himself " A hearty well-wisher to Scotland," alludes to a satisfactory increase and improvement in that branch of manufacture, and states that " the increase and *improvement* lately made in the linen manufacture of *Scotland*, has afforded the most solid satisfaction to every friend of the interest of *Great Britain*. And the quantities of *fine* cloth that have been sent hither of late hath very much altered the judgment of people here, who, from the large parcels of *slight goods* you have hitherto sent us, were apt to conclude you incapable of furnishing linen of any considerable fineness." [1] He goes on to recommend the establishment of a society in Edinburgh for the prosecution and encouragement of the trade. As we shall see, this idea was realised a few years later, though on somewhat different lines from those suggested.

Meanwhile the rebellion of 1745 broke out, and thoughts of mercantile and financial progress gave place to the instincts of safety. All the records seem to show that the sympathies of the Lowland middle class and the townspeople generally were on the side of the reigning power. The little progress they had made was owing to the security and peace they had enjoyed at home (the almost continual foreign wars were borne as a chronic evil immeasurably preferable to the constant unrest at home from which the nation formerly suffered), so they were little disposed to rejoice at the advent of their legitimate sovereign, although his efforts were aimed at their unloved English rulers. Accordingly, we find that the approach of the rebels upon Edinburgh was regarded with dread by the citizens ; and the banks and some private persons, as well as the Government departments, removed their effects into the Castle for safety. This was about the 14th September.

Three days later the Pretender's army took possession of the city. In a contemporary account, it is recorded

[1] *Scots Magazine*, 1739, p. 361.

that on the 25th September " a proclamation was issued, in which, upon a narrative that great inconveniences had attended the removal of the two banks into the Castle, and from an opinion industriously spread, as if the Chevalier intended to seize on money wherever it was to be found ; he declared that the money lodged in the banks should be entirely sure under his protection, and free from all contribution to be exacted by him in any time coming, so that the banks might return to their former business with safety ; and that he himself should contribute so far in the re-establishment of publick credit, as to receive and issue bank-notes in payments." Notwithstanding this polite, but by no means disinterested, manifesto, the bank directors continued to regard the security of stone walls and cannon as more reliable than the words of a prince.

They were not left undisturbed, however, for, finding invitations and assurances of no avail, Prince Charles Edward sent his officers to the bank managers, demanding payment of a considerable amount of their notes in specie. Many interviews took place, and eventually it was agreed that, if safe access could be got to the Castle, payment would be made. To understand the position aright, it must be remembered that the Prince's power extended from Holyrood House to the city end of the Castle esplanade, and intermittent conflict raged between that point and the fortress. A truce having been arranged between the Government forces and the rebels, the bank managers, with their assistants, advanced under a white flag, and were admitted to the Castle. Having counted out the necessary amount of coin, they proceeded to utilise the opportunity by destroying notes which they had deposited with the coin ; but it would seem that the authorities of the Castle were anxious to get rid of them, and so hastened them that they had time only to tear the notes in pieces instead of burning them. Perhaps the Government commanders disliked this wholesale destruction of negotiable securities, which, at some turn of Fortune's wheel, might prove useful to them. These visits were repeated on several occasions, as the rebels were doubtless anxious to convert the Scotch notes they possessed into a more marketable commodity, in prospect of their advance into England. It seems a little curious that the Government authorities should have allowed the Prince thus to secure the sinews of war ; but, perhaps, their object was to avoid reprisals on the city.

The battle of Prestonpans took place on the 21st September, five days after the Prince entered Edinburgh ; and on the 31st October he left it with his army for the south. By the middle of November, the law officers and other Government authorities had returned to the city from Berwick, where they had sought safety, and the banks resumed business. It was not until February of the succeeding year, however, that affairs were so far settled as to allow of the full resumption of their operations by the banks.

On the 16th April 1746 the rebellion practically ended with the battle of Culloden ; and soon thereafter we find that the suspended proceedings in connection with the linen trade were resumed. This manufacture had for long been the most important in Scotland ; but it would seem that at the time of the formation of the Board of Trustees for Manufactures (1727) it had very largely fallen off. By a system of premiums and bounties, they endeavoured to encourage it in a similar way to that pursued in Ireland, although not at a proportionate cost to the State. Whether owing to this nursing, or to the more satisfactory process of spontaneous energy on the part of the people, a gradual improvement mani- fested itself. During the five years, 1727–32, the value of linen cloth stamped for sale within Scotland is stated to have amounted to £662,938 ; and so rapidly did the trade increase that, in the five years 1746–51, it had risen to £1,607,680. In this latter period, several manufacturing companies were formed for the prosecution of trades hardly attempted previously. Among these were rope and sailcloth manufactories, ironworks, gold and silver lace companies, sugar refineries, herring and whale fisheries. We are, however, principally concerned with the establishment of a corporation for the encouragement of the linen trade, but which has for about a hundred and fifty years been better, if not exclusively, known as a bank.

The British Linen Company was incorporated by charter of George II., dated 5th July 1746. The authorised capital was £100,000, but of this only £50,000 was offered for subscription at the outset. No decisive movement appears to have been made until 17th September, when a general court of the proprietors (presumably few in number) was held to settle " the method of proceedings at elections, the forms of oaths, and several other rules and bye-laws." It was agreed " that a seal be made for the company in the figure of a Pallas," and that the subscription books for the capital should be kept open at Edinburgh and London until £50,000 were subscribed for. Of these subscriptions 10 per cent was to be paid by 1st December, and the court of directors was authorised to borrow money, " in case of need," on bills or bonds under the company's seal, and they were required to meet at least once a week. The first managers appointed were Ebenezer Macculloh and William Tod, merchants in Edinburgh. In the warehouse there were to be " a book-keeper and an accomptant, two staplers to give out the yarn and receive the cloth, and a porter." These four officers were endowed with " salaries not exceeding £150 in whole " ; and they were prohibited from receiving gratuities or keeping public-houses or pawnshops.

In the disposal of profits a more liberal system was adopted, and it was evident that the projectors calculated on a very remunerative business from the outset. The proprietors were to get 5 per cent per annum on their paid-up stock preferentially. The managers were to get 2 per cent, and the directors $\frac{1}{2}$ per cent, on the sales, and losses were to be provided for out of the remainder.[1] To our modern ideas these arrangements savour of reckoning without the host ; but doubtless the company knew very well what they were about. They gradually engrafted banking on to their original business. In 1750 they began issuing their own notes, and they doubtless engaged in general financial business from an early period ; but, although their name occurs in the earliest lists of Edinburgh bankers, their banking business seems to have been (until a comparatively late period) of a semi-private nature, and to have resembled that of contemporary private bankers. They gradually withdrew from all mercantile and manufacturing operations, which were brought to a close in the year 1763. But it was not until 19th March 1849, when they obtained a new charter, that they were formally recognised as a banking corporation.

Ten years later than Messrs. Mansfield & Co., another important private banking house arose. It was that of Messrs. Thomas Kinnear & Sons, who first began their business as bankers in 1748. The house maintained a good position during all the private banking era, but signs of weakness seem to have shown themselves towards the close of their career. They passed through the fiery trial of the Douglas, Heron, & Co. period, when almost all the private banks in Edinburgh were swept away ; but they could not withstand the current of the public mind towards joint-stock banking, which became strongly developed in the first quarter of last century. In 1831 they were joined by the much younger firm of Donald Smith & Co., as Kinnears, Smith & Co. ; but the amalgamation was of little avail, for on the 24th July 1834 the firm closed their doors. They did not issue their own notes, but used those of the Bank of Scotland.

[1] Report of meeting, *Scots Magazine*, 1746, p. 624.

About this period forgeries of bank notes appear to have been frequent. The punishment inflicted was usually transportation to the plantations; but occasionally the more summary and effective preventative of hanging was inflicted. In the former case, if the convict returned to the country, he was to be whipped periodically until re-transported. These forgeries seem, however, to have been poorly executed and readily detected.

CHAPTER VII

DEVELOPMENT OF BANKING IN GLASGOW AND THE PROVINCES

Up to the time when Thomas Kinnear & Sons commenced business, the banking business of Scotland was entirely confined to Edinburgh. It was not until the succeeding year that the first attempt at provincial banking was made. Owing to the jealous and vindictive policy of the two public banks it proved unsuccessful. The first country bank was erected in Aberdeen (1749), by Messrs. Livingston, Mowat, Bremner & Dingwall, as the Banking Company at Aberdeen. (They were the first private company to issue bank notes in Scotland.[1]) This movement was well timed, and was calculated to be of great service to the important district of Aberdeenshire. The Scottish Jacobite troubles were practically settled for ever, by the discountenance shown to the Stuarts subsequently to the Treaty of Aix-la-Chapelle; and the conclusion of the Austrian war of succession gave a period of peace to the harassed European Powers. This satisfactory state of matters permitted attention to be devoted to the encouragement of British industry, and the country ceased to be drained of its blood and treasure. Circumstances looked favourable for the extension to the provinces of Scotland of those banking facilities which were so beneficial to the metropolis. But the wisdom of the ever-intelligent and enterprising Aberdonians was

---

[1] Fleming.

destined, in this matter, to be thwarted at the outset by the narrow monopolistic views of the financial magnates of the capital.

It does not appear, however, that the Edinburgh banks paid much attention to the Aberdeen bankers, until they showed symptoms of proving formidable rivals in the matter of circulation of notes, and until a similar danger manifested itself in Glasgow. The Bank of Scotland and the Royal Bank then established an agent in Aberdeen, to encourage the circulation of their own notes, and to collect those of the new company, and to get them retired for specie or Edinburgh notes. The scarcity of coin in the country proved the ruin of the Aberdeen Company. They could not long sustain the drain on their resources, and accordingly towards the close of 1753—after little more than four years' existence—they gave public notice of the dissolution of their partnership and their cessation of the issue of notes.

The biassed author of the narrative of their downfall attributes their inability to withstand the assault of the Edinburgh banks to their own inherent want of strength, without reflecting that the Bank of Scotland itself had more than once given way from want of specie in its coffers. It may be that the Aberdeen adventurers were injudicious in the extent to which they pushed their issues in proportion to their metallic reserves ; but the fierce attack of the comparatively wealthy, and wholly unsympathetic, Edinburgh banks was of itself sufficient to put a stop to their operations. As it is, there is no assertion that they at any time failed to meet demands made on them, and their retirement from business was entirely voluntary. Elsewhere, it is true, there is record of an application to the Clerks of Session to register a protest of the Aberdeen bankers' notes, in order that summary diligence might pass on them, which was referred to the Judges, and unanimously refused as incompetent ; but it does not seem that whatever delay may have occurred through the unworthy tactics of the public banks, that the partners' credit was at any time doubted. A disinterested judgment must, in the absence of further evidence, ascribe the failure of this, the earliest attempt to establish that magnificent system of country banking which has proved one of the distinguishing features of Scottish banking, to the prejudice and short-sighted self-interest of the two oldest banks.

But a greater danger in the matter of competition was engrossing the attention of the Edinburgh banks ; and, flushed with their success in the north, they soon bent their energies to the suppression of formidable rivals who had arisen in the western capital. Up to the year 1749, the merchants of Glasgow were entirely dependent on the Edinburgh banks for banking accommodation ; and, notwithstanding the competition between the two banks, cash-credits were very sparingly granted, and capriciously withdrawn. The Glasgow merchants favoured the New in preference to the Old Bank (they were always so distinguished in those days), and this had favoured the circulation of the notes of the former. The increasing business of the city made this dependence inconvenient ; and the merchants made a proposal to the two banks to establish an office in Glasgow for the transaction of their local business. Whether from mutual jealousy, or from a mistake in judgment as to the effect of such action, this opportunity of preserving their monopoly of the banking business of Glasgow was, happily for the prosperity of that city, lost to the Edinburgh banks.

In order, however, to improve its position among the Glasgow merchants, the Bank of Scotland, in the same year that the bank at Aberdeen was started, promoted the establishment of a banking company in Glasgow, under the designation of the Ship Bank, the

5

firm being Dunlop, Houston & Co.[1] Not to have the wind taken out of their sails, the Royal Bank next year got up the Glasgow Arms Bank of Cochran, Murdoch & Co. Each of the new companies got cash credits from their respective patrons. Self-confident in the superiority of their resources, and over-estimating the dependence of the western traders, who themselves appear to have been unconscious of their own powers, the Edinburgh banks regarded these new bankers merely as agencies for the conservation and encouragement of their business. With true Glasgow precocity, however, the banking chickens had hardly chipped the shell ere they began to forage on their own account.

At last, realising the gravity of the case, the two old banks united their efforts to crush their *protégés* ere years should give them strength. They withdrew

---

[1] In Campbell's *Historical Sketches of Greenock* an interesting story is told of an imposition on this bank early last century. A man, purporting to be Sir Thomas Maitland, Admiral and Lieut.-General, drove up to the bank, in a magnificent hired equipage, and presented his order on Smith, Payne & Smith for £90. Both writing and spelling were defective; but Mr. Rowand, the manager, seems not to have expected proficiency in such matters from a distinguished sailor and soldier. He was particular enough, however, never to discount to a stranger without an introduction. As Sir Thomas professed to know the minister of the Gorbals, he was referred to him for an endorsement. In due time he returned with the reverend gentleman's name on the back of the draft, and got the cash with a superfluity of deference. Doubts having presented themselves to the mind of the chief clerk, he submitted them to the manager, who sent to the clergyman to ask him to verify his signature, when it was discovered to be a forgery. The " admiral " was then sought for, and eventually found in the Highlands, whither, discarding his grand get-up, he had fled. He confessed that he was a discharged soldier who had lost an arm at Badajoz. The banker was so badgered at the trial by the prisoner's counsel—Erle Monteith—that he declared he would rather have lost the money than have come through such an ordeal. The prisoner was sentenced to be hanged ; but Mr. Rowand exerted himself so strongly in his favour that the sentence was commuted to transportation. There is a smack of the sea and piracy, appropriate to a reference to the Ship Bank, about a statement in *Banking in Glasgow* that " it was the duty of the youngest apprentice to protect the treasure during the night, for which purpose he was armed with a gun, powder-horn, and a few charges of slugs, and locked in till morning. A bugle lay beside him to sound an alarm. For this dangerous service he received a present of £1 : 10 : 6 yearly."

the credits granted, and ordered the two firms to give up their business. But the Glasgow merchants were not to be thus browbeaten ; and, while desirous to maintain amicable relationships, declined to do as they were told. In this action they were well supported by the public spirit of the inhabitants. The Edinburgh banks then commenced a series of those persecutions with which they had formerly afflicted each other and the Aberdeen company. For this purpose they employed Mr. Archibald Trotter, once a partner in the house of John Coutts & Co., who had settled in Glasgow in 1757, to collect notes of the new firms and present them for payment in considerable sums. They had, however, heavy metal to deal with. The Glasgow bankers were not slow to adopt the petty tricks for delaying payment which had been taught them by their oppressors. It would even seem that, in several cases of delayed payment of notes which occurred, they acted not so much from want of cash, as with the object of tantalising their quondam patrons. The strife drifted into litigation, and was not closed for several years ; but the independence of the new banks was secured. The older of the two—the Ship Bank—maintained an active career until 1838, when it merged in the Glasgow Union Bank, having, in the year previous, amalgamated with the Glasgow Banking Company, as the Glasgow and Ship Bank. The Glasgow Arms Bank, which was the one that Trotter had most trouble with, was not so fortunate, for it got into difficulties, and was sequestrated in 1793. The partners eventually paid their liabilities in full, without interest.

About this time private banking seems to have advanced apace in Edinburgh. Between 1750 and 1760 some ten private firms appear to have come into existence ; so that with those previously in business, there appear to have been about twenty private banks in operation at the last-named date. The most im-

portant of those not already referred to were the houses
of Adam & Thomas Fairholme, Wm. Cuming & Sons,
Wm. Alexander & Sons, and Seton & Houston. Of
these, all but the Cumings, and perhaps Seton & Houston,
engaged in corn and other commission businesses as well
as banking—a combination which proved their ruin
some years later.

It was about this time (1761) that, as Sir William
Forbes tells us, his firm gave up speculation and devoted
themselves exclusively to banking, to which action he
rightly attributes their further success. Other firms
which arose in the decade, 1750 to 1760, or immediately
previous to it, were William Hogg & Son, in whose house
the afterwards eminent Dr. Robert Hamilton spent some
of his earlier years ; Johnstone & Smith [1] (afterwards
Johnstone, Smith & Co.), Fordyce, Malcolm & Co.,
Arbuthnot & Guthrie, Gibson & Hogg (subsequently
Gibson & Balfour), Scott, Moncrieffe & Ferguson, and
Andrew Sinclair & Co.[2] Of individual bankers, George
Chalmers, Samuel Foggo, John Fyffe, and William Hogg,
jun., probably complete the list. Most of these had
passed away by 1772. They were mainly mercantile
houses, but dealt in exchange business, and banking
generally, as occasion offered.

From a curious paper published at Edinburgh in
1778, entitled " Bank Disputes," reference is made to
a " convulsion of credit 1761 and odd years, in which
the Royal Bank took no part." What is meant is not
exactly apparent ; for, although the Seven Years' War
(1756–63) disturbed the circulation of specie in Scotland,
we are unaware of any special crisis which occurred in
consequence beyond the action of the banks (including

---

[1] The two partners, Robert Johnstone and Donald Smith, styled
merchants in Edinburgh, each appear in 1766 as subscribers for £500
of the capital of The Banking Company in Aberdeen.

[2] Sir W. Forbes (followed by Mr. Richardson) styles this firm
W. Sinclair & Co. No confirmation of this has been found. Perhaps
it was a misprint.

the Royal) in December 1761, in reducing cash accounts by one-fourth. This proceeding seems to have been absolutely necessary, in order to replenish the reserves of coin. A contemporary account states that " exchange has risen so high that bills on London, at a short date, sell at Edinburgh at four and a half and even five per cent, a rate considerably higher than exchange has amounted to for forty years." One of the causes contributing to this condition of the money market appears to have been the realisation of funds in Scotland by proprietors desiring to purchase the public funds, which were then at very low prices, consols being quoted, even after the peace in 1764, at 45 per cent. This money was paid in Scottish bank notes ; and, it being necessary, in order to remit the funds to London, to exchange them, there arose an extraordinary demand for cash or bills upon London on all the banking companies in Scotland.[1] The year 1761 appears to be in the natural series of periodic crises.

In January 1762, the Edinburgh banks made a further restriction on holders of cash-credits, prohibiting them from paying in and drawing out money on the same day. This provision appears to have been aimed at the private bankers, whose practice was to draw out a supply of cash every morning, and re-deposit the balance on hand in the afternoon. The prohibition must have been afterwards withdrawn, for the practice continued till the close of private banking. In March following, the banks took a further step to strengthen their position, for we find them advertising as follows : " Both the banks at Edinburgh, established by Parliamentary authority, hereby give notice, that they have resolved to receive in money at their respective offices, in the way of borrowing, on the treasurer or cashier's receipts, for six months certain, or longer, as shall be agreed on, at the rate of five per cent per annum ; and at four

[1] Logan, *Scottish Banker*, 2nd ed. p. 79.

per cent per annum repayable on demand, on cash accounts, free of all charges. That this measure is taken to avoid the inconvenience of a sudden call upon their debtors, and towards the support of public credit, trade, and manufactures, which have always been the care of the banks."

At this time the notes of the Bank of Scotland bore the well-known optional clause, an option of which they seem to have taken the benefit in some instances (for the first time, it was believed) by marking notes presented for payment ; [1] but those of the Royal Bank were payable on demand. The exchange on London had now fallen considerably, and by April the rate was only ¾ per cent ; and so the crisis passed away. Next year the banks gave notice that they had resolved to repay the deposits taken at 5 per cent, as they were unable to make a profitable use of the money.

In passing, we may refer to a few points worthy of notice which occurred during the period we have just gone over. By the year 1750 the metallic currency of Scotland had become almost entirely replaced by the notes of the public banks. The country was always deficient in coin, so the circulating medium supplied by the banks was readily appreciated ; and, as there was an almost incessant drain of specie to England, the tendency of paper to drive out coin was accelerated. In 1752 the Bank of Scotland and the Royal Bank commenced the system of note exchanges [2] which has (with modifications) continued to the present time, and to which must be greatly attributed the high character for convertibility always attaching to the issues of the banks in Scotland. Guinea notes were first issued by the Royal Bank in 1758, and bore the date 24th March.

The success of the two Glasgow banks does not seem to have furthered the development of country banking for some time, as we find that no other bankers entered

[1] *Scots Magazine*, April 1762.   [2] Reid's *Manual*. Also Logan.

the field out of Edinburgh up till 1761, a period of eleven
years from the establishment of the Glasgow Arms Bank.
In that year (3rd November), however, the Thistle Bank
Company of Sir Walter Maxwell of Pollock, Bart., James
Ritchie & Co. commenced business. This firm merged
in the Glasgow Union Bank in 1836, after a prosperous
career of seventy-five years. David Watson, whose firm
became afterwards James & Robert Watson, also founded
a private banking house in Glasgow about this time ;
but the business appears to have been more an agency
for other banks than an independent one.

Dundee was the next town to take up the business
of banking. In 1763 the firm of George Dempster, Esq.,
& Company commenced as bankers, under the designation of the Dundee Banking Company. Unlike the
Glasgow banks, this was (in form at least) a regular
joint-stock company, the original partners in which
numbered thirty-six, with a nominal capital of £12,600
in 63 shares of £200 each. Of this, only one-tenth
was called up at first. The bank got into difficulties
in later years ; but it was restored to a prosperous
career by the discretion of the late Mr. C. W. Boase,
who was appointed manager. While still under his
management, the bank, which had then a capital of
£100,000 paid up, and a large business, was amalgamated
with the Royal Bank of Scotland in 1864.[1]

Another incident which deserves notice within this
period was the failure, in March 1764, of Messrs. Adam
& Thomas Fairholme. They had not been long established as bankers ; but Sir William Forbes states that
" the family of Fairholme had for some generations been
considered as of distinguished credit and reputation."
He adds, " They dealt largely in corn like their neighbours, in receiving money on deposit, and in exchanges."
During the Seven Years' War, Government stocks were

[1] *A Century of Banking in Dundee*, C. W. Boase, Edinburgh, 1864
and 1867.

depressed in price, and Adam Fairholme speculated largely in them. Prices rose in prospect of peace, and he might have secured a large profit (estimated at £70,000). But, eager to make still larger gains, the play was continued until not only was the profit lost, but the firm was crushed under an overload of obligations.

No other banking failure occurred at this time, but the effects of this crisis, while not serious, are described as " extremely unpleasant." The rates of exchange on London ruled from 3 to 5 per cent premium, occasioning a heavy demand for gold for remittance to the south. To protect themselves, the banks restricted their advances, and thus kept down the amounts of their note issues. There was, consequently, both a severe strain on the banks and great inconvenience to the general business community. But the difficulties of the situation were satisfactorily overcome.

CHAPTER VIII

NOTE-ISSUING MANIA AND THE ACT OF 1765

THE year 1765 is notable, in Scottish banking, on account
of the first Act specially regulating the business having
been then passed. Previous to that date, there were no
restrictions on the proceedings of the various establishments, other than those embodied in their individual
constitutions, or imposed by the common law of the
land; and it was only in the case of the three oldest
banks that the constitutions were prescribed by competent authority; the others being entirely free to lay
down, or abstain from laying down, such rules as to the
partners seemed fit. In point of fact, however, the old
establishments set the example, and moulded the general
principles, which were adopted throughout the country,
for the conduct of banking business. That they should
have survived, while the majority of their imitators
have passed away, is to be attributed to the fact that
the younger establishments, in the eagerness of their
rivalry, forgot the principles they nominally adhered to,
while they had not sufficient strength and credit to
carry them through trials which were met by their
powerful competitors with comparative ease.

The practical immunity from legislative interference
which characterises banking in Scotland until the year
1844 has been an unmistakable blessing to the country,
and has saved the banks from those vexatious and
unnecessary distinctions and restrictions which have

hampered and distorted English banking. In Scotland, banking was permitted to develop as the country advanced in wealth and in intelligence. Nay, it was even enabled to lead the nation on the path of prosperity, and to evolve, from practical experience, a natural and healthy system of banking, which would have been impossible under close State control similar to that followed in other countries. Despite the manifest errors and stains conspicuous in the history of Scottish banking, the system matured by Scottish bankers is justly acknowledged to be a model one. Freedom, however, has its limits ; and, at the time we are now dealing with, it had become absolutely necessary to impose some check on the indiscriminate issue of notes, which had been pushed to an extent which produced the pardonable, but not strictly accurate, contemporary exclamation of a writer in the *Edinburgh Advertiser* : " Since the beginning of the world there never was a nation so much abused by banking as Scotland is at present, and probably never will again till the end of time."

The grievance was not that there was an over-issue of notes (although that was freely stated), for with the system of periodical exchanges, which even then was pretty systematically carried out, that was impossible except to a small extent. The main evil lay in the pernicious practice devised, as we have already seen, by the Bank of Scotland during its early troubles with the Royal Bank (1730), of inserting in the bank notes a clause making them repayable at a term after presentation (usually six months) in the option of the issuers. Although it was stipulated that, in such circumstances, interest should accrue on the principal sum at 5 per cent per annum, the option was entirely inconsistent with the nature of bank notes, whose legitimate character is that they should be convertible into specie on demand. The action was, besides, of the nature of a forced loan, in regard to which the lender had no say.

Moreover, by this means, persons of little or no substantiality were enabled to raise money by an unadvisably easy method, which was availed of to a very large extent as far as the number of issuers was concerned.

This phase of the note circulation was greatly aggravated, by the practice of issuing notes for very trifling sums, varying from one shilling Scots upwards. The regular bankers do not seem ever to have adopted a smaller issue than five shillings ; but a multiplicity of business firms, and small partnerships organised for the purpose, thrust their worthless paper on the public. This appears to have been accomplished, mainly, by employers of labour paying wages in this personally convenient form. It would probably be impossible to enumerate all the instances of this species of note issues, but the following examples may be both interesting and amusing. James Smiton, seemingly a coffee-house keeper in Edinburgh, obliges himself " to pay the bearer, on demand, in money or drink, two shillings and sixpence sterling," on the backs of which notes, it is stated, " are sometimes marked receipts for one or more mugs of porter, or bottles of strong ale, &c., in part [payment]." P. Williamson, Edinburgh, under the designation of the Ready - Money Bank, promises " to pay to Sir John Falstaff, or bearer on demand, in books, coffee, or ready-money, according to the option of the Director (!), One shilling sterling, value received." The Mason Barrowman Company of Edinburgh issued a lengthily-worded and formidable-looking document for the value of one shilling Scots (one penny sterling).

Perth, however, was the great seat of this industry. There, notes were issued by the " Wright Journiman Company " for one shilling Scots ; by the " Tannery Company " (Stewart, Richardson & Co.) ; by the " Craigie Company " (John Ramsay & Co.) ; John Stewart & Co. ; Blacklaws, Wedderspoon & Co. ; and MacKeith,

Rintoull & Co.[1] But, while the epidemic was most
virulent in the old town of St. Johnston, it was general
throughout the country. Even in Stornoway, in the
Lews, there was an issue by the local proprietor. In
this case, however, it is probable that no smaller denomination than £1 was used, and that the issue was
justified by the want of currency.[2] George Kellor & Co.,
wine and spirit merchants in Glasgow, Martinson & Co.
at Falkirk, James Scrimgeour & Son at Borrowstounness,
and Alex. Fleming & Company at Kirkliston, issued
similar notes. These, together with the Perth notes,
were made retirable in Edinburgh, when public opinion
became clamant against this species of imposition. The
position of this matter was rather piquantly hit off by
a print, purporting to be a note dated Glasgow, 16th
January 1765, promising to pay one penny sterling, or,
in the option of the directors, in three ballads, six days
after demand. The border was ornamented with figures
of wasps, and the note bore the motto, " We swarm."

Although this state of matters was highly objection-
able, and justified the futile endeavours of county
magnates to refuse such notes in payment of rents,
taxes, etc., the existence of these notes was occasioned
by a severely felt public want of a medium for small
payments. The metallic currency of Scotland was, and
had been for an indefinite period, in a chronic state of
insufficiency. Some theorists may hold that the paper
drove out the coin ; but, although this is a sound theory
in general, it will not hold in the present case, for the
want of coin was felt before any notes existed, and the
denominations of the notes were only lowered below £1
as the necessity for small change became pronounced.
Moreover, it is clear that there was a distinct suction of
coin to England, to assist in meeting war expenditure
abroad ; and during the intervals of peace, English

[1] Boase, p. 56.
[2] This issue may not have commenced until a later period.

investments in Scotland were withdrawn for employment at home, where a state of war prevented so profitable a use of capital as the poverty of Scotland at all times admitted of.

From innumerable statements, it is evident that the silver coinage in Scotland (gold had been almost entirely replaced by notes) was altogether inadequate to meet the requirements of the people. Even the large banks experienced great difficulty in maintaining their reserves. This scarcity of coin was the cause both of the optional clause and of the issue of small notes. Indeed, some contemporary writers held that the optional clause was a necessary counteraction to the tricks of English bullion jobbers, who drew fictitious bills on London, at 30 days' currency, which they sold in Edinburgh at a premium for notes payable on demand. These in turn being converted into gold, the proceeds were sent to London to meet the bills which would fall due a few days after the arrival of the remittance.

In response to the agitated condition of the public mind in regard to the note circulation, the Bank of Scotland and the Royal Bank induced the then Lord Advocate, Thomas Miller, Esq., of Barskimming, after-wards Lord President of the Court of Session and a Baronet, to bring in a bill dealing with the subject.[1] The result of this representation was the Act of George III. cap. 49, entitled, " An Act to prevent the inconveniences arising from the present method of issuing notes and bills by the banks, banking companies, and bankers, in that part of Great Britain called Scotland." The provisions of this Act were : (1) That from and after 15th May 1766, it should not be lawful to issue " any note, ticket, token, or other writing for money, of the nature of a bank-note circulated, or to be circulated as specie,

---

[1] The *Scots Magazine*, October 1769, states that the credit for this Act is chiefly due to the Earl of Eglinton, whose murder they then record.

but such as shall be payable on demand in lawful money
of Great Britain, and without reserving any power or
option of delaying payment thereof for any time or term
whatever." Also, that such as were in circulation at
that date, should thenceforward be deemed payable on
demand. (2) That summary execution might proceed
on all bank notes not paid on demand—one protest
being allowed to include any number of notes. (3) That
from and after the 1st day of June 1765, no bank note
should be issued for any sum of money less than 20s.
sterling; and that those which had been issued up to
that date might be allowed to circulate for one year
thereafter. The penalty attached to infringement of
the provisions of this Act was a fine of £500 with costs
of suit, payable to informers.

The delays prescribed for the full enforcement of the
provisions of the Act were doubtless intended to allow
time for the accumulation of reserves of coin, and for an
increase in the metallic circulation; but it does not
seem that the Government took any steps towards
practically assisting this movement. Indeed, it is probable that unless the banks had themselves moved in
the matter, the abuses of the circulation would have
gone on unheeded by the rulers of the land, whose heads
were always more engrossed, in those days, with foreign
dynastic intrigues, and the raising of loans and taxes at
home, than with the social questions which distressed
their subjects.

The issue of guinea notes appears to have begun in
1758, but the Royal Bank, at least, did not continue
them in 1759. However, the issue of 20s. notes is stated
to have been discontinued by August 1768, guinea notes
being substituted. Those of the Royal Bank then
issued were dated 24th March 1758, evidently of the
original preparation, or plate at least.

A minor effect of this Act was an alteration of the
hours during which the banks were open for business.

Formerly they were open forenoon and afternoon, with an interval for refreshment : (we read of the worthy citizens going for their " meridian " when the " gill-bells " rang at half-past eleven from St. Giles, just as in the afternoon they took their " four hours' penny," *i.e.* a penny glass of ale). This arrangement was changed to a continuous period from nine to three o'clock ; these being the hours during which notes not paid on demand might be protested. It need not be supposed that total abstinence during these hours supervened ; doubtless a luncheon hour (whatever it might be termed) would be arranged on some system of relays.

We are now approaching the great Scottish banking crisis of 1772, which will fall to be treated of in our next chapter ; but meanwhile we may note some of the principal incidents which occurred from 1763 till that date, other than those already dealt with. In our last chapter we alluded to the establishment of the Dundee Banking Company of George Dempster & Co., which commenced business on 1st August 1763, with a paid-up capital of £12,600. Although during the century of its existence, terminating with its amalgamation with the Royal Bank of Scotland in February 1864, it gradually developed into an institution of no small moment, having a paid-up capital of £100,000, deposits to the amount of £685,000, and a note circulation of £41,000, it was in its early years classed with the note societies of which we have been treating. It was, however, from the first in all respects a bank ; and although about the year 1837 it was actually in a state of insolvency, from which it was only rescued by systematic good management, it played a most important part in developing the industries of Dundee and Forfarshire ; and as the first bank formed in Dundee, and one of the earliest and most successful of the provincial banks, it possesses a peculiar interest. Its progress has been fully chronicled in a series of valuable statistics and notes (a quarry of information) by its last manager, Mr. C. W. Boase, who, while managing partner of the Dundee New Bank, was called on to readjust its embarrassed finances, which, as we have seen, he amply succeeded in doing.

The private firm of John Macadam & Co., in Ayr (or Air, as it was then spelled), was also established in 1763. The business was purchased eight years later by Douglas, Heron & Co. The year 1766 witnessed the formation of the Perth United Company. It was dissolved on 6th May 1787, its notes being retired and the banking business carried on by a new company under the firm-name of the Perth Banking Company, which existed until 1st August 1857, when it joined the Union Bank of Scotland. The firm of Alex. Johnston, Hugh Lawson & Co. in Dumfries,[1] which was another of Douglas, Heron & Co's bad bargains, also commenced in this year (29th October).

In the succeeding year (1767), the long-headed Aberdonians made up for their abortive scheme of 1749 by establishing The Banking Company in Aberdeen, which proved a most wonderful success. It was organised as a regular joint-stock company. The contract of copartnery, which took effect as from 1st January 1767, ascribes the formation of the company to the great scarcity of all kinds of specie in the north of Scotland, and the dangers of " the extensive and industrious circulation of a variety of bank-notes issued and signed by people unknown in this part of the country," as well as for the promotion of local industries. It defines the business to be engaged in as " issuing notes of hand, lending money on cash-accounts, bills, or permanent securities, purchasing bills of exchange, and discounting inland bills or notes." The capital subscribed was £72,000, in shares of £500 each, of which £200 was to be paid up. This seems to have been immediately completed to

---

[1] A specimen of their £1 notes (which must be very rare) is in the Museum, Chambers' Institution, Peebles.

£75,000, with £30,000 paid up. An absolute prohibition against engaging in any other business was carefully prescribed ; and the other regulations were similarly judicious. The company appears to have been managed with consummate ability during the greater part of its career. Over a series of years its dividends averaged 8 per cent per annum, besides occasional large bonuses added to paid-up stock. In 1836 the paid-up capital was £200,000, of which £170,000 was accumulated from profits, in addition to a reserve of £50,000. The shares, bearing £150 paid, sold in 1821 at £1400, and in 1836 they were worth £3000. This singularly prosperous concern was merged in the Union Bank in 1849.[1] About this time—the spring of 1769—the smaller traders in Glasgow started a new bank, called The Merchant Banking Company of Glasgow.

The only important banking incident which falls to be recorded at this time is the failure, in August 1769, of William Hogg & Son, who had been established in Edinburgh for about twenty years. They had temporarily suspended payment previously, when the senior partner was alive. After his death the business was continued by his son Thomas. The failure was connected with advances to a lead-mine speculator. Although the business was not extensive, the liquidation seems to have been a prolonged one, as notices of meetings appear as late as 1793. The depositors were not paid in full. The surviving partner died in Edinburgh on 12th April 1784. This bankruptcy had little effect on the general position. In the same year the miserable three years' fiasco of Douglas, Heron & Co. commenced its ruinous career.

There is a certain quaint interest in the following report of an otherwise commonplace incident which, as illustrative of the time, may excuse its insertion.

[1] *Theory and Practice of Joint-Stock Banking*, Peter Watt, Edinburgh, 1836.

" In the morning of Saturday, Aug. 13, the door of the counting-house of Mess. Johnston & Smith, bankers in the Exchange, Edinburgh, was found to have been opened by a false key, and 830l. in notes of different banks were carried off. An advertisement was published by them in the papers of that day, offering a reward of £5 for every £100 that should be recovered of the sum carried off ; & in the evening of next day, Sunday the 14th, a gray-paper parcel was found by a porter at the council-chamber door, containing £225 in notes, which he delivered to the magistrates, and they gave to Mess. Johnston & Smith, they paying the porter the promised reward." [1]

[1] *Scots Magazine*, September 1768.

CHAPTER IX

THE action of our history for the years 1769–72 centres and culminates in the rise and fall of the banking house of Douglas, Heron & Co., trading under the designation of the Ayr Bank. With the exception of the Darien Scheme, the failure of which is attributable in great measure to circumstances independent of its constitution and management, there has never been in the history of Scotland so signal an instance of financial mania. We do not mean that the contract of copartnery was framed on erroneous principles, or that the operations of the bank were absolutely prejudicial to the country. On the contrary, the constitution of the company was carefully drawn, and provided the usual preventatives to mismanagement ; while advances made to customers had a very stimulating effect on the agricultural and other industries of the nation. The madness consisted in the unwritten principles on which the promoters started and carried on the concern. The promoters were, seemingly, men who thought that the old banks selfishly studied their own interests to an extent both unnecessary and injurious to the progress of the industries of the country; and that, at the same time, they were monopolising a lucrative trade, which could be profitably competed for by men of larger views.

They, therefore (to quote their own words), " considering that the business of banking, when carried on on proper principles, is of great public utility, particularly to the commerce, manufactures, and agriculture of a country, at the same time that it may yield a reasonable profit to the bankers concerned in it ; and likewise considering the necessity there is in the present situation of the country, that a Banking Company should be created on proper principles at this juncture . . . resolved to establish a Banking Company upon a solid, creditable, and respectable footing." The contract of copartnery is dated 24th August 1769, and provided for a capital of £150,000. Among the original shareholders, whose subscriptions amounted to £96,000, were the Duke of Queensberry and Dover, Governor ; the Duke of Buccleuch ; the Earl of Dumfries, Director ; the Earl of March and Ruglen ; the Hon. Archibald Douglas of that Ilk ; Patrick Heron of that Ilk, and several other distinguished and respected names. The list numbers 136 in all, and embraces men of " rank and fortune," lawyers, merchants, shopkeepers, etc., but no bankers.

The advent of this great company was the occasion of general congratulation, of which the following may serve as a specimen : " The utility and advantage of a Bank of this kind to the country is too obvious to require any commentary. Its influence upon the commercial part of this nation, the evident tendency it must have to forward the improvement of the country, and the aid and support which it must naturally afford to its manufactures, were the inducements of those concerned to establish it, and are the benefits expected to be derived from it—events wished for by all who are lovers of their country." This was a euphonious, perhaps inspired, declaration of the origin of the bank, which is more plainly and authoritatively described by Sir William Forbes. " Some of the houses which carried on the banking business in Edinburgh, having embarked in extensive speculations for the purchase and cultivation of lands in the newly acquired West India Islands, required a larger capital than their own resources could command. To this must be added, the rage which then began to take place for building larger and more expensive houses than had been customary in Edinburgh before the plan of the New Town was set on foot ; and larger houses led to more extensive establishments, as to furniture, servants, and equipages. At the same time those projectors and improvers, flattering themselves with the prospect of the immense advantage to be derived from their speculations, launched into a style of living up to their expected profits, as if they had already realised them. Such causes combined had induced those gentlemen to have recourse to the ruinous mode of raising money by a chain of bills on London ; and when the established banks declined to continue a system of which they began to be suspicious, the Ayr bank was erected."

On 6th November 1769, the head office was opened at Ayr, and soon afterwards branches were opened at Edinburgh (in Canongate, 31st January 1770) and Dumfries. Each of these offices exercised independent powers in the conduct of business, under separate boards. Agencies were established at Glasgow, Inverness, Kelso, Montrose, Campbeltown, and elsewhere. Among the partners were many members of trading firms, who immediately secured for the new bank an extensive advance business. Indeed so large were their demands, and so accommodating were the directors, especially at Ayr, that the coffers of the company were speedily emptied. This circumstance, however, occasioned no uneasiness. When the capital and deposit money were exhausted, they had an inexhaustible treasury from which to feed the insatiable demands of their customers. They had paper money " for the makin'," and they proceeded to manufacture it right heartily.

Before long, however, their inexhaustible treasury began to manifest symptoms on which they seem never to have calculated. The notes came back on them for payment almost as quickly as they were issued. The directors had little specie to pay them with, and the partners were paying up the periodical instalments of their subscriptions in an unsatisfactory manner. Difficulty, however, is the opportunity of genius. A banker of merely average ability would, in such circumstances, restrict his advances and endeavour to replenish his cash reserves. But the directors of the Ayr Bank, like those of two long-to-be-remembered Glasgow banks, breathed the upper strata of the economic atmosphere. Their mission, like that of their predecessor, John Law, was that of the " eye-opener "; and it must be admitted that if, in a purely literal and technical sense, they failed, in another and hardly less literal sense, they achieved their object a couple of years later.

Instead of contracting their business as they ran out of funds, they increased their engagements. To provide themselves with funds, they arranged with certain firms in London to accept bills on their account at a commission ; and with their notes they purchased bills of exchange on London from the Edinburgh bankers to replenish their account with their London correspondents. Thus assisted, and aided by a call of 20 per cent on the shareholders, the affairs of the company proceeded pretty smoothly for some time during the year 1770, though the London debt stood at £85,000. Bills maturing were met by renewals, which were readily granted, as the commission was tempting, and the liability of a wealthy proprietary was unlimited ; and further requirements were similarly provided for. But early next year the London debt assumed a threatening aspect. Dimsdale & Co., the London correspondents, refused further assistance. A deputation to London, however, overcame obstacles and arranged for further credits.

Meantime the management went from bad to worse. Irregular advances were made to privileged individuals ; the circulation of notes was forced by means of paid

agents scouring the country for specie and notes of
other banks ; the affairs of the company were represented
to the shareholders as in a flourishing condition ; and a
dividend was declared in May 1771. The business of
John Macadam & Co., bankers in Ayr (the Air Bank),
was purchased on 1st January of that year for £18,000 ;
and, on the following 29th October, that of Alex. Johnston,
Hugh Lawson & Co., in Dumfries, was acquired for
£7350. Neither of these houses seems to have been in a
satisfactory condition ; and Johnston, Lawson & Co.
were virtually insolvent. Meanwhile the capital had
been increased beyond the originally designed £150,000,
the old directors were regularly re-elected, and affairs
went on in the usual way.

In May 1772, the directors began to realise the gravity
of the situation, and resolved on retrenchment. But
the opportunity for such a course had passed, and irre-
trievable ruin stared them in the face. Even if they
had had the moral courage (which they had not) to put
their resolution into force, their power of doing so was
gone. They were so hopelessly involved in the web
they had themselves woven, that they could only passively
submit to the fate that awaited them in a few weeks.
Their bills on London had rapidly augmented until they
amounted to about £400,000 ; they had more than
£200,000 of notes in the circle, and £300,000 of deposits,
and but small available funds. The Edinburgh banks
had refused to hold their paper, and even their hitherto
fertile genius was at last unable to devise an alleviation
for their distress. They struggled on, nevertheless, and,
aided by the general ignorance of their position, managed
wonderfully to maintain their credit.

But in the afternoon of Friday, the 12th of June, a
horseman, in extreme haste, rode into Edinburgh. He had
travelled from London in the extraordinary space of forty-
three hours. The news he brought accounted for his speed.
The banking house of Neale, James, Fordyce & Downe

had failed, and dragged down other firms with it, from which a terrible panic had ensued. These were dire tidings for the financial houses of the Scottish metropolis. All, except the few who had preserved the even tenor of their way, unallured by will-o'-the-wisp dreams of suddenly-got wealth, read their doom in the message. To none must the news have had more purport than to the Edinburgh Board of the Ayr Bank, who, although not at the chief seat of management, were perhaps even more involved than the Ayr Board in maturing and carrying out the credit and exchange transactions. They had intimate relationships with most of the private banking houses in Edinburgh, in order to assist the floating of their paper.

The first of these firms to collapse was Fordyce, Malcolm & Co., who stopped payment three days after the arrival of the news from London. Next day, the 16th, Arbuthnot & Guthrie followed suit. These failures, and fears of more to follow, seem to have raised the first excitement to a considerable pitch. A rumour got abroad that the bills of the Ayr Bank were refused for discount in London. " Terrified with the apprehension that an immediate stoppage would be the consequence, the common people ran in crowds to draw specie for their notes ; and on Tuesday evening the following advertisement was handed about in Edinburgh : ' BANK OFFICE, CANONGATE, *June* 16, 1772.—Whereas the Branch of Douglas, Heron & Co., here, have for these two days past had an immense demand for specie, from the lower class of people, in exchange for notes, owing, as it is suspected, to some ill-grounded reports raised by foolish or malicious persons respecting said branch, a reward is therefore offered of one hundred pounds sterling, to any one who will discover the person or persons who have been concerned in raising such an infamous report ; the reward to be paid by Mr. Hogg, cashier, upon conviction of the offenders. For Douglas, Heron & Co., Tho. Hogg, cashier.' This advertisement, joined with the knowledge of the solid foundation of that company, in a good measure quieted the minds of people, and the ferment had greatly subsided. But new failures continuing to happen, the demands on them for specie became greater than ever." On the 24th June, the important firm of Wm. Alexander & Sons, with Gibson & Balfour, Andrew Sinclair & Co., Johnstone & Smith, and Garbet & Co.— all well-known houses—suspended payment.[1]

The demands on the Ayr Bank had now become too great for their restricted treasury ; and on the morning of the 26th they issued the following circular : " AIR, *June* 25, 1772.—The company of Douglas, Heron & Co., Bankers in Air, taking into their consideration the present state of the credit of this country, and the uncommon demands that have been made upon them for specie, owing to causes sufficiently well known, have come to a resolution to give over, for some time, paying specie for their notes. But as the country, who have received the most liberal aids from this company, cannot entertain the smallest doubt of the solidity of its foundation, it is hoped that, on occasion of a national emergency of this kind, the holders of their notes will not be under any alarm." The circular, which was signed by John Christian, cashier, proceeded to declare that interest at 5 per cent per annum would be allowed on notes remaining in the circle, for which a bond was duly executed on 4th July succeeding. The Ayr office appears to have closed on 22nd June.

Thus passed away in a thunderstorm, originated, or at least greatly aggravated (so far as Scotland was concerned), by their own actions, a great house who

---

[1] Sir William Forbes mentions (p. 42), in a list of firms which failed in consequence of the Ayr Bank collapse, an Anthony Ferguson. All the other names are those of bankers, and it may be that Ferguson was also engaged, more or less, in banking business ; but his name does not appear in other lists of Edinburgh bankers. Sir William does not, moreover, give his list explicitly as that of bankers.

had promised much, and of whom much had been expected. Their hopes of resuming business speedily vanished amid the engrossing difficulties of providing for their outstanding liabilities. The Bank of England had refused assistance,—they had probably enough on hand with their clients in London, for the crisis there was of the gravest nature, and they had already £150,000 of Ayr Bank paper on their books,—so the directors, who had been sent to London to negotiate a loan, were at their wits' end how to accomplish their mission, notwithstanding they had two noble dukes and many other influential and interested friends to assist them. Eventually they succeeded in raising £356,715 on most exorbitant terms, viz. at the rates of an annuity of £100 a year for life on payment of £700 or on two lives for £800, with the fortunate proviso of option of redemption at the purchase price *plus* a half year's payment. The total sum raised, as afterwards redeemed under authority of a special Act of Parliament, was £457,570.

These events were productive of much hardship to the public, for, although the shareholders of the Ayr Bank were, for the most part, well able to meet their losses, the failure of so many bankers produced a general distrust, which for a time paralysed the note circulation of most if not of all the banks. In this connection it is gratifying to note the position of the three public banks and the leading private bankers in Edinburgh. These, or at least the two old banks, had for some time previous to the crisis been expecting and providing for it. They had refused dealings with Douglas, Heron & Co., and had made ample provision for the catastrophe which they anticipated as the consequence of that company's proceedings. The result is recorded by Sir William Forbes. " Besides the Bank of Scotland, Royal Bank, and British Linen Company, which were established by public authority, the only private companies that continued solvent were Mansfield, Hunter & Co., William Cuming &

Sons, and our own." From other records, it would appear that two or three individual bankers also survived the crisis ; but it is probable, from the omission of reference to them by Sir William, that they temporarily suspended payment, or that their banking business was of small extent. " On Monday, [presumably the 29th June], a very smart demand for money took place on us all, just as had happened the preceding week in London [Black Monday, the 22nd]. This was a new and unexpected circumstance ; but as neither our house nor any of those others had been engaged in the circulation carried on from Scotland, and were sufficiently provided with funds to answer promptly all the demands that were made on them, the panic abated after two o'clock on Monday, and the public confidence in their solidity was restored."

Glasgow and the provinces of Scotland suffered but little, in comparison with Edinburgh, in this crisis ; as, with the exception of Douglas, Heron & Co.'s connections in Ayr and Dumfries, they were not involved in the fictitious exchange business to any great extent. The Merchant Banking Company of Glasgow, however, was forced to suspend payment on the 9th of July. They announced on that day that they would resume on the 9th of October, and they appear to have been able to do so sooner. As confidence was felt in their solvency, their notes, together with those of the other local banks, remained in free currency. Similar confidence was shown in other banks throughout the provinces. William Alexander & Sons resumed business in Edinburgh on the 13th of July ; but whether they retained their banking as well as their mercantile business does not appear.

It was a fortunate circumstance in connection with this crisis that an Act of Parliament, amending the bankruptcy laws of Scotland, had been passed just in time (the Royal assent was given June 1772) to preserve the equality of rights of creditors in the numerous bankruptcies that occurred. Previously, creditors ranked by priority of arrestment, and thus debtors could give and creditors secure undue preferences. The Act 12 Geo. III. cap. 72 abolished this system, and made several salutary provisions for securing the rights of creditors.

At the time of stoppage, the Ayr Bank had a capital stock of £160,000, of which £130,000 was called up ; but, of course, the partners were unlimitedly liable for the debts of the company. The number of shareholders, shortly before the crisis, was 241. The total liabilities, including the capital, were not less than £1,250,000. These are specified in round numbers as capital stock, £130,000 ; private loans (deposits), £300,000 ; note circulation, £220,000 ; and current bills on London correspondents, £600,000. The assets consisted of (1) advances of various kinds at Ayr, Edinburgh, and Dumfries, amounting to £694,175 : 19s. ; (2) advances at agencies which had been established at Glasgow, Inveraray, Inverness, Kelso, Montrose, and Campbeltown, £133,788 : 0 : 11 ; (3) bills of exchange, principally held at Edinburgh, £409,079 : 7 : 2 ; making a total of banking debts, £1,237,043 : 7 : 1 ; and (4) an unascertained amount of fixed capital, such as buildings and furniture in use for the business. Of the debts due to the bank, about £400,000 consisted of advances made to partners.

On 28th September following, the bank offices were reopened, but notes were payable in specie only at Ayr. At Edinburgh, interest was paid on notes for the period of suspension, in specie when less than 20s., and in notes when amounting to that sum. For the convenience of holders of large notes, small notes were given in exchange. The Edinburgh banks and private bankers would not receive Ayr bank notes. The bank continued to struggle on in this fashion for nearly a year after resuming, but at a general meeting of the partners in August 1773, it was unanimously resolved to give up business. The liquidation was conducted in Edinburgh. Although the shareholders were well able to bear the strain of meeting the liabilities of the partnership, the losses were felt very severely. No less than £750,000 of landed property is stated to have been forced into the market through the failure of the bank, and the ultimate loss to the partners is estimated at £663,396 : 18 : 6.[1]

The shareholders were very indignant at the outcome of the brilliant essay at banking into which they had been drawn, and this feeling was much intensified when revelations were made of gross irregularities and reckless mismanagement. A committee was appointed to investigate the affairs of the company ; and their report, presented in August 1777, and subsequently printed as a thick folio volume, gives details which fully corroborate the accusations made, and forms a detailed history of the bank.[2] The book, although now but little read, is also valuable for the lessons it teaches. In almost all their transactions, the directors appear to have acted in the wildest manner. Advances for the development of agriculture were made profusely far beyond the ability of the country at that time to sustain, and still further beyond the resources of the bank ; and worse still, the requirements of speculative customers were freely met by the discount of bills. As their resources failed, the directors pressed their notes into circulation, in the false hope that they would remain in the hands of the public. As they found that their notes came back upon them very speedily, they resorted to raising an ever-increasing amount of money in London by bills, until the amount of the London debt was so great that their credit in that quarter gave way. But worse than recklessness was proved against them. Privileged persons got advances

---

[1] *Scotch Banks and System of Issue*, R. Somers, Edinburgh, 1873, p. 103.

[2] *The Precipitation and Fall of Messrs. Douglas, Heron & Company, late Bankers in Air*, Edinburgh, 1778.

either without security, or on worthless cash-credit bonds and bills, to the extent of £361,611 : 17 : 6. Even after the failure, mismanagement continued. The raising of money on annuities, to which we have referred, was conducted on ruinous terms, and it appears that some of the funds so obtained were misapplied in several cases, and a sum of £6220 was not accounted for.

In reviewing this crisis, it is evident that much of its intensity was due to the unadvisable conjunction of mercantile with banking business, which had always been a prominent feature of private banking. It may be thought that an over-issue of notes was a leading feature in the failure of the bank. But this was not so. A vigorous and sustained effort at over-issue was made all along ; but the effort failed by the physical impossibility of making the public hold more notes than they required. The system of exchanges, moreover, expedited the return of the notes for payment. All the Edinburgh houses which fell, with the exception of the branch of the Ayr Bank, were general traders and speculators, as well as bankers. Although Douglas, Heron & Co. were not directly engaged in mercantile pursuits, they were entirely under the influence of the mercantile spirit. Their existence began, and their business was conducted, in close alliance with merchant banking. The collapse of 1772 effected a thorough revolution in this matter ; and, although private banking again assumed a very active existence, its subsequent career witnessed a complete severance of the hitherto somewhat indistinctly defined departments of banking and commerce.

The essential errors of the Ayr Bank were—trading beyond their means ; divided control by permitting branches to act independently ; forcing the circulation of their notes ; giving credit too easily ; ignorance of the principles of business ; and carelessness or iniquity of officers.

CHAPTER X

RESUSCITATION OF PRIVATE BANKING AND RAPID DEVELOPMENT OF JOINT-STOCK BANKS

THE crisis of 1772, which formed the subject of our last chapter, although sharp and disastrous in its immediate effects, passed off more quickly and easily than might have been expected. Several causes conduced to this. The old banks, and the three private banking houses of Forbes, Mansfield, and Cuming, who were almost the sole surviving representatives of what had been a large community of financial establishments, had foreseen and provided for the approaching catastrophe; and, being themselves unentangled in the speculations and grotesque banking indulged in by Douglas, Heron & Co. and their clique, they not only themselves rose lightly on the wave of adversity, but were able to afford the necessary banking accommodation to *bona fide* traders and the public. It was remarked at the time that the forbearance of creditors largely aided the recovery from the crisis; but this was only an unphilosophic way of stating that business was in the main sound, and that money was fairly plentiful. Coin, it is true, was scarce, but the notes of the public banks were in full credit. The crisis was essentially a banking one; and although it was necessarily directly associated with trade, it would appear that that connection was, as far as Scotland was concerned, limited to a comparatively small section of the community. The resolution of the banks, in 1773, to accept the notes of the Ayr Bank in payments, when that establishment finally agreed to give up business, was a further assistance in the restoration of confidence. The harvest of 1773 was fairly good, the fisheries excellent, the cattle trade active, and money cheap.

Hardly had affairs resumed a satisfactory aspect, when the dark cloud of war cast its shadow over the land. Complications with the American Colonies arose, and rapidly drifted into open rupture. In January 1774 hostilities commenced which did not end until 1782, when the independence of the United States, who had formally thrown off their allegiance to their tyrannical parent six years previously, was acknowledged by Great Britain. Meanwhile the latter country was at war with France, Spain, and Holland ; had to sustain repeated reverses in India, at the hands of the victorious Hyder Ali ; had to stamp out sedition and open rebellion in Ireland ; and had to check discontent and riots within its own borders. It does not concern us here to discuss the policy of the British Government during those events ; but the events themselves are potent factors in the history of banking. The national expenditure had assumed enormous proportions ; and although increased taxes were laid on the much-suffering public, the warlike and aggressive rulers of a commercial people year by year dragged their subjects deeper into debt. The American war alone cost 129 millions sterling, besides the loss of 50,000 men. The financial result of the eight years of warfare, ending with the peace of January 1783, was that the national debt was increased from 136 to 238 millions sterling, even after exhausting efforts to balance expenditure and income.

Although Scotland had to bear her share of the burden of the national foreign policy, she, as usual, suffered less from its effects than her more wealthy and powerful neighbour. England being much further advanced in its social condition, relied greatly on its foreign trade, which was crippled by a state of war; while Scotland, in its comparatively backward state, had enough to occupy its attention in the development of its agricultural and other industries. The scarcity of specie, moreover, from which it was a chronic sufferer, but which was aggravated by the foreign expenditure for military and political purposes, was largely counterbalanced by the readiness with which paper money circulated. For sums of £1 and upward there was practically no want of currency, but it must be admitted that for smaller payments there was great lack of a medium. It would seem, nevertheless, that about the year 1776, loanable capital was more abundant, and the value of land vastly greater than at any former period. As regards the banks—both corporate and private—the national difficulties were actually a source of great advantage, as they readily invested in British Government securities, and Bank of England stock, at greatly depreciated prices, from which they realised large profits when these securities rose in value on the return of peace. So much was this the case, that serious accusations were made against them from time to time for diverting the funds, which should have been employed in the nourishment of the national industries, to stock-jobbing purposes. As Sir William Forbes explains the matter, however, they seem really to have been more shrewd and prudent in the management of their own affairs than neglectful of their public duties.

Almost immediately after the collapse of private banking in Edinburgh, in 1772, it arose as a Phœnix from its ashes, renewed in vitality, and purified from the evils which had attached to its former condition. The houses of Sir William Forbes, J. Hunter & Co., and Mansfield, Hunter & Co., who were destined for long and honourable careers, and who, together with the firm of William Cuming & Sons, and presumably that of Thomas Kinnear & Sons,[1] had easily survived the trials

[1] Sir William Forbes expressly says that, besides the public banks,

which ruined their imprudent brethren, were not long
left undisturbed by rivals. In 1773, the firm of Donald
Smith & Co.[1] commenced business ; and three years
later (1776) Robert Allan and Alex. Allan (they were
not, if we are rightly informed, relations) established the
houses which were well known in the earlier part of the
last century, as Robert Allan & Son, and Alexander
Allan & Co. About this time the firms of Bertram,
Gardner & Co., and Allan & Steuart, and one or two
individual bankers, began their career. Wm. Scott was
in business in 1778 ; John Wordie is included in a list of
bankers in the same year ; and, as he was Dean of Guild
in the Edinburgh Town Council previous to 1769, it
is probable that his business was of older standing. It
continued for a few years, but his name drops out of the
roll in 1781 ; and, on 25th September 1782, his creditors
were advertised to lodge their claims, in anticipation of
a division of the proceeds of lands sold. He is designated
" merchant " in the notice. He seems to have died in
India.[2]

In the provinces, a few new private banks were started.
Mr. Hunter, who had been cashier in Ayr for Douglas,
Heron & Co., founded (1773) the successful business of
Hunters & Co., which exists still as the Ayr office of the

---

only the three first-named banking firms continued solvent. We are
unaware, however, of any other authority for supposing that the
Kinnears suspended payment at that time. The house continued
until 1834.

[1] It is possible that the senior partner was the junior partner of
Johnstone & Smith who failed 24th June 1772. This is the more
probable as their failure was deemed unfortunate rather than discreditable. The Trustee in sequestration advertised that he was
fully satisfied that the firm carried on business with much regularity,
diligence, and frugality, and that the failure was occasioned by connection with other houses. They are said to have had a flourishing
trade. Apart from the trust estate an arrangement was made for payment of 15s. per pound on their notes from 15th December subsequent
to the stoppage (*Scots Magazine*, 1772, p. 515). Donald Smith was
for long in the Town Council of Edinburgh as Bailie, Dean of Guild,
Treasurer, etc. The firm's office was in front of the Royal Exchange.

[2] *Caledonian Mercury*, 5th April 1786.

Union Bank of Scotland. The Stirling Banking Company and the Commercial Banking Company of Aberdeen were formed soon afterwards (1777 and 1778). Sir Wm. Forbes, James Hunter & Co., took an important step in the development of their business at this time, by beginning, on 1st January 1782, to issue notes of their own house in the same manner as the public banks in Edinburgh. Previously they had used the paper of the Royal Bank, with whom they had a cash-credit, and of which bank Mr. John Coutts was a director. During this period (1772-82) two banking failures occurred, but they were not of much moment. We allude to the temporary suspension (20th August 1773) of John Fyffe, Edinburgh, who was probably more an agent for country banks than a banker on his own account ; and the collapse (1774) of the Merchant Banking Company of Glasgow, who had closed their doors during the difficulties of 1772, but who were resuscitated by the public spirit of the western metropolis. The creditors were paid in full.[1] John Fyffe continued in business till 1790. He died in 1799. The Merchant Bank seems to have perished amid the disasters of 1793.

In 1774 the Bank of Scotland made a third and successful attempt to establish a branch system in the provinces. The localities first selected were Dumfries and Kelso. Next year an office was opened in Ayr ; and shortly thereafter, their operations were extended to Kilmarnock, Inverness, Aberdeen, and Stirling. That at this time their funds were accumulating in their hands seems to be indicated by an advertisement they issued on 3rd May

---

[1] Boase is the only authority for their stoppage in 1774, when, he says, they were compelled to wind up. Somers erroneously indicates that they did not survive 1772. We find, however, that in a shipping advertisement in the *Mercury* of 10th July 1784, reference is made " to James Robertson, Merchant Bank, Glasgow " ; and they advertised on 30th August 1788 a forgery of their £1 notes, dated 2nd February 1782. If, therefore, they stopped again in 1774 they must have resumed, for they do not finally disappear until the commercial crisis of 1793. The estate, however, was sequestrated.

1775, offering to lend money at Whitsunday on heritable
security.   This loan, we are told, was soon completed.
The improvement of the gold coinage also occupied the
attention of the Bank at this time.   That reform had
been prescribed in 1773 (Act 13, Geo. III. cap. 71).   That
it was much needed is evident from the fact that, including
both England and Scotland, it entailed a loss of upwards
of one million sterling, £300,000 of which fell on the
holders of light coin.   Silver coins, in sums of £25 and
upward, were ordered to be taken at 5s. 2d. per oz.   At
the same time the Mint price of gold was fixed at
£3 : 17 : 10½.   The Bank of Scotland seems to have
bought light gold at £3 : 17s. per oz., which price they
subsequently reduced to £3 : 16s.   The Royal Bank
was appointed to give out new coin for the light coin
called in.[1]

By a second Act of Parliament, obtained in 1774,
the Bank of Scotland was authorised to increase its
capital from £100,000 to £200,000.   It would appear that
up to 1773 the amount of capital called up was 80 per
cent ; and in that year " it was resolved to make a call
for the remaining two-tenths of their capital not yet paid
up, by which the bank will be enabled to give an aid
more effectually to the country, now that Messrs. Douglas,
Heron & Co. have given up the banking business."
According to a pamphlet which appeared in 1778, but for
the accuracy of which we cannot vouch, the Bank of
Scotland attempted in a discreditable manner to acquire,
through the agency of a private banking firm, a secret
influence in the management of the Royal Bank.   Their
mode of doing this was to enable their friends to purchase
the stock of that bank in sufficient quantities.   This
plot, if it was actually ever laid, does not appear to have
had any effect on the policy of the intended victim.   But

[1] Boase, p. 92.   From a notice in the *Scots Magazine*, 1773, p. 443,
however, the Bank of Scotland appears to have begun giving the Mint
price on 20th August 1773.

if one pamphleteer abused the Bank of Scotland, another who appeared about the same time was not less animated (although less effective) in his reflections on the Royal Bank.

About the same time there was a rumour of a projected union between the two banks, which had perhaps some connection with the incident to which we have just referred ; but it does not appear that open overtures were made on the subject. It is more than probable that any desire which may have existed on the part of the Bank of Scotland for the accomplishment of this object—the Royal Bank appears to have been entirely passive in this drama—never assumed a very definite shape. At this time an animated warfare was also being carried on between the Glasgow and Aberdeen bankers.

About this time there appears to have been a project for establishing a bank in Kincardine-on-Forth. From its name—Farming Banking Company—it seems to have been designed to foster the agricultural interests. It may have originated in connection with large land improvement works which were being carried out in the neighbourhood—a great bog was washed piecemeal off the underlying soil into the river—but information is wanting meantime. The proposal seems, however, to have taken tangible shape, as an engraved form of note for £1 : 10s., dated 12th January 1782, with motto, " God speed the plough," is extant. But there is no reason to suppose that the bank ever commenced business.

We get a glimpse of the internal relationships of the banks at this time from the records of the Dundee Bank.[1] Wm. Cuming & Sons, their agents in Edinburgh, had demanded a salary of £200 a year, with a commission of $\frac{1}{4}$ per cent, besides interest, on any advance beyond £3000. They refused £150 salary, and $\frac{1}{8}$ per cent commission on advances. Bertram, Gardner & Co., however, undertook the agency on these terms ; agreeing also to

[1] Boase, p. 117.

allow interest at 3 per cent, and to charge at 5 per cent,
on the balance of the account, as it happened to be in
favour of or against the Dundee Bank.   Their position
was not so good as that of the Cumings.   They failed in
1793, at which time they still retained the agency ; but,
although they did not pay their creditors in full, it is
probable that no loss occurred to the Dundee Bank,
as the balances seem to have been running against the
latter.   As at this time the assets of the bank were little
over £50,000, and the payments through the Edinburgh
agents about £100,000 per annum, the terms look sufficiently liberal to occasion surprise that the Cumings
should have been so stiff.

With the advent of peace in January 1783, there
dawned on Britain a period of comparative prosperity,
during which mechanical science made considerable
progress.   The utilisation of steam as a motive power ;
the improvements of Arkwright and others, on machinery
for the manufacture of textile fabrics ;   and the improvement in the means of communication throughout the
country, by the regular organisation of mail-coach routes,
and by the formation of canals, at once evidenced a
material advance in the intelligence of the nation (of
which the resolution come to a few years later to abolish
the slave trade was one of the earliest fruits), and provided
the means for carrying out their enlarged views.

Alluding to this satisfactory change, the directors of
the Royal Bank, in the course of an unfortunate rupture
which occurred between them and an important private
banking house some thirty years later, make the following
statement : " The fact is, that during the times to which
Messrs. Ramsays, Bonars, & Co. allude, more especially
from 1783 to 1792, the circumstances of the country under-
went a more favourable change than they had ever done
in so short a period at any former time.   The improving
agriculture and trade of the country at this time required
a much greater circulation.   Hence the banking business

became more profitable, and the Royal Bank among others shared in the prosperity of the times." During the same period the average dividend of the Bank of Scotland, on an enlarged capital, was higher than for some time previously ; and a great increase occurred in the amount of capital devoted to banking in Scotland. The latter movement appears to have been inaugurated by the Royal Bank, who, in March 1783, added to their original capital of £111,347 : 19 : 10$\frac{5}{12}$ a sum of £38,652 : 0 : 1$\frac{7}{12}$, thereby raising it to £150,000. In this year also they opened a branch in Glasgow.

In June following they obtained their fourth charter, which authorised a further increase to £300,000. This operation was carried out at Midsummer, 1784. Under the authority of a fifth charter, dated 5th June 1788, they again doubled their capital. The former increases, and £100,000 of the increase in 1788, were made out of profits, without any payment on the part of the proprietors. In this connection the following contemporary newspaper notice is interesting : " The public will be happy to be informed that the Royal Bank of Scotland has just obtained a new charter from the Crown, empowering the proprietors to double their capital. . . . It will now be no less than £600,000. When it is considered how liberal this bank has been for these many years past, in the manner of transacting business ; what facilities they have given to the landed, mercantile and manufacturing interests of the kingdom ; and how much they have done, on the present emergency, for the support of public and private credit, every person must rejoice at their prosperity, as it will enable them to do still more for the advantage, not only of the proprietors, but of the nation at large." [1]   At Christmas 1793, the capital was further enlarged from £600,000 to £1,000,000, but without any transference from profits.

The Bank of Scotland was not long in following suit.

[1] *Caledonian Mercury*, 12th June 1788.

As we have already seen, they had doubled their capital in 1774. In 1784 they obtained their third Act of Parliament, authorising an increase from £200,000 to £300,000. Only proprietors holding two shares or more were permitted to apply for the new capital. They were entitled to one new share for every two old shares held. This seems unfair to holders of single and odd shares; but, although the terms of the notice are obscure, it would seem that holders could obtain the value of their proportions by transferring their right to subscribe. Subscription was limited to three months from 27th July 1784. A call of 20 per cent was made, payable 15th December. In 1792 they got a fourth Act to permit an addition of £600,000, and in 1794 the capital was further raised to £1,000,000. Unlike the Royal Bank, however, the subscriptions were not fully called. How they amalgamated the original £100,000, which, as we saw, was fully called, with the subsequently created capital, does not appear; but it is probable that the 20 per cent called in 1773 was repaid to the stockholders.

But it was not only in Edinburgh that long steps in the development of banking were being taken. Although on a much smaller scale, the provinces also were making decided advances. Full details regarding the country banks are awanting; but the following particulars relating to the Dundee Banking Company are significant. In 1784 the paid-up capital was increased, out of profits, from £8560 to £10,700; in 1786 a call was made, raising it to £21,400; and in 1794 a further addition was made, which raised it to £31,700. About three-fourths of the last-mentioned sum was, however, partly repaid to the partners, and partly written off as lost, and it was not until 1839 that this decline was fully made up again. The profits, during the period with which we are dealing, do not seem to have kept pace with the increase of capital. It may be presumed that other provincial banks contributed a share in the increase of banking capital; but, at any rate, there was a striking tendency to the erection of new banks. The Paisley Banking Company was established in 1783 ; the Merchant Banking Company of Stirling in 1784 ; the Greenock Banking Company, and Andrew, George & Andrew Thomson, a small banking house in Glasgow,[1] in 1785 ; Campbell, Thomson & Co., Stirling, 6th January 1787 ; the Falkirk Banking Company in 1787 ; the Paisley Union Bank Company in 1788 ; the Dundee Commercial Banking Company, and the Leith Banking Company, in 1792.

At this time a somewhat curious advertisement [2] was issued by the Stirling Banking Company which is interesting as throwing a sidelight on the circumstances of the period. It is as follows : " The Directors of the Stirling Banking Company think it incumbent on them to give this notice to the public,—That of late, some notes, dated at Stirling, and signed by Robert Belch and James Drysdale, have appeared, and probably may be artfully passed upon simple people, by some interested persons, for notes of the said Banking Company, which must be considered not only as an imposition on the public, but also an injury done to the said Company. No public intimation of those concerned in the business has been given, nor of any bond of security to the public being lodged ; but it is reported that the company for which Robert Belch acts, consists of a Country School-master near Glasgow, and a Farmer at Calder, who, it is said, has absconded. The business is in the hands of some boys who are minors, and not answerable for their transactions. The Directors therefore give this notice

---

[1] This firm were the victims of a remarkable robbery narrated in *Banking in Glasgow*, p. 16. " On Friday night, 29th October 1791, a mahogany box containing £1600 in guinea and twenty shilling notes of Messrs. Thomson's issue, and twelve bills, which had been put in a small sack, and sent on a carrier's cart from Cumnock to Glasgow, was stolen in going along the streets. A reward of £200 was advertised, and ' no questions asked.' On the 17th November following, the box was found in a dunghill in Saltmarket. It had not been opened. The reward was paid to the lucky finder."

[2] It appeared in the *Caledonian Mercury* of 27th November 1784.

to put people on their guard, and appoint their Cashier
to get this advertisement inserted in the public papers,
and to sign the same.

"DAVID ROBERTSON, *Cashier*.

"STIRLING, 25*th November* 1784."

Of course, none of these banks were corporate bodies ;
for at that time, and for many years thereafter, the only
way of obtaining corporate privileges was by obtaining
the special consideration of the Crown or of Parliament.
They were all, therefore, private partnerships ; but most
of them were on the joint-stock principle, having a definite
amount of transferable capital divided into shares.   Some
of them, however, were nothing more than banking firms,
consisting of a very few individuals, although taking a
local designation.   The only banking corporations existing
at that time were the Bank of Scotland, and the Royal
Bank of Scotland.   The British Linen Company, although
also a corporation, and actively carrying on banking
business, were not nominally authorised to act as bankers
until 1849.

It is worthy of notice, in connection with the chronic
agitation regarding the rights and privileges of banks,
that the essential difference between the old banks as
public corporations, and the new banking companies
as private partnerships, was, until comparatively recent
times, invariably taken for granted.   When, however,
incorporation became attainable by simple registration
under a general statute, the distinction was to a large
extent lost.   The subsequent growth of the younger
banks, to dimensions similar to those of their older rivals,
has now almost obliterated the distinction to all but
those who have carefully studied the subject.   This
leads many to assert, that the old banks have had special
privileges conferred on them.   The truth is, that the
old banks started under the only conditions that were
possible at the time they were formed.   Since then they

have grown in proportion to the progress of the work they commenced and carried on to the benefit of the public ; but they have not otherwise altered, nor have they had any further special privileges conferred on them. The change which has taken place is entirely on the part of the other banks, who have, from time to time, reaped the benefit of subsequent legislation, which has gradually extended to them all, or nearly all, the advantages which could only be bestowed formerly by the special interposition of the sovereign individually, or by concurrence with the legislature.

It is not out of place here to refer specially to the question of limitation of liability of members of corporations, for contemporary records are full of references to the subject. These references, however, are never connected with any questioning of what is now a sometimes debated point. They never have any other phase than simply pointing out the difference existing, in this and other respects, between the " public banks " and the " new banking companies,"—for so they were usually respectively designated.

The profitableness of the banking business at this time is indicated by the high value of Royal Bank stock, £900 of which, with the benefit of the new subscription, sold in April 1784 at from £375 to £393 per cent. " This is by far the greatest price ever given for any bank stock in this country." [1]

[1] *Mercury*, 12th April 1784.

CHAPTER XI

FORGERIES AND ILLICIT COINAGE

Among crimes connected with banking in Scotland, forgery of the notes of the various banks appears to have been the favourite. So far as one can judge, however, practice did not make perfection ; for the imitations do not seem to have been clever, and many of them must have been clumsy work, hardly calculated to deceive any but the most ignorant people. But, perhaps, in those days, that class of person, common enough at all times, formed a considerable portion of the community. Forgeries began soon after the first issue of bank notes ; but the period during which the crime was most common appears to have been the second half of the eighteenth century. The first quarter of the nineteenth century was also, however, an active time in this special industry. But, if the testimony of an author who, although anonymous, shows extensive knowledge of banking and mercantile finance, may be accepted, the loss entailed was trivial. He writes : " From every enquiry, the loss sustained by the banks and the public, from forgeries of Scots notes, betwixt 1815 and 1820, did not exceed £500 in all, or £100 annually." [1] On detection, the culprits were dealt with in the drastic fashion of the good old times. The usual penalty was hanging ; but that sentence was sometimes modified to whipping and transportation for life. It need

[1] *A Review of the Banking System of Britain*, Edinburgh, 1821, pp. 79, 80.

not be supposed that this alternative was dictated by the
" quality of mercy." There is more reason to suppose
that the physical condition of the prisoner would influence
the judgment of the court, whether he should patriotically
die for or " leave his country for his country's good " as
a prospective sturdy labourer in His Majesty's plantations.
It is noticeable that the forgeries were almost, if not
entirely, confined to the small notes ; doubtless because
of the greater ease with which these could be passed.
While the number of forgeries was large, it does not
appear that either the banks or the public suffered heavily
by them.

We are indebted to the writer of the *Historical Account
of the Bank of Scotland* for the earliest notices of forgeries.
The first of the four cases he mentions occurred about the
end of February 1700. " One Thomas Macghie, who was
bred a Scholar, but poor, of a good Genius and ready Wit,
of an aspiring Temper, and desirous to make an Appearance in the World, but wanting a Fund convenient for his
Purpose, was tempted to try his Hand upon Bank-notes.
. . . By artful Razing, he altered the Word Five, in the
Five Pound Note, and made it Fifty." But the " Check-
book and Record " were so carefully kept that the villainy
was soon discovered. The villain himself, however, escaped
to try his aspiring scholarship in foreign countries.

" In September 1710, one Robert Fleming, a very poor
Man, who taught an English School at Hamilton, was
taken up for cheating some poor People with Twenty
Shilling's Notes, all wrote with his own Hand, and a dark
Impression made like the Seal of the Bank. He was
prosecuted for the Forgery ; and on his own Confession
found guilty, and condemned to Death ; but, having been
reprived by Her late Majesty several Times, and at last
during Pleasure, he after Her Majesty's death obtained
a Remission." What inspired Queen Anne's great
clemency on this occasion does not appear.

A new forgery of 20s. notes appeared in January 1723 ;

" but tho the Directors took all Pains to discover the Author, and that they had Jealousy of some, yet they could never fix upon any particular Person as guilty."

Another forgery of 20s. notes was discovered about the middle of November 1726. Before announcing the forgery, the bank got a " List of all the Engravers, and such as keep Tailliedouce Printing-Presses in and about the City, and obtained a Warrant from my Lord Justice-clerk for a Search." The search, however, discovered nothing. " But on Sabbath Evening, 25th December said year, Information being brought to the Secretary of the Bank that there was good Ground to believe, that one John Currie, a Bookbinder, was the Forger, at least accessory and privy thereto ; and a Bit of Paper being shown him, which Currie's servant found in his Work-house, with an Impression on it . . . of these Words BANK OF SCOTLAND he was thereby convinced." Further search supplied more evidence. Currie was arrested, and eventually confessed to " having done the whole Forgery." His trial, however, had seemingly not been concluded at the time our author wrote, for he closes the incident by remarking, " But whether Currie will be subjected to the Pain of Death, or an arbitrary Punishment, I cannot say."

The absence of a special chronicler occasions a hiatus of twenty-one years in our record ; for there is but little reason to suppose that that period was unmarked by experiences similar to those immediately preceding and following it.

The next case of which we have details is that of Archibald Currie, a wright, who was tried, in 1747, by the Court of Session for forging notes of the Royal Bank, and, being remitted to the Justiciary Court, was, on his own petition, with consent of the Lord Advocate, ordered to be banished to the plantations, with certification that, if he return, he shall be whipped monthly till retrans-ported. Three years later, John Young, who had been " a serjeant in Col. Rich's foot " (as he is concisely designated), was executed in the Grassmarket, Edinburgh, for " forging and fabricating " notes of the same bank, and " uttering them as true." Some months afterwards a fellow-soldier and accomplice was allowed to elect banishment to New England, with the usual notice of the welcome which would await him should he give way to homesickness. He loved his country, however, not wisely but too well ; for we find that he was again apprehended in Edinburgh and duly whipped through that city.

There is record, without particulars, of " a precognition at Banff, in 1765, about a *vitiate Note* of the Dundee Bank." An advertisement regarding a forged note of the British Linen Company appeared that same year ; during which also there was a prosecution of a James Baillie, in Dundee, who was pilloried and transported for forging bank notes. The Thistle Bank notes appear to have been repeatedly forged ; for, in 1768, what is described as " another forgery " was discovered, for which offence Wm. Herries, Ayr, was taken up on suspicion, tried and hanged. Another man, John Raybould, was, at Edinburgh, also hanged for forging this bank's notes. Mr. Boase states that he had issued 452 £1 notes, and had in his possession 9677 more, which were burned after his trial. In 1774 both the Bank of Scotland and the British Linen Company advertised forgeries of their notes, and offered £100 rewards for discovery of the offenders. The subjects were the guinea and £1 plates respectively. Next year there was a curious case in London, when Thomas Bell was charged with intending to forge notes of the Bank of Scotland. It is said that he got paper made with the bank's watermark, and asked an engraver to print the notes. The latter, however, being as canny as the Scot, made a preliminary inquiry which stopped the game. The prisoner was, however, acquitted.

The Royal Bank guinea notes were forged in 1776 ; and, a few years later, the same denomination of the Bank of Scotland was similarly treated. For the latter crime, David Reid, merchant in Manchester, was arrested, and, after a prolonged trial in the Court of Session and High Court of Justiciary, in Edinburgh, found guilty. The execution took place in the Grassmarket, 13th September 1780, on which occasion he made a full confession, delivered a long and solemn warning to the crowd, and generally conducted himself in a manner which is stated to have been " decent and becoming in a very uncommon degree," concluding with particularly appropriate devotions.[1] Next year another forgery of the same bank's guinea notes was dealt with at the trial of a journeyman watchmaker from Falkirk, John Brown. The jury found it proven that he engraved the " brass plate," but not proven that he adhibited the subscriptions to, or issued any of the three notes produced. The judges " animadverted very severely on the verdict, but," pursues the recorder,[2] " the jury bore it with truly Christian patience."

We now come to a case in which one is apt to feel that the prisoner got more justice than mercy. The culprit, John Macafee, was an ignorant soldier of the 77th regiment, then quartered in Ireland, and appears to have become the tool of some Irish blackguards. He was apprehended at Campbeltown, in 1782, for passing four forged notes in imitation of a British Linen £1 plate of 13th May 1774, the date being altered to 1776. He confessed that he was employed by people in Ireland who professed to have successfully committed forgeries on several of the other banks in Scotland. What is specified as " a bundle " of the forged notes, which he had got a boy to secrete, was found. The paper was coarse and ill-coloured. " We have seen one of them," says the narrator,[3] " and do not think the Public run any risque of being deceived by them." Macafee was tried at the circuit court at Inveraray, before Lord Garden-

---

[1] *Caledonian Mercury*, 24th June to 13th September 1780.
[2] *Ibid.*, 10th, 12th, and 14th March 1781.   [3] *Ibid.*, 6th July 1782.

stone. The jury, by a majority, found him guilty of the forgery or being accessory to it (the former proposition was quite improbable) and, unanimously, of issuing the four notes ; which verdict the judge reported to the High Court at Edinburgh. After a careful consideration of his case, he was sentenced to be hanged ; and, six months after his capture, was executed in the Grassmarket, in a spirit of contrition and resignation.

A forgery of the 20s. note (2nd May 1781) of the Aberdeen Banking Company was discovered in 1783, the notes being uttered in Paisley.[1] In the following May a man named Steven, and his two sons, were tried at Glasgow for the crime. They escaped, however, owing to " a principal evidence " not having come from Ireland, while they were " running their letters " (the Scottish form of *habeas corpus*), which ran out the day after the trial. The father and the eldest son were, however, recommitted for theft.[2] The sequel to this incident is striking. The " principal evidence " was an accomplice, Thomas Moreton, who had decamped. He appears to have been murdered a year or two later, and one of the younger Stevens, Thomas, was hanged at Glasgow, in 1785, as the culprit. He persisted to the last in denying the crime. He walked to the place of execution dressed in black clothes, with " weepers " and a crape hat-band ; and his body was delivered to Professor Hamilton for dissection. This was the ninth execution in Glasgow within twelve months.

The guinea note of the Bank of Scotland was again the subject of forgery in 1784. It was dated 1st March 1780, and appears to have been a good imitation. But the paper was common, and there were several small differences from the original. The Bank offered a reward of one hundred guineas. Either the same or another forgery of this note appeared the next year.

---

[1] *Caledonian Mercury*, 15th November 1783.
[2] *Ibid* , 17th May 1784.

At this time there seems to have been much counterfeit copper in circulation, which occasioned a prevalent
refusal of halfpence, to the great inconvenience of the
poor. By an advertisement,[1] thirty Edinburgh merchants intimated their intention to accept all genuine
halfpence, but no larger payment than 5½d. in copper at
a time. Along with this appeared a supporting notice
by the magistrates. The Procurator Fiscal at the same
time warned persons refusing " halfpence of his present
Majesty's [George III.] coin " that they are bound to
receive such in payments up to the amount stated in
the statutes, and that they will be prosecuted for refusal.
Similar action was taken by the shop-keepers of Leith,
who had at first resolved to accept only the Old Scots
halfpence, King William's, and those of Kings George I.
and II. Notwithstanding all exertions, however, the
poorer people were so alarmed that they refused George
III. halfpence in payments or in change, and penalties
had to be repeatedly inflicted before the erroneous notion
that all these were bad could be removed.

In this year (1785) Neil M'Lean was executed at
Glasgow, in the Castle Yard, for uttering forged notes
of the Glasgow Arms Bank. We are told that " he
appeared penitent, and went to the place of execution
with great composure, but laboured under a miscon-
ception of the nature of his crime." What the mis-
conception was we are tantalisingly not informed ; but
if, as seems probable, M'Lean was an illiterate High-
lander, he might not understand the Sassenach's meta-
physical distinction between good and spurious pieces
of printed paper ; and perhaps felt that a less severe
penalty might have sufficed.

Another imitation of the British Linen Company's
£1 note, dated 2nd August 1781, and another of their
guinea note dated 1st August 1683 [sic, but presumably

---

[1] *Caledonian Mercury*, 23rd February 1785. For further particulars
see *Scots Magazine*, 1789, pp. 202 and 256.

meant for 1783], appeared later in the year. " They were both wholly done with a pen, and written on common paper, whereas the real notes, except the number and names, are all copper-plate impressions printed on the Company's own paper bearing the water-mark *British Linen Co.* on the £1 notes, and *B. Linen Co.* on the guinea note." The usual reward, one hundred guineas, was offered, but we hear of no result.

A somewhat serious forgery of another kind was discovered about this time in Edinburgh. Thomas Mercer, a writer, got three bills of £200 each discounted, one at the Bank of Scotland, another at the Royal Bank, and the third at Forbes' Bank ; all of which were subsequently found to have been forged by Mercer.

Hunters & Co., Ayr, advertised a forgery of their guinea note in 1789. " The note is dated 1st August 1781, the written figures in the date and number were very ill done, the features of the impression of the king's head are very unlike the original ; it is printed on thinner and coarser paper, of a bluish colour, and without any water-mark, by which it is easily distinguished from the real notes of the Company." [1] The usual reward seems to have failed to discover the authors.

Earlier in the year a forgery of Bank of Scotland notes came to light. Thomas Watling, a painter or limner in Dumfries, was accused of the crime. Probably dreading the death penalty he petitioned for transportation, to which fate he was sentenced for fourteen years under certification of whipping and retransportation in case of return before the expiry of the period.[2] About the same time Daniel Aldridge, alias Baldridge, a tailor, was, at Glasgow, banished for life for coining or counterfeiting current coin of the realm.[2]

An unsatisfactory case also occurred in this year. At a fair in Kilmarnock a countryman sold his horse,

---

[1] *Caledonian Mercury*, 19th January 1789.
[2] *Scots Magazine*, 1789, p. 255.

and when he was to receive payment he objected to the most part of the notes offered. The purchaser, thus challenged, stept to the door, and did not return. The notes, which purported to be the guinea issue of the Paisley Bank, proved to be forgeries. John Brown, a farmer in Ayrshire, being suspected of the offence, was committed to jail ; but there seems to have been some doubt of his identity with the impostor. He was, however, sentenced to be hanged at Glasgow, which fate he met with great firmness and devout behaviour.[1]

Early in 1790, William Robertson was tried for forgery, or uttering knowingly a guinea note of the Bank of Scotland, and attempting to utter another. He pleaded guilty, and, as a mitigated punishment, owing to his confession, was sentenced to be " banished beyond the seas for fourteen years, and to suffer death without benefit of clergy, in case of his returning before the lapse of that time." Whether the sentence was carried out or not is uncertain, for it appears that he had to be sent to the Royal Infirmary, where the death with which he was threatened may have overtaken him, in which case let us hope that he was afforded all the consolations that man can permit or withhold.

Forged guinea notes of the Glasgow Arms Bank appeared about this time. They were dated 1st April 1784. The paper was of a coarser quality than the genuine, of softer texture, with a bluish cast in the colour. The ink was brownish, and there were other defects. For this crime Wm. Carsewell was tried. A somewhat exceptional case was that of Millesius Roderick McCuillen, who was tried in 1797 for forging guinea notes of the Paisley Bank. He is described as not twenty-four years old, and evincing the manners of a gentleman. He made an unsuccessful attempt to escape, and tried twice to poison himself. He was found guilty and, on 6th December, hanged at the west end of the Tolbooth,

[1] *Caledonian Mercury*, 19th November 1789. *Courant*, 3rd May 1790.

Edinburgh. His name appears to have been assumed, but he refused to reveal his true one. He showed great composure at the execution.[1] In 1798, a number of notes purporting to be guinea notes of " The Company of the Bank of Aberdeen," a company which had no existence, were in circulation. By this artifice the accusation of forgery was avoided ; but, of course, it was a case of wilful imposition. As, however, the ingenious culprits were clever enough to preserve their incognito, the courts had no opportunity of discussing the interesting questions connected with their action.

A rather absurd case is recorded by Mr. Boase. " On 25th August 1800, a forgery of the 5s. notes of the Dundee Commercial Bank, all executed with a pen, by one James Martin, was discovered. On the bank applying to the Procurator-Fiscal to prosecute him, the answer was that the prosecution of such offenders was always left to the banks themselves. This the bank declined, on the ground that only eight notes had appeared, and these so badly done, that no person familiar with the genuine notes could be deceived by them." Royal Bank notes seem to have been forged in June 1800. Robert Barr, " late of Lanark," was accused of the crime, but discharged on a verdict of not proven.[2] On 3rd September of this year Samuel Bell was hanged for forgery of Ship Bank notes.[3]

The annoyance caused by so many forgeries led to " an agreement being entered into by the Bank of Scotland and the Royal Bank that if forgeries were attempted upon the notes of either of them, the trials should be carried on at the joint-expense of both these banks, and it is said they determined to let no offender pass against whom they could bring proof." [4] Forgeries of the guinea notes of both the Renfrewshire Bank and the Commercial Bank appeared in 1822 ; and the Dundee Union

---

[1] *Scots Magazine*, 1797, p. 928.
[2] *Ibid.*, 1800, p. 373.
[3] *Ibid.*, 1800, p. 496.
[4] *Ibid.*, 1800, p. 574.

Bank's £1 notes were forged in 1824 ; but no particulars are supplied regarding these cases.

A specimen in the author's possession shows a well-executed forgery of the Royal Bank £1 issue dated 1st December 1823. The heavy engraving is fairly good, but the lighter work is imperfect. The bank's seal is represented with considerable minuteness ; and the signatures, written date, and numbers are good and natural. The paper, however, is hard, unlike what is used for bank notes, and does not show a watermark. This must have been a dangerous fraud, likely to impose readily on the public. Perhaps owing to this incident, we find a genuine note of 9th May 1832 of a totally different design ; while one of 9th November of that year again shows a change to what, in general aspect, is similar to the current issues ; the principal differences being that the custom of stating the amount in the body as " Twenty Shillings " was still continued, and the printing had not yet been changed to colour.

There were many other forgeries, some of which were audacious and well executed, during the nineteenth century ; but we must rest content meantime with having dealt thus fully with what may be called the mediæval period of Scottish banking.

CHAPTER XII

THE CRISES OF 1793 AND 1797

THE Treaty of Paris, concluded between Britain, France, and Spain, in January 1783, inaugurated a period of ten years' peace. This was abruptly and terribly ended by the great French Revolution, which appears to have been only the most hideous manifestation of an almost world-wide disturbance in all departments of the civilised economy. Great changes had taken place in men's views; and with the progress of knowledge, and the increase of wealth, there spread a desire for liberty which rapidly developed into license. Comparatively isolated as Scotland was, it reflected in a marked degree the tendencies of the time. The rude and simple-living Scot had become luxurious as his wealth increased; and the vices of advanced civilisation manifested themselves in a corresponding ratio. This was particularly the case in Edinburgh, which had always been far ahead of the rest of Scotland. The city had spread out its borders to a large extent; and with the exodus of the higher classes from their pent-up alleys and courts to the spacious streets and squares of the New Town, a complete change occurred in the manners and customs of the citizens. Scotland, like the rest of the European nations, had awakened to a sense of its inherent power. It cannot occasion wonder that this social revolution was accompanied by excesses; and it is matter for congratulation, that the natural good sense of the people kept them within comparatively moderate bounds.

In Chapter X. we traced the rapid development of banking in Scotland, which accompanied this progress of the nation in material prosperity. It remains for us on the present occasion to bring down our narrative to the close of the century, which terminated with the consolidation of the empire as the United Kingdom of Great Britain and Ireland.

In 1783, simultaneously with a large increase in their capital, the Royal Bank (who had refused in 1780 a proposal to open a branch in Paisley) for the first time departed from their policy of confining their operations to the Metropolis, by opening an office in Glasgow. It would appear, however, that this desirable and too long delayed operation was performed in a very humble manner. According to an interesting record of banking events in Glasgow, " their first office was on the one side of a small shop in ' Hopkirk's Land,' east side of High Street, five doors north from the corner at the Cross. Their agent carried on his ordinary business of a linen-draper on the other side of the shop. The rent paid by the bank was £2 : 10s. annually. The agent had been originally a herdboy, afterwards a weaver in Paisley, Hamilton, and Cambuslang, thereafter a clerk to a silk-mercer in Glasgow, and at the time the bank employed him, he was, as already said, a linen-draper on his own account." [1] If this account of the commencement of their direct connection with Glasgow be correct, it is evident that they had no great faith in its success. Their subsequent policy in regard to branch extension shows a strict adherence to conservative views. It was not until the collapse of the Western Bank, in 1857, that they adopted in earnest the theory of a branch system.

[1] *Banking in Glasgow during the Olden Time*, Glasgow, 1862, p. 23, note. Also 2nd edition, 1884, p. 15. His name, it is elsewhere stated, was Dale, and it seems that he had prospered beyond the loom by the time he lived in Cambuslang.

With the exception of a slight panic which seized the depositors with private bankers in Edinburgh in 1788—a consequence of several severe failures among corn merchants and distillers, with whom they were involved—few incidents of importance fall to be considered until the year 1793. The private banking house of Seton, Wallace & Co. was established in Edinburgh in 1791. It does not seem to have existed for more than fifteen years, as the firm is not mentioned after 1805 ; probably owing to the death of Mr. Alex. Wallace on 12th June 1804. The firm of Robert Anderson & Co. appear as bankers in the Edinburgh Directory of 1796–97 with address " opposite Luckenbooths."

Bank stock seems to have commanded a high price at this time, as it is recorded in 1792, that " three shares of the capital stock of the Bank of Scotland, with the benefit of the new subscription, were sold at £740, which is £246 : 13 : 4 a share. Besides this, the purchaser pays the auction duty, which makes it above £254 for each original share of £1000 Scots, or £83 : 6 : 8 sterling." About the same time the new stock of the Royal Bank sold at £240 per cent.

The rapid advance of the country in industrial projects, to which we have already referred, seems to have proceeded with more activity than discretion. The political disturbances in connection with the French Revolution, and the renewal of hostilities with France, gave a severe shake to the unduly extended system of credit. Numerous bankruptcies occurred throughout the country. These told heavily on the banks. This was more particularly the case in Glasgow, where the crisis led to the failure of the Glasgow Arms Bank (Murdoch, Robertson & Co.), the Merchant Bank of Glasgow, and the house of Andrew, George, & Andrew Thomson, which had been formed in 1785. The former bank stopped payment on 14th March, with liabilities to the extent of £183,000. These were eventually met in full without interest. The failure of the Messrs. Thomson did not take place until 5th November. Their debts, which are stated at £64,564 by one authority, and at £47,000 by another, were ultimately paid in full.

The private bankers in Edinburgh were greatly pressed for money. Sir William Forbes says : " The check to circulation, and the consequent demands for money, began to be felt by us, as well as by our neighbours, very early in the year 1793, and rose to such an alarming height as put the demands on the house that took place in the year 1788 totally out of remembrance." After referring to the failure of the Glasgow Arms Bank, and to the bankruptcy of " James Dunlop, of Glasgow, who was supposed to be one of the most opulent and cautious men of business in the West," he proceeds to state that " on the 23rd April, the house of Bertram, Gardner & Co., of Edinburgh, also stopped payment, and to complete the confusion, the four banks of New-castle, which were known to be opulent, were forced to shut up on the 12th April, owing to their not having had the precaution to keep in readiness sufficient funds to meet the demands that were made upon them. Their stoppage was accompanied by that of a great many country banks in England." Sir William is, doubtless, correct in giving 23rd April as the date of the stoppage of Bertram, Gardner & Co., but it is somewhat curious that their actual bankruptcy did not occur until 10th December following. Their creditors had granted a " deed of *supersedere*," under which, " followed by a very liberal subscription of guarantee in aid of the funds of the house," and the direction of a committee, they continued to conduct their business.[1] Sanguine expectations were, however, disappointed ; for the firm failed again on 10th November, and were made bankrupt a month later. They were the only bankers in Edin-

---

[1] *Courant*, 2nd May 1793. It is probable that the Merchant Bank of Glasgow also ceased at or about this time.

burgh who succumbed at this crisis. Their liabilities were about £145,000, of which their estates liquidated 17s. 6d. per pound. The provincial bankers seem to have all stood this trial.

An interesting project, which unfortunately proved abortive, was formed about this time, for the establishment of a new bank at Glasgow. Recognising the superiority of corporate banks over banking companies, its promoters proposed that it should be erected under Act of Parliament. It was to have been modelled on the constitution of the Bank of England ; but, had it been formed, it would probably have more nearly resembled the two Edinburgh banks. On 12th June 1793, just when financial affairs were assuming a more satisfactory character, a meeting was held in Glasgow to consider the proposal. The decision appears to have been favourable, and steps were taken to carry out the project. But, whether from want of sufficient support, or on account of the unfavourable condition of commercial affairs in the West of Scotland, or refusal of Government recognition, or other impediment, the scheme fell through. This gives cause for some regret, for had the Glasgow Royal Bank—for so it was to have been styled—been actually established on the high-class footing which was sketched out, there is reason to believe that it might have been very successful, not only in a financial sense, but as fostering legitimate trade, and imparting a high tone to banking in the West of Scotland. It might have done much to mitigate, if not to avert, the consequences of the recklessness and speculativeness which have always been too characteristic of banking as conducted in Glasgow, more especially, but also elsewhere, by banking companies dominated by the mercantile spirit. Nearly, we might almost say absolutely, all the banking disasters in Scotland can be clearly traced to too intimate a connection between the management of banks and the mercantile section of the community. Such a bank as was here designed would have been sufficiently independent.

The continuance of the war with France and the dread of invasion were the immediate causes of another crisis in 1797. This was a more general disturbance than that we have just referred to.[1] A continuous and heavy drain of gold to meet expenditure abroad, and loans to foreign allies, had exhausted the bullion reserve of the Bank of England, and curtailed the metallic circulation throughout the country. The wants of the community led to extensive issues of local coins, tokens, and notes for small payments. Year by year the withdrawal of coin from the country had grown worse, prices had risen excessively, and at last the Bank of England was brought within a few days of stopping payment. Roused to action by the representations, often repeated, of the Bank Board, the Privy Council, on 26th of February, directed the Bank of England to suspend payment in specie. On the following day, in accordance with this order, the Bank Directors issued a circular declaring " the affluent and prosperous situation of the general concerns of the Bank," and stating that they would continue " their usual discounts for the accommodation of the commercial interest, paying the amount in bank notes." The suspension of specie payments was confirmed by Parliament, and lasted until 1821.

The news of this important event arrived in Edinburgh on the 1st March, by an express sent to the Bank of Scotland. The demands on all the banks in Edinburgh for specie were continually pressing ; but they had hitherto maintained their ability to meet them. Now that access to the ultimate bullion reserve had been cut off, however, it was imperative that they should protect themselves by immediate action of an unusual kind.

---

[1] It was not, however, in the so-called " decennial " series. That occurred four years earlier—1793 being in the true periodical rotation. The present was a currency crisis.

Sir William Forbes supplies a graphic and interesting account of the proceedings which took place. It was generally believed that " the nation was ruined beyond redemption." The public banks and private bankers met, and consulted with one another, " for all ceremony and etiquette of public or private banks was now out of the question, when it had become necessary to think of what was to be done for our joint preservation on such an emergency." It was resolved to follow the example of the Bank of England by suspending all payments in specie. The local authorities supported this resolution, and information of the fact was sent throughout the country. Sir William adds that " the instant this resolution of paying no more specie was known in the street, a scene of confusion and uproar took place, of which it is utterly impossible for those who did not witness it to form an idea."

Another contemporary account states that, " in consequence of the measures adopted by the banks, of refusing to give out specie for notes, resolutions have been entered into by a great number of gentlemen to receive bank notes in all payments ; for this purpose, subscription papers lay open for several days in the Merchants' Hall. There seems little doubt that the great scarcity of specie in this part of the island is occasioned by the fear of an invasion, operating too powerfully on the ignorant and desponding part of the community. The responsibility of the Banks, joined to a renewal of confidence, from a short trial, will, we doubt not, set all to right very soon. While individuals hoard up, and deprive the banks of their usual supplies, it cannot be expected that they should exchange in their usual way. A little more liberality, in giving small sums to such as they know, we think would be right and proper." [1]

One of the most distressing features of the situation was the want of small currency. For sums of £1 and

[1] *Scots Magazine*, 1797, p. 212.

upward the bank notes were still available, but for smaller sums there was no medium of payment. The commonalty, and indeed the whole community, were thereby placed in a most painful situation. Tradesmen could not pay wages, and small purchases could not be made. People resorted to the expedient of tearing £1 notes into halves and quarters, a practice which appears to have been tacitly recognised by the banks. Eventually an Act was passed to permit banks to issue notes of less than 20s. value for a limited period. Under the provisions of this Act, the Bank of Scotland, Royal Bank of Scotland, and British Linen Company (who are specifically mentioned), and all other banks or banking companies in Scotland, in operation, and issuing notes on or before 1st March 1797, but no other persons, were empowered to " issue notes, bills, or tickets, in the nature of bank-notes, payable to the bearer on demand, for any sum whatever, under the sum of 20s. sterling." The banks were indemnified for having so issued before the passing of the Act ; but the powers of issue conferred by the Act were to cease on 15th May following. By a subsequent Act the latter provision was extended to 5th July 1799. In accordance with the powers thus given, the three old banks, and probably many of the other banks, made an issue of 5s. notes, and the excitement gradually subsided. It does not appear that any other denomination of fractional notes was issued. Indeed, it is probable that the banks were reluctant to do more in this matter than was absolutely required in the public interest. For, while the expense of making these notes would be as great as for larger denominations, the profit from them would be proportionally smaller.

The action of the Scotch bankers in suspending payment in specie was, of course, quite illegal, and any creditor could have prosecuted his claim for payment in legal tender. The authority granted, or rather the order given, to the Bank of England did not extend to other bankers. It is noticeable, however, that notwithstanding the public excitement which ensued on the promulgation of the resolution, no attempt was made to enforce claims by appeal to the law courts. It would appear, moreover, that while the notes of the Bank of England fell to a discount, the Scotch circulation always maintained its par value. In fact, after the first excitement had worn off, the public accepted the notes of the banks in an inconvertible form as readily as they had formerly done when they were exchangeable for specie on demand. Such a circumstance would be impossible now ; and rightly so, for an inconvertible note is essentially an abomination. But it was not ignorance on the part of the public that tided the banks over this dangerous epoch. It was that spirit of true national patriotism which, relying with confidence on the solidity of the banks, recognised that the action of the latter was occasioned by a common emergency, and called for the support and not for the opposition of their creditors. We now live under more selfish, if more logical conditions ; but to the repeated forbearance of our ancestors in regard to the conduct of the Scotch banks, and to their sometimes overtaxed confidence in their respectability, Scotland owes no small part of its subsequent prosperity. Had our forefathers overturned the banking system whenever it went a little agee, the industrial life of the nation would have been subjected to repeated paralytic strokes, which would have dwarfed and stunted the national growth.

It would seem that up to this period the impression of the duty stamps on bank notes, newspapers, etc., had to be performed in London ; for it is stated that, in September 1785, there was an agitation to have arrangements made for carrying out that part of revenue work in Edinburgh instead of requiring papers to be sent to London. The agitation was renewed in 1805, and some time before 1812 the Edinburgh Stamp Office seems to have been authorised to impress. At least this may be inferred from the narrative of an unsuccessful attempt then made to exact new license dues on changes of partners in banking companies.

It may be interesting to note how the various Edinburgh banking offices were grouped at this time, *circa* 1796. The Bank of Scotland was located at the middle of the Lawnmarket (properly Inland Market), on the south side, about the present Melbourne Place, where their elaborate safe arrangements were still in evidence some years ago. The Royal Bank was in the High Street, opposite the Mercat Cross, in the close that still runs beside the Police Office. The British Linen Company were in Tweeddale's Court, Canongate. Robert Allan was in the High Street, as also were Alexander Allan & Co. Robert Anderson & Co. were near St. Giles' Church, on the north side of the street. Sir William Forbes & Co. were in Parliament Close, while congregated together in the Royal Exchange were Thomas Kinnear & Sons ; Mansfield, Ramsay & Co. ; Scott, Smith, Stein & Co. ; Seton, Wallace & Co. ; and Donald Smith & Co. Subsequently the Bank of Scotland built a new office on their present site which is incorporated in the great pile which constitutes a dominating object in the city ; the Royal Bank migrated to Mr. Crosbie's house [1] in St. Andrew Square until they acquired, in 1820, the old Excise Office next door (a handsome Italian villa designed by Sir William Chambers for Sir Lawrence Dundas), where they still are ; and the British Linen Company later built their present fine office in the same square.

[1] Now the Head Office of the Scottish Union and National Insurance Company.

CHAPTER XIII

CONFLICT OF JOINT-STOCK AND PRIVATE BANKING—
THE COMMERCIAL BANK OF SCOTLAND

On the first day of the first year of the last century, the United Kingdom of Great Britain and Ireland commenced its career as a consolidated constitutional empire. But, notwithstanding this great step towards peace and civilisation, there succeeded a period of fifteen years, during which the nation was engaged in exhaustive warfare with most of the nations of Europe, with the United States of America, with the native princes of India, and with the colonies and dependencies of European nations in various parts of the world. France, Russia, Denmark, Sweden, Spain, Turkey, and the United States, were all grappled with severally or in combinations. But this does not indicate the total difficulties of the country. Trade, as was natural in such circumstances, was depressed and almost paralysed; Ireland was openly disaffected; great distress existed among the working classes; and, in England and Scotland, the corn-laws were made the occasion of serious and widespread disturbances and riots. Taxation was oppressive, and yet so insufficient to meet expenditure, that the national debt was increased to the extent of about £200,000,000. The French War, lasting practically from 1793 to 1815, is estimated to have cost Great Britain £1,427,219,964. These events culminated in 1815, when the power of Napoleon was finally shattered, and the commercial equilibrium was re-established after the throes of a crisis which, if not of the first magnitude, was widespread in its incidence.

The period was not, however, destitute of important features of a favourable character. If industry was depressed, the means for its improvement and extension were considerably developed. Mechanical science continued to advance; so much so, indeed, that the supersession of manual labour by machinery occasioned, in the unfavourable state of the country, a bitter opposition by the working classes, who imagined that their means of livelihood were being taken from them, and led to serious outbreaks of popular fury. In 1812, moreover, steam navigation was inaugurated by the success of Bell's *Comet* on the Clyde. Thus, in a period of deepest gloom, one of the most potent factors in the development of commerce and the advancement of civilisation was placed at the service of mankind.

The crisis which closed the period which may be considered to have commenced about the middle of 1797 appears to have been a gradual one, extending from 1810 for about five years. It fell with great severity on the English country bankers—141 provincial banking houses being reported as having succumbed. This was doubtless due in great measure to the unfortunate state of banking legislation, which fostered a plurality of small firms, and prohibited the formation of large joint-stock banks. Scotland did not suffer to the same extent as England, owing to its comparatively backward condition giving scope for its industries within its own borders.

As regards banking, this period was one of much activity. At least sixteen new banks were started; and the Bank of Scotland and the Royal Bank both obtained power to increase their capitals to one million and a half. Of the new banks, which date from 1802, the most important is the Fife Banking Company, who commenced with a capital of £30,000, and after a career of a quarter of a century, collapsed in 1829, through mismanagement and dishonesty, entailing total loss, and liability for £5500 per share, on the partners. Another bankrupt born in this year was the Renfrewshire Banking Company. They managed, however, to pull on for forty years, when they made a disgraceful failure. The Cupar Banking Company was also formed in 1802, and is said to have retired from business nine years later ; but the dissolution of copartnership did not take place until 1820. The Falkirk Union Banking Company was another unfortunate venture. Established in 1803, with a capital of £12,000, held by fourteen partners, it existed for thirteen years, and was sequestrated on 18th October 1816. The liabilities were about £60,000. Malachi Malagrowther cites it as one of the few instances of bank failures in Scotland, and states that it " paid up its engagements without much loss to its creditors." Another authority, however, states the deficiency at 10s. 6d. per pound.

John Wardrop & Co. began business in Edinburgh in or shortly before this year, and dropped out of sight some twenty years later. The principal, perhaps sole, partner was John Wardrop of Sharpsbanks, whose marriage is recorded in the *Scots Magazine* for 1808, p. 878. At this time the affairs of the Dundee Commercial Bank having got into gross disorder, the business was reorganised as the Dundee New Bank, on 14th January 1802, with a capital of £58,000, in shares of £2000 each, of which one-tenth was paid up. It does not seem to have been a satisfactory concern during its earlier years. Its business was purchased by the Dundee Banking Company in 1838. We should also mention David Paterson of Costerton, who at this time commenced a ten years' banking career in Edinburgh, which ended in sequestration in 1813. He appears to have had thirteen years' training in the Kinnears' office when, on 5th January 1782, he commenced business as an insurance broker in the Old Assembly Close. He must soon have removed, for in 1785 his office address is given as Milne Square, where it seems to have continued. In 1796 his house address was 5 St. Andrew Street. He began the banking business about 1803 or 1804, but it only lasted till 1813, when he failed with liabilities of £118,047 : 6 : 2 and assets of about £90,000 which yielded a dividend of about 14s. per pound. The liquidation was protracted, as in February 1824 a dividend was announced. The Kilmarnock Banking Company, which was established 10th June 1802, continued till October 1821, when it was absorbed by Hunters & Co., Ayr. The house suffered from a forgery which is recorded as unimportant in the *Scots Magazine* of 21st March 1808.

This rapid extension of banking naturally occasioned anxiety to the Edinburgh banks, who, in order to check it, intimated that they would not receive the notes of any new country banks that might be established. Either as the result of this opposition, or more probably from the circumstances of the country, the growth of new banks was somewhat restricted for several years subsequently. With the exception of a wretched attempt at Dumfries, where James Grace, with the assistance of his son and another partner, started the Dumfries Commercial Bank in 1804, only to succumb four years later with a deficiency of 10s. per pound, and of the firm of Belsh & Co. who commenced business in Stirling, in 1804, but failed two years later, only two banking houses, and those not of great importance, were established up till 1809. These were Inglis, Borthwick, Gilchrist & Co., in Edinburgh ; and the Galloway Banking Co. of Douglas, Napier & Co. The former firm began business in 1805, and continued for ten years, when, on the death of Archibald Borthwick, 13th July 1815, it became James Inglis & Co., who failed in 1834, with liabilities amounting to £23,000. The Galloway Banking Company, established in the following year at Castle-Douglas, was a more important firm ; but it had a career of only fifteen years, when it withdrew from business. The banking mania now broke out afresh. In 1809 the Dundee Union Banking Company and the Glasgow Banking Company were started. The former, which subsequently amalgamated with the Western Bank, appears to have been somewhat energetic in the establishment of branches—for, not content with eight offices in the immediate neighbourhood of Dundee, it is recorded that the experiment of a branch in London was made, though without success. It had a nominal capital of £100,000, of which £60,000 was paid up. It was absorbed by the Western Bank on 31st March 1844. The Glasgow Bank was an offshoot of the Dundee New Bank, and started with a fully paid capital of £100,000. It afterwards joined the Ship Bank as the Glasgow and Ship Bank, and the conjoined business was, in 1838, merged in that large collection of banking companies, the Union Bank of Scotland.

The Glasgow Commercial Bank was established in 1810, but it does not seem ever to have risen into much notice, and it ceased to do business in 1820. A more noteworthy production of the same year was the East Lothian Banking Company, whose head office was at Dunbar. It had a capital of £80,000, in 400 shares of £200 each. Malachi Malagrowther speaks of it as a company " whose affairs had been very ill-conducted by a villanous manager." This model banker was William Borthwick, the cashier, whose career forms quite a romance of crime. The bank stopped payment in 1822, with liabilities amounting to £129,191 : 16 : 7, which were subsequently met in full.

The Perth Union Banking Company was also established in 1810. In 1821 it had branches at Dunkeld, Coupar-Angus, and Alloa. It amalgamated with the National Bank of Scotland in 1836. In 1812, the Caithness Banking Company was formed at Wick, as a private partnership. They are said to have been the only

Scottish bank who had no agents in Edinburgh.[1] The anonymous author adds, " their circulation, though in excellent credit, is consequently local." The firm got into difficulties in 1825, and the business was taken up by the Commercial Bank of Scotland. Another provincial bank was the Montrose Banking Company, established in May 1814, with a capital of £15,000 in £100 shares. It was merged in the Dundee Union Bank in 1829. The private firm of Thomsons & Co. was established in Edinburgh in 1811, but it is probable that they may more properly be classed as financial agents than as bankers. If they were actually bankers their career, as such, would seem to date from the year mentioned, when they took up lottery business. But, as James Thomson & Sons, they appear in 1793, becoming Thomsons & Co. in 1811, and Thomson, Pollock & Rhind in 1815. After 1820 they drop out of the Edinburgh Directory.

By far the most important banking establishment which came into existence at this time was the Commercial Banking Company of Scotland. It was formed in November 1810, and was on the joint-stock principle, although not incorporated until some years later.[2] It has been remarked that it was the first bank not established by public authority which assumed the national designation implied in the addition to its name proper— a practice which has been followed to a large extent since. It was not long, however, in justifying its adoption of the designation, for it speedily spread itself over the land with much spirit and success. Its comparatively large capital—£3,000,000 nominal, divided into 6000 shares of £500 each, of which £2,250,000, with £450,000 paid up, was issued at first—enabled it to do this with ease. From the outset, it appears to have been designed on a large-minded plan, and to have met a decided want.

[1] *Review of the Banking System of Britain*, p. 55.
[2] For some interesting details regarding the origin of this bank see *Some Edinburgh Shops*, Josiah Livingstone, Edin. 1894, p. 64 *et seq.*

The old chartered banks were not then, as now, banks of the general public. Their business was for the most part among capitalists—small, doubtless, as well as large, but who, as financiers, were distinct from the body of the people. They occupied, to a considerable extent, a position similar, though of course on a much smaller scale, to that at present held by the Bank of England. They did, doubtless, as occasion offered, deal directly with the general public; but the practice then was, for private individuals to transact their business with private bankers. The private Edinburgh firms were each in close—sometimes, as we shall presently see, too close—connection with one or other of the old banks. This arrangement had sprung up at a very early period, and had been always continued. It saved the banks both from danger and from trouble; for the middlemen managed all the details of small deposits and discounts, and assisted in extending the circulation; and it paid the private bankers (who were very like the modern bill discounters), for they exacted heavier terms from their clients than they were charged by the banks.

The connection between the Bank of Scotland and the Royal Bank on the one hand, and their respective sets of banking customers on the other hand, became more and more intimate, until partners of private banking firms not only got seats on the bank boards, but actually to a large extent controlled the proceedings of the latter. Business men then began to find it irksome to have to pass their business through the strait gate of the private bank, where toll had to be paid, as the only practical way of obtaining the benefit of the public banks' accommodation; for they believed, rightly or wrongly, that the private banker would refuse at the board meeting to approve of paper which he would readily discount in his own office. It was one great feature of the Commercial Bank to counteract this state of matters; and accordingly it was made a rule of their constitution that no private banker could hold the office of director. This was practically the death-blow to private banking in Edinburgh; for, although many firms continued to exist for years afterwards, the system was ever on the wane.

The new establishment was very popular, but it was also very discreet; for while it studied the best interests of the public, it imitated the wisest provisions of the old banks' practice. In short, the founders of the Commercial Bank evinced an amount of true wisdom, which, while it produced great advantage to themselves, was at the same time largely beneficial to the general community. It must not be supposed, however, that the new bank at once sprang into the position of a compeer of the old banks. It commenced on a scale much inferior to their resources, and although it had public favour, it was destitute of the prestige and influence, and accumulated wealth, which placed the old banks in those days on a distinctly elevated platform.

Another circumstance which aided the progress of the Commercial Bank was the practice of speculating in the Government funds—which in the depressed state of the country fell to a very low price—indulged in by the old banks. This was a very safe kind of speculation for persons who could afford to lie out of their money for an indefinite time; as, with a declaration of peace, Government securities were sure to rise in value. But the banks were accused of yielding to the temptation to such an extent as to seriously neglect their duties towards trade. The Commercial Bank got credit for devoting due attention to this matter. There is good reason for believing that the competition of this bank had a good influence in bringing the old banks into more direct contact with the public, and in breaking down their rather selfish ideas of aggrandisement. They had relegated into the hands of private bankers, to an undue extent, those duties to the community which they were erected for the purpose of performing, and were devoting their attention mainly to their own pecuniary interests. From this golden trance they were aroused by the advent of the Commercial Bank. It may have been partly owing to this circumstance that the rate of interest on deposit receipts was raised from 3 per cent to 4 per cent at this time.

The estimation in which the Commercial Bank was held during its earlier years is amusingly shown by a paragraph in a tract [1] dealing with the joint-stock excitement which culminated in 1825, in which the writer says : " In our own city [Edinburgh], every one admits that all the old chartered banks and private banking companies are just as liberal as any reasonable man could wish, and even the Commercial stripling, which, like all young folks, should at least not be rash, has never yet been accused of a close or niggardly spirit. On the contrary, Firebrass himself told me that he had never heard a single complaint uttered against that bank, excepting one,—and that was for keeping a huge mastiff somewhere about their premises, which, with its vehement nocturnal howlings, broke in upon the balmy slumbers of all the hypochondriacal nymphs and nervous sootbrokers in the neighbourhood."

Lord Cockburn is even more complimentary to the new bank, but not so complaisant to the chartered banks : " The rise of the Commercial Bank marks the growth of the public mind. . . . No men were more devoid of public spirit, and even of the proper spirit of their trade, than our old Edinburgh bankers. Respectable men they were, but without talent, general knowledge, or any liberal objects, they were the conspicuous sycophants of existing power. . . . They all combined banking with politics. . . . A demand for a bank founded on more liberal principles was the

---

[1] *Three Letters on the Speculative Schemes of the Present Times, and the Projected Banks.* Anthony Romney. Edinburgh, 1825.

natural result of this state of things. Hence the origin of the Commercial, professing to be the bank of the citizens." [1]

The Merchant Bank of Stirling failed in 1813 with liabilities of £50,140. The redoubtable Malagrowther states that it never was in high credit, having been known almost from its commencement by the ominous nickname of Black in the West. But, for such a dark character, its outcome was not so bad as that of some banks which were better spoken of. Notwithstanding specially heavy liquidation expenses, dividends of at least 14s. 9d. per pound were paid, and it is probable that by 1820, when the final payment was made, the total was somewhat more. [2]

The relationship which existed between the chartered banks and the private bankers in Edinburgh is graphically illustrated by an incident which occurred early in the year 1816. This was a rupture between the Royal Bank and the private house of Messrs. Ramsays, Bonars & Co., who had for many years been their principal auxiliaries (although previously clients of the Bank of Scotland), two of the partners of the firm being at the time directors of the bank. It appears from the printed documents which were issued during the course of the dispute, that the majority of the directors accused the firm of unadvisedly availing themselves of their long and intimate connection with the bank to obtain, without proper authority, large advances. There never was any question as to the sufficiency of the security, but the irregular manner in which the loans had been obtained, and a supposition that the firm were endeavouring to increase their already considerable influence in the direction of the bank's affairs, were made the basis of an appeal to the proprietors by the board. In their defence the firm

[1] *Memorials of His Own Times*, Edinburgh, 1856, pp. 252-3.
[2] Both John Reid and Boase say that 20s. per pound was paid, and they are good authorities.

state that " the account current of our house with the Royal Bank rests on much stronger grounds than the form of applying for a credit, and obtaining it at any recent date from a board of directors. It rests on the best understanding and usage of near half a century, grounded on the close connection of having been of the greatest mutual advantage to each other for the last thirty-four years. . . . Mr. Ramsay, the senior partner of our house, . . . devoted his whole attention to the concerns of the Royal Bank, and placed it in a train of management that has produced greater prosperity than, we believe, ever attended any chartered company in the same period [1781 – 1807]—not excepting even the Bank of England — in proportion to their respective capitals."

An important point in connection with this matter is, that the money so obtained was understood to be employed in purchasing Government stocks at a low price, with the object of realising them at an enhanced figure. Thus the money was not used for banking purposes. The directors do not seem to have disapproved of this practice in itself, but to have considered that it would have been more advantageous for the bank if the money had been so invested directly for behoof of the bank. In fact, they considered that the firm were diverting to themselves a profit which the bank would have obtained, had they been aware that Messrs. Ramsays, Bonars & Co. were operating on their account to so large an extent. For they were fully aware of the profitableness of this style of investment, and habitually availed themselves of it. It would seem that the firm had acquired, and held for years, a controlling influence in the direction which was prejudicial to the independent and safe management of the bank. One writer on the subject refers to it as " the thraldom under which the bank has long languished," and points out that the then market price of the stock—185 per cent—was much below the figure twenty-eight years before.[1] This latter circumstance he attributes to the exercise of the firm's influence in availing themselves of the use of the bank's funds to an excessive extent; and he asserted that the previous prosperity of the bank, referred to by Messrs. Ramsays, Bonars & Co., was principally due to the improved circumstances of the country.

It is evident that such a relationship between banks and their customers is fraught with much danger; but there can be no doubt that the above-narrated incident was the outcome of a long-established and not intentionally evil system peculiar to banking in Edinburgh. Its exposure at this time, and the competition of new joint-stock banks, effected a cure. This result, however, was attended with the rapid decay of private banking. Indeed, it was only in Edinburgh that private banking, pure and simple, was still in active operation. Of course, all the banking companies, other than the incorporated banks, were merely partnerships; but, from the least to the greatest, they were more and more assuming the appearance and functions of public banks, except in the metropolis.

In closing our review of this period (1800–15), it may be advisable to refer briefly to some minor details. Although, as we have already seen, the Bank of Scotland early essayed the formation of branches, and at the close of the eighteenth century had several in operation, it was not until 1804 that it opened in Glasgow. This is the more extraordinary, as their great rivals, the Royal Bank, who otherwise abstained entirely from branch extension, had opened in Glasgow twenty years before. It has, however, been supposed that a tacit agreement had existed between the two banks, that the former should have the provinces (excluding Glasgow), and the latter

---

[1] In August 1788, a sum of £3592 : 6 : 8 of Royal Bank stock was purchased in London by a banker at £209 : 6 : 8 per cent, and three years later the price was 240 per cent.

Glasgow as their respective spheres of influence. In this same year the quotation of Bank of Scotland stock was altered from Scots to Sterling by Act of Parliament. Previously, the stock was only transferable in shares of £1000 Scots (= £83 : 6 : 8 Sterling). By the Act of 1804 this practice was discontinued and the stock could be transferred " in any sums or parcels without regard to the above division." To the Bank of Scotland we are indebted for inaugurating the present system of deposit receipts in 1810. This movement was doubtless made in contemplation of the competition of the new joint-stock bank. About this time there were sixty bank offices in Scotland. Interest was usually allowed at from 3 per cent to 4 per cent, and charged at 5 per cent. The par of exchange between Edinburgh and London was forty days. In 1813 the British Linen Company obtained—despite great opposition on the part of the older banks—a supplementary charter authorising an increase of their capital from £200,000 to £500,000 ; but, although they were to all intents bankers, the legal right to be so considered was still withheld from them.[1]

We may fitly conclude this chapter by referring to the inauguration of savings banks, which occurred at this time. Daniel Defoe is credited with the original suggestion of such a scheme, and it is said that institutions of this nature were formed on the continent of Europe towards the end of the seventeenth century. The earliest movement in this direction in Britain appears to have been that of the Rev. Joseph Smith at Wendover in England in 1799, and it was followed by the Charitable

---

[1] It would appear that the practice of granting licenses to issue notes was commenced at this time. By a Stamp Act passed in 1808 (48 Geo. III. c. 149), every issuing bank was required to take out a license, costing £20, for its head office and all branches previously established ; while every branch subsequently opened necessitated another license. By a later Act (55 Geo. III. c. 184,—year 1815), the cost of such licenses was raised to £30 ; but banks in Scotland were not required to take out more than four licenses whatever the number of their branches.

Bank at Tottenham, both of which were of primitive character. It is understood that the first regularly organised savings bank in this country was established by the Rev. Henry Duncan, D.D., in his parish of Ruthwell, Dumfriesshire, on 20th May 1810. It was called " The Parish Bank Friendly Society of Ruthwell." The idea was rapidly taken up in other parts of the country ; the first attempt on an extended basis being made in Edinburgh in 1814 ; but details regarding it are wanting. On 19th June of the succeeding year, a similar establishment, which was styled the Provident Bank, was formed in Glasgow. The Savings Bank of the County and City of Perth began business on 22nd May 1815, and was followed on 23rd September of the same year by the Greenock Provident Bank. A Provident Bank was established in Port Glasgow, under the patronage of the Corporation, in 1818.[1]

The banks formed in Edinburgh and Glasgow were unable to resist the competition of new Savings Banks established locally under Acts of Parliament (9 Geo. IV. cap. 92, and 5 & 6 Will. IV. cap. 57) regulating such institutions. The Port Glasgow Provident Bank also passed away. It is, however, particularly interesting to know that the Perth and Greenock societies have continued their beneficent operations, with steadily progressive success, till the present time, having registered under the public statutes. They seem to have allowed interest on deposits at the rate of 4 per cent per annum, the second named being aided in this by being able to lend their funds to three municipal trusts. The Perth society used to lodge deposits accumulated to £10 on deposit receipts in the depositors' own names with the Perth Banking Company. Both of these Savings Banks celebrated their centenaries by publishing histories of their careers which are interesting narratives.

[1] The Greenock and Port Glasgow Banks are mentioned in the New Statistical Account, vol. vii. pp. 478 and 72.

The practice of the Scottish banks allowing interest on deposits materially facilitated the savings banks movement. There has been much legislation in regard to these banks. The English Act of 1828 was made applicable to Scotland in 1835, when the banks were placed under the supervision of the National Debt Commissioners. They were reconstructed as National Security Savings Banks at that time. It is stated that the Church of St. John's Parish, Edinburgh, was largely built by a grant from the directors of the Edinburgh Savings Bank of unclaimed deposits, etc., when its operations ceased through supercession by the new organisation. A consolidation Act was passed in 1863. More recent legislation, by extending the amounts of deposits receivable, has largely altered the character of savings banks ; the customers of which now include a large proportion of the middle classes as well as the working classes. This point is usually overlooked in discussions on labour economics. Thus was laid the foundation of a system for improving the condition of the poorer classes, which has since successfully developed to such an extent as to supply no small portion of the national resources.

CHAPTER XIV

MURDER AND ROBBERY

To persons who are not directly interested in, or, to speak more correctly, who do not devote attention to, economic subjects, the history of banking sometimes seems rather a dry subject. Unlike political history, it does not present an absorbing series of national and world-wide convulsions, involving wholesale slaughter and indescribable misery, and producing innumerable instances of heroism and intellectual greatness. Even ecclesiastical history supplies thrilling narratives of cruelty and oppression, which rival romance, and, at all times, enlists the liveliest enthusiasm in the battle of the creeds. The records of geographical and scientific discovery are also more powerful in riveting the attention and exciting the imagination. But, if our subjects deal in the main with the peaceful progress and economic well-being of nations, and are outside the realm of the startling and the sanguinary, they do at times supply material for stories which might interest the most devoted students of Newgate calendars and detectives' experiences. As illustrating this phase of banking, we shall narrate a few conspicuous instances of crime which occurred towards the close of the eighteenth and in the early part of last century, merely premising that the full details of the second story were never judicially established.

Crimes in connection with banking in Scotland are mostly confined to forgeries ; but, although robberies have not been very numerous, some of those which have occurred are rather remarkable. While not an event of the " first magnitude," the robbery of the head office of the Dundee Banking Company was attended by some remarkable features, not least of which was the number of persons tried, condemned, and punished for the offence, while, from beginning to end, the question of their guilt was matter of grave doubt.

The building in which the bank office was situated served a triple purpose, being primarily the public jail, but also containing the guildhall, as well as accommodating the bank. A common entrance gave access to them from the street, the bank being on the street level, with the guildhall immediately above it. The utilitarianism of this conjoint arrangement was surpassed by the Arcadian simplicity which dispensed with any nightly resident on the premises. When the bank closed on Saturday, 16th February 1788, the premises were left under the charge of the jailor, who, having subsequently shut up his prisoners as sheep in their fold, locked the outer door at ten o'clock, and betook himself to more felicitous scenes. The bank office was thus left to solitude, and the proximity of the imprisoned, but unguarded, rascality of the town.

Next morning (Sunday) Peter Stewart, the said jailor, was roused from his balmy slumbers " about eight o'clock, by two boys, to look at a woman who was making a great noise," when he experienced a sensation similar to that of the keeper of the prison at Philippi when he awakened out of his sleep and saw the prison doors open. But like him, also, the Dundee jailor had assurance that his charges were safe. As stated in his evidence at the trial, " he found one leaf of the great gate forced open, which made him afraid lest the prison was broke ; but he found it safe. He, however, found the door of the guildhall half open, and a hole made in the floor. He also saw an iron pinch at the side of the hole. He immediately went and told the keeper of the guildhall and the deputy-cashier (or teller) of the bank." On proceeding to the scene, the teller (William Watson) looked through the hole in the floor, which was immediately above the bank, and saw that his drawers in the office below had been broken open. In these drawers he had left about £1000, which is another illustration of the happy-go-lucky way in which they managed affairs in the good old times.

Mr. Robert Jobson, the cashier (or manager), was then called, and an examination of the bank office made. Of the teller's cash, amounting to £998 : 13s., notes, gold, silver, and copper, to the amount of £423 : 7 : 6 were gone ; but apparently the rest had been overlooked. The manager's room, which constituted the treasure vault, was found locked ; but the key, "which was usually left in the teller's room " (another happy instance of sublime confidence), "was carried off." The door being of iron, " they were obliged to get a smith, with a mason, to force it open, which took up about two hours." Fortunately all was right within.

The bank immediately advertised the robbery, and offered a reward of £50 for information ; but it was not immediately forthcoming. According to their minutes, as quoted by the historian of the bank, the directors, " finding as yet no prospect of a recovery of the money, nor even of a discovery of the perpetrators, ordered the above sum to be placed to the debit of profit and loss." However, a tailor called Macdonald, who afterwards played the rôle of chief informer, professed to be able to reveal the mystery ; but, owing to his reticence, nothing could at the time be made of him. One man, Harris or Herries, was arrested, but, being found innocent, was liberated. In the August following, two men, Bruce and Falconar, were tried in the High Court of Justiciary, Edinburgh, for the crime. The jury having by a majority found them guilty, they were sentenced to be hanged.

Owing to doubts regarding their guilt, the sentence was twice respited. Meantime, other three men, Dick, Willox, and Howie, were arrested, and tried at Edinburgh in November. The libel was found not proven against Willox and Howie, but Dick was found guilty and sentenced to be hanged. Doubts again arising, however, a respite was given in his case also to allow of further inquiry.

Alexander Macdonald, the original informant, whose character was, at both trials, spoken of as very bad, was examined at great length. He asserted that the plot had been hatching from the middle of the previous year, when Dick, Willox, Falconar, and Bruce, " complaining of want of money, Falconar proposed to break into Jobson's chest," as they facetiously called the bank office. Consultations went on from time to time, and they made him take an oath which, he was told, they had all sworn, to wit,—" If I make a discovery, may I never have any share in the blood of Christ." On the night of the robbery they made him promise to go with them ; but he made an excuse to return first to his house, " having nothing on him but his shirt." Later, along with a woman and two men, he went to the place, and going up the stair of the guildhall, saw all the men named, and Howie in the hall. Dick and Bruce were lowering Falconar, by means of a rope, through the hole in the floor. He narrated other details which tended to confirm his evidence, but which must be passed over here. " During the time they were all laughing like to split their sides." Returning to the street, Macdonald and the people with him, from the shadow of the pillars, watched the five thieves leave the premises. They had apparently been scared by a woman screaming ; but whether this was the disturbance which caused the boys to rouse the jailor from his well-earned repose or not we are not informed.

A great amount of evidence was taken which seemed

to confirm Macdonald's tale, but it does not appear that the others who saw the proceedings explicitly identified the prisoners. Notwithstanding the respites which had been granted, the sentence on Bruce and Falconar was carried out at Edinburgh, on 24th December. Consistently throughout they denied all knowledge of the crime. According to a contemporary account, " their behaviour on the scaffold was devout, serious, and becoming ; and in their address to the Almighty they implored forgiveness to those by whose testimony they had been untimely cut off." Dick was fortunate enough to obtain a pardon. The witness Macdonald soon came to a bad end. He was tried and condemned to transportation a year later for forging a bill. This raised doubts as to his former evidence ; but he vehemently asserted in Court that Bruce and Falconar had been guilty of the robbery. On his way to Botany Bay he was hanged on board ship for mutiny. Nearly a year later another malefactor, under sentence of death for robbery, asserted that he was the actual perpetrator of the Dundee Bank robbery. A respite was granted for three weeks to allow of inquiry ; but as it appeared he had fabricated the story to escape his fate, his sentence was carried out. With his latest breath, however, he asserted that Falconar, Bruce, and Dick were innocent of the robbery.

So ended this melancholy episode, regarding which one has an uneasy feeling of uncertainty as to the justice of the sentence on the unhappy prisoners.

Late in the afternoon of the 13th November 1806, a young Edinburgh sailor, whose ship had come into Leith, started from the latter town to visit his mother and sister in the Netherbow. Although described at a later period as " a very industrious good man," on the present occasion he displayed that elasticity of conscience which is too frequently shown by people in their dealings with the revenue departments. He was taking home " a small present " from foreign parts, of a contraband description. Leith Walk, which formed the main part of his route, was very different then from what it is now. Its location and extent were precisely the same, but it was dark and desolate. As he walked on, he saw two men before him. One was tall, and carried a yellow bag ; the other was dressed in black. The men were not together. The last mentioned was " dogging " the other—crossing from one side of the Walk to the other, as occasion might require, to avoid notice. So steadily did he pursue his game, that he never observed our sailor lad behind him. The latter's conscience immediately divined that the carrier of the bag was a smuggler, who was being tracked by a custom-house officer. His own guilt, unfortunately, distorted his vision, and enforced on him such precautions for his own safety as prevented him from detecting— perhaps preventing—a diabolical crime.

The first man was no smuggler. He was William Begbie, messenger of the British Linen Company, and was, in accordance with his usual practice, carrying notes of the various banks, to the value of £4392, from the Leith branch to the head office, to be exchanged next day. There is reason to believe that the man who was following him was James Mackcoull, a London villain of the blackest dye ; but of such dexterity that, even in his grossest and most daring crimes, he almost invariably escaped detection. He seemed to find the comparatively unsophisticated people of Edinburgh as good game ; for he paid them repeated visits, which only terminated when his quarters got too hot for him. On the present occasion he had lodgings in New Street, Canongate, but usually spent the day among the Leith taverns. He was now on his way home ; but, whether or not he had previously planned the scheme, he turned his present opportunity to the uses of his profession, which was that of pickpocket, thief, receiver of stolen goods, and vendor of stolen bank notes.

The three *dramatis personæ*, at respectful distances from one another, proceeded up the Walk and up Leith Street. Here Begbie appears to have at once crossed Princes Street, to go up the North Bridge. Mackcoull was too great a professor of the light-fingered art to seem to follow. The east end of Princes Street, although then a quiet place as compared with its present bustle, was not a spot for privacy. The Theatre Royal stood where the General Post Office now stands ; and Shakespeare Square, with its roystering taverns and oyster cellars, was built around it. Instead of following his victim directly, he turned along Princes Street, in front of the Register Office. It may be that his guilty thoughts pictured a tragic scene, of which he might well be aware from his frequent visits to the city, enacted within a stone's throw of the spot where he stood and gazed around, to make sure he was unobserved ; for in that thoroughfare which is now called West Register Street, but which then was a Kirk Lane, a tutor had cruelly murdered his two young charges. He thought himself unseen—although he was a licentiate of the Church, it may be presumed he did not think of his Maker's eye— but his deed was witnessed from Moultrie's Hill, on which St. James' Square was afterwards built, the view being at that time uninterrupted by buildings. Taken red-handed, he was lynched on the spot, which, after him, was named Gabriel's Place.[1]

When our sailor friend observed the " custom-house officer " look about him, " he hove-to and watched him " (to use his own words), as he feared he might be looking for him. However, the " officer " shortly followed his victim up the bridge, and both were soon lost to sight in the darkness ; for it must be remembered that the streets were then very ineffectually lighted with oil lamps.

[1] Part of the roadway still exists, and bears the name Gabriel's Road. A tree under which, according to tradition, the deed was done, stood in the south-east corner of the grounds of the Royal Bank, until it was blown down about thirty years ago.

The sailor then slowly pursued his way, which lay in the same direction, and saw nothing of the two men. He reached the High Street, and turned down towards the Canongate. When he came to Tweeddale's Close, in which the office of the British Linen Co. was situated, he was surprised and alarmed by seeing the " custom-house officer " run out of the entry with something under his coat. In the excitement of the moment, he seems to have lost his presence of mind ; for he could not after-wards tell which way the " officer " went. Rushing to his mother's house, which was close at hand, he stayed only to leave his contraband present, which had so dis-turbed his peace of mind, and hastily returned to his ship, imagining he had narrowly escaped detection of his smuggling.

Next day the city learnt that William Begbie, messenger of the British Linen Company's Bank, had been fatally stabbed in Tweeddale's Close, and robbed of bank notes to the value of £4392. Lord Cockburn, who was counsel for the Paisley Union Bank in a sub-sequent action against Mackcoull, says, " he was found with a knife in his heart, and a piece of paper, through which it had been thrust, interposed between the murderer's hand and the blood "—so premeditated was the deed. Fear of the discovery of his own illegal doings seems to have sealed the sailor's lips. His ship left Leith within a few days, and he did not return to Scotland for years. Various apprehensions were made, but the guilty person was never identified. Later investigations tended to point out Mackcoull as the perpetrator ; but his death appears to have interrupted the successful prosecution of these inquiries. The large notes of which Begbie had been robbed were subsequently found in a hole in a wall in the grounds of Bellevue. It is supposed they were placed there by Mackcoull on his return to Edinburgh—he had left his lodgings in New Street immediately after the murder occurred—when he felt himself unable safely to dispose of them for value. It is, perhaps, but just to add that Lord Cockburn's judicial mind was not satisfied with the evidence as to Mackcoull's guilt.

Some years after the sad event we have just narrated, a still more extraordinary, though happily less horrible, crime was perpetrated on the banking community. Early in May 1811, three travellers arrived in Glasgow. The oldest, and seemingly the ruling spirit of the party, was a man under fifty years of age, of average height, stout, with ruddy round face, in which were set large, sharp, dark eyes. He gave his name as James Moffat, and is said to have been " somewhat like a gentleman." Neither of his companions was so striking in appearance. The more respectable-looking of the two was about Moffat's height ; the other was thinner and taller, and was dressed like a mechanic. They answered respectively to the names of Stone and Down. Moffat said they were his cousins. The three had left London by post-chaise, and finished their journey by mail coach. Presenting themselves at the house of a widow, named Stewart, who kept lodgings at the Broomielaw, where she lived with her son and niece, they secured rooms for a fortnight, and seemed to live a quiet and retired life.

They early contracted a habit of leaving the house about ten o'clock at night, for about a couple of hours. This, it would seem, was at that period a very unusual time for citizens of St. Mungo to be abroad ; but, our friends being Londoners, and seemingly of irreproachable character, no surprise was excited. In these circumstances, it can hardly be wondered that the mysterious disappearance of a small chamber organ from the house should have been attributed by the good widow to some inscrutable dispensation of providence, which had no connection with her respected English guests. We do not mean to say they stole it. Such an insignificant article could not excite their cupidity. But, having a use for its pewter pipes, or rather for the metal itself, they simply did as all great men have done since the world began—they made use of the materials that lay readiest to their hands. However, at best, this is a mere minor part of the business.

As our readers will suspect the character and intentions of our heroes, and as they are already acquainted with the most important member of the party, it is as well, perhaps, that we should introduce each *in propriâ personâ*. James Moffat, then, was no other than the old custom-house officer who gave the sailor boy such a fright, and did worse damage still, if all tales be true, to his own soul and poor Begbie's body on the same occasion. He had formed a great plan, and taken to himself two other spirits, who, if less wicked than he, were only so from want of similar natural talents. Their real names, or those at least by which they were principally known to the police, were Harry French and Houghton (or Huffey, as he was colloquially termed) White. They were as precious a pair of villains as remained unhanged. Indeed, White (the " Down " of the present episode) had been specially rescued from the hulks, for the purposes of the present expedition, on account of his mechanical knowledge. The great design which Mackcoull had elaborated was the robbery of the Glasgow Branch of the Paisley Union Bank.

The office which formed the subject of the trio's attentions was situated in Ingram Street, occupying the street floor of a corner house, there being separate warerooms above, and cellars below. It consisted of two rooms, in the inner of which was a vault or closet, with an iron door, which formed the strong room of the branch. Many a time, during May and June, had the three robbers reconnoitred the premises—more particularly during the silent time after ten o'clock at night, when the worthy and unsophisticated inhabitants had retired to rest. At first they had thought that a fortnight would suffice to effect their purpose ; but the keys which they had pro-

cured from a confederate locksmith in London would not
suit. The old-fashioned simple locks baffled burglars who
were accustomed to more scientific guards, so Mackcoull
set off for London (under pretence of going to Liverpool),
to have keys made under his own supervision. White
manufactured a key from the pewter pipes of the musical
box, probably to get the impression of the wards of the
locks. After Mackcoull's return, a little adjustment of
the keys seems to have given complete command of the
premises. It was now the beginning of July, and, according to notice they had previously given, they left their
lodgings, with the ostensible object of going to Bristol.
Where they did go does not appear. It would seem,
however, that they purposely delayed the execution of
the robbery until the Fair week, when the presence of a
heterogeneous crowd of questionable characters might
serve to divert attention from them.

On Saturday, 13th July 1811, business went on as
usual at the branch office. Four o'clock came. Mr.
Likely, the cashier, and other officers, had taken their
departure ; and Mr. Hamilton, the teller, handed over
his cash to John Thomson, the porter. On the arrival
of a box of retired notes, amounting to about £4000,
from the bank's correspondents in Edinburgh—Sir Wm.
Forbes & Co.—the porter locked it, with the teller's cash,
into the safe, shut up the office, and took the keys to the
house of Mr. Templeton, the manager. We have here a
charming glimpse of bank office management in the
olden time. One does not know whether most to admire
the mutual confidence displayed by the staff from the
highest to the lowest, or to envy the social conditions
that permitted the total absence of supervision in the
transference of cash. Sunday passed, no doubt with
prolonged doctrinal disquisitions, slightly interspersed
with discordant tunes, and added to by domestic cate-
chisings in semi-solitary confinement, amid repressed
desires for the return of Monday. The morning came

at last, and John Thomson got the bank keys, and opened the office as usual. He unlocked the safe to get out the teller's cash, and then he witnessed a spectacle which must have produced in him sensations more easy to imagine than to describe. The lid of the Edinburgh box was broken, and the remittance had disappeared. The cash drawers had been forced, and their contents abstracted. Everything in the shape of cash, including some base coin, was gone. The bank since Saturday was *minus* £19,753 : 4s.

Sunday morning had been a busy time with the interesting trio ; but it is left to the imagination to picture their *modus operandi*. They had been seen in the Gallowgate on Friday the 12th July—the day preceding the robbery—but there is no other record of their movements until after the great event was accomplished. A certain David Clachar, who was early astir, saw the three " sitting on a dyke at the corner of Stirling's Road," not far from the bank. They had a large bundle with them, from which they took a parcel of notes, and counted them. They also counted silver coin ; and then packing up, proceeded towards the heart of the city. There they procured, with some difficulty, a post-chaise, in which they left for Edinburgh, urging the postboy to speed, on the plea that Mackcoull had a brother at the point of death, whom he earnestly desired to see. Posting thus, early on the Sunday morning, and changing horses at Airdrie and Uphall, they drove into Edinburgh. They dismissed the chaise at the west end of Princes Street— just where Dean Ramsay's monument now stands— being anxious to throw pursuers off the scent. And pursued they speedily were ; for no sooner was the news of the robbery circulated, than Clachar and others put the bank authorities on the trail. But the robbers had a good start, of which they did not fail to avail themselves. They were not the sort, however, to neglect their personal comfort. They had regaled themselves, at each stage, with drinking and smoking. Mackcoull, who was well acquainted with Edinburgh, led the way to M'Cousland's St. Andrew Tavern in Rose Street, which he had formerly frequented when he lodged in that street. There they dined — no doubt sumptuously. During afternoon church services they appear to have slipped unnoticed, through the deserted streets, to the Black Bull Inn in Leith Street, then the great centre of the mail coach routes. There they hired another chaise, and proceeded by Haddington and the usual stages to London, taking four horses after they crossed the Border.

Their pursuers followed them with great activity; but the necessity for inquiry at every stage gave the villains more than the full advantage of their start. Mackcoull and his associates got to their villainous haunts without interruption. The London police, however, succeeded in arresting French and White; but, by a most extraordinary system of negotiation, Mackcoull managed to save himself, and secure about £8000 of the booty. Through his wife he negotiated a treaty with the authorities, by which he agreed to give up what was left of the money, on condition that the offence would be overlooked, and that his accomplices would be saved from the sentence of death to which they were liable for escaping from the hulks. The amount he gave up, however, was only £11,941. He had the audacity, some years later, to come to Leith and purchase bills on London with the stolen notes, and, when arrested, to sue the Paisley Union Bank for the amount of the bills then taken from him. Strange to say, after prolonged litigation, he very nearly won his case. But, at last, his guilt was fully established at the concluding sederunt of his case; and he was arrested, tried, and condemned to death on the criminal charge. A reprieve was granted, however, and he died in the county jail in Edinburgh, on 22nd December 1820, after enduring a period of great mental agony. White was afterwards executed for robbing a mail coach.

Another robbery,[1] bearing some resemblances to the one just narrated, occurred seventeen years later. In this case, too, the operators were London burglars, whose *modus operandi* shows a scientific finish contrasting strikingly with the criminal manners of the natives as exemplified by the Dundee Bank robbery already described. Indeed, it must be admitted that in all departments of the light-fingered arts, the Scotch could not hold a candle to their metropolitan *confrères* ; and, seemingly, the latter do not appear ever to have considered it worth their while to seek their assistance.

This crime was the robbery of the Greenock Bank on Sunday, 9th March 1828. The office consisted of two apartments on the street floor of the Assembly Rooms, entering by the first door on the right hand of the hall of the building. Further in, on the left, was a newsroom, which, even at that early period of the century, was open on the Sabbath day—a circumstance which facilitated the depredation ; for, had the outer door of the building been shut, the scheme would have required even bolder and more precarious efforts than the policy of the " open door " necessitated.

The enterprise was very carefully arranged. Having paid Greenock the compliment of selection for their attentions, the thieves, in the preceding June, deputed one of their number—Henry Sanders, or Saunders (which, it must be confessed, has a somewhat Scottish sound)—to reconnoitre. For the occasion, however, he assumed the name of Eldin, perhaps out of regard for a facetious Edinburgh judge of the time. His practised eye readily saw that the weak points of the Greenock Bank's position rendered it the most suitable for their attentions. Having satisfied himself as to the object of attack, he departed from the scene, probably to consult with his colleagues ; but doubtless also because the early and late sunlight of the northern summer made it necessary to delay proceedings until the winter supplied the facility of darkness for their enterprise.

We accordingly find that, on 23rd November 1827, Mr. Eldin returned to his old landlady, bringing a companion with him. They were received joyfully, for Mr. Eldin had been a most quiet, regular, and respectably living man. This style of life was resumed. The lodgers were evidently men of the most sedate—not to say stoical—character. They went to bed at 10, and rose at 5.30, going out every morning to bathe in the salt sea waves at 6 o'clock although it was winter-time ; at least they said so—it is not recorded that they were ever seen in the water. Indeed, traducers of their characters insinuate that they employed these early hours to take impressions of the bank locks. It seems that was the only time when no one was on the premises ; the messenger, Robert Love, after sleeping in the bank, with his bed against the safe door, going to his home round the corner, probably to get his breakfast ; but, as it is more touchingly expressed in the history of the transaction, " to say good-morning to his wife." However that may be, he had a further expedition in view—for every morning, Sunday included, he attended to his interests as contractor for the mail communications between Greenock and Largs, by seeing to the starting of his gig with a small boy as driver. This then was the only time our interesting acquaintances had for making their bank inspection. It was not perhaps as thorough an inspection as official inspectors are wont to make ; but, if they did not overhaul the securities for advances to customers, they secured an advance themselves, and verified the cash balance.

But we are anticipating. For after a stay of seventeen days the two scoundrels left Greenock, for the purpose, it was conjectured, of improving their false keys. Their absence was, however, of short duration, and on their

return to their old landlady they stayed until 7th January
1828.   The worthy lady was confirmed in her good opinion
of her lodgers by discovering that they were ironmongers ;
for, from a cupboard, she heard them filing and clinking
metal most industriously.   It remained, however, a
subject of debate between her and a gossip whether they
were in the cutlery or Britannia metal line.   But the
ladies seem to have had no shadow of doubt as to their
being true as steel.   They now took to rather a roving
life, staying sometimes at one inn and sometimes at
another ; with occasional disappearances from the town.
Thus, laboriously, did they study their enterprise, moving
from place to place that they might more thoroughly
observe the movements of the denizens of the building,
and visiting accomplices to get their keys more delicately
adjusted.

At last, after about nine months' preparation, the
great enterprise is fixed for the morning of Sabbath, 9th
March.   On the preceding evening the conspirators bade
adieu to their host of the George Inn, but they could
not tear themselves away from the town of their adoption
without some keepsake for remembrance.   So they lay
perdu in the town until early morn.   The same evening
two confederates arrived in separate gigs ; and, no doubt,
a full council of war would be held to settle final details.
The weather was propitious, in so far that it was of so
boisterous a description that people were too much
absorbed in looking to their own protection to pay heed
to the movements of the couple, even if the good people
of Greenock had been of a suspicious turn of mind.

On the eventful morning, Robert Love arose from
his sentinel slumbers.   The conscientious historian relates
that he dressed himself, which might almost have been
taken for granted ; but he says not a word as to ablutions,
a detail for which a voucher would not have been amiss.
The porter was, however, of sufficiently tidy habits to
tuck away his bed and bedding into a corner where they

were wont to lie out of sight during the hours of business. Leaving the key of the bank at his house round the corner, he proceeded to his duties in connection with His Majesty's mails, and to conversation with his friends, which the comparative freedom of the Sabbath permitted.

Meanwhile the opportunity for which the miscreants had plotted for nine months had come, and the preconceived arrangements were put in action. The two gigs were in waiting in different streets adjacent to, but out of sight of the bank. The second of the two chief actors (who was endowed with a squint, which seems to have been his principal recommendation, as it enabled him to see things when it was supposed he was looking in a different direction, and who is represented as a lily-livered creature) went in trembling to the newsroom and kept the attendant there looking up the Jamaica papers for a report of a fictitious accident to an imaginary relative, whose ship, he said, had foundered in the Gulf of Mexico. Under cover of this feint, the judge's name-sake opened the bank door with his false key; and, entering, soon got access to the treasure of the bank. Not content with the coin, amounting to £1661 : 15 : 6, Mr. Eldin annexed all the notes in the chest. These amounted to £28,354 of the bank's own issue, and £4100 : 13s. of notes of other banks. These he crammed into two great travelling bags; and, throwing a large cloak about him, carrying booty to the value of £34,116 : 8 : 6, he evacuated the premises. Gaining one of the gigs he stowed cargo, and jumping up beside the confederate driver they started, at a rapid rate, for Glasgow. His craven-hearted lieutenant, leaving his phantom relative's fate to the further researches of the kindly librarian, followed so hastily that his gig actually overtook that of his chief.

Reaching Edinburgh, they succeeded early on Monday morning in cashing some of the notes at Sir William

Forbes', the Royal, and the British Linen Banks to the amount of about £4800. The teller at the Bank of Scotland, however, was not so easily hoodwinked, and refused the business. So, fearing that further delay might be dangerous, they hired a post-chaise and made for the south with their plunder. Arrived in London they declared a dividend of the entire profits of the undertaking, and dissolved partnership ; rejoicing doubtless no less in the pride of their skill than in the material result of so perilous an expedition. And it must be admitted that, if an evil deed can be so described, it was well done.

The sequel was very remarkable. By private negotiations, through a thieves' lawyer, more than half of the stolen money was recovered. It was arranged that a single representative of the bank was to wait in a hackney coach at a secluded spot. This was done, and there a porter delivered to him a box which was afterwards found to contain about £20,000 of the stolen notes. The consideration for this restitution (which, it may be noticed, was the giving up by the thieves of what entailed more danger than prospective profit in the retention) was that prosecution proceedings, on the part of the bank, should be dropped. Here the matter would have ended had not the Lord Advocate instituted inquiries. As it was, our friend Mr. Eldin was laid by the heels, brought to Glasgow, and tried six months after the robbery. The jury, however, brought in a verdict of " not proven," and the prisoner was discharged ; Lord Meadowbank, who presided, clearly indicating his suspicions. Indeed, the evidence, though circumstantial, reads so clearly adverse to the prisoner, that it is surprising that he escaped. But he was a clever rogue.

CHAPTER XV

THE period of about ten years, from the close of the
Napoleonic wars in 1815 to the great crisis of 1825–6,
which forms the subject of the present chapter, was one
of almost profound peace. During the first year, the
bitter effects of the terrible international struggle which
had convulsed the world were severely felt in Britain.
Commercial enterprise was in a state of great prostration ;
provisions were scarce and dear ; and the sufferings of
the labouring classes broke out in disturbances which were
not always quashed without bloodshed. In 1817, however, symptoms of improvement manifested themselves.
Commerce revived, the national industries showed greater
signs of life, and financial ventures were indulged in.
Steamboats began to ply on all the great rivers ; and
steam power was applied to printing and manufactures.
Foreign loans, also, became popular, and much British
capital was thus profitably employed in ameliorating the
distresses of the European nations.

In 1816, the Government issued a new silver coinage.
This had become an absolute necessity owing to the
worn condition of the metallic currency. This was so bad
that it is recorded that, in some districts, the greatest surprise was manifested at the liberality of the Government
in supplying for general currency beautifully - executed
" medals " in place of the smooth discs in circulation.

Early in the following year, the gold coinage was also renewed ; and in the autumn, the Bank of England partially resumed payment in specie. Before the death of George III., on 29th January 1820, considerable advances had been made in the national prosperity. Some great public works—such as the Edinburgh and Glasgow Canal in Scotland—were completed ; ocean steam navigation was developed ; and a healthy amount of national industry was displayed. The two great questions of Free Trade and Parliamentary Reform were much agitated at this time.

In a work [1] published in 1821 it is stated that, as the notes of the Scottish banks were found to be preferred in the north of England to those of the English provincial banks, a proposal had been made, some years previously, " to six of the most respectable partners of an Edinburgh bank of large capital, that they should, on their own account and in their own names, transact business at Berwick, under the guarantee of the Edinburgh bank." The project was not, however, carried out. The author subsequently remarks [2] that " some of the respectable banks in Newcastle, etc., have agents in Edinburgh, for exchanging their notes, and it is proper to state that they pass very currently also in all parts of Scotland."

The year 1820 would seem to have been the turning point of the period, when the feverish stage commenced. In the middle of that year a great commercial and financial crisis occurred in Ireland, whereby private banking— which had, for the most part, been conducted on most unsatisfactory principles — was virtually extinguished. Some twenty banking and note-issuing firms were swept away. This crisis did not, however, extend to Britain. There, enterprise and industry were proceeding apace, in buoyancy and hope. In 1821, the Bank of England was permitted fully to resume specie payments ; and, during

[1] *Review of the Banking System of Britain*, p. 15, see *ante*.
[2] *Ibid.* p. 55.

the three succeeding years, the condition of the country was one of much prosperity, combined with which the spirit of speculation was largely developed. After that came the inevitable crisis.

As regards banking in Scotland during the greater part of this period, the leading characteristics would seem to have been, the continued development of the large banks, and the withdrawal or failure of purely local establishments. Previous to 1825, only two new firms commenced business. The first of these was the Exchange and Deposit Bank of John Maberly & Co., with offices at Aberdeen, Montrose, Dundee, Edinburgh, and Glasgow. They were properly an English linen manufacturing firm, with flax spinning mills in Scotland. In 1818 they established themselves as bankers in Scotland, with the object of profiting by the high rate of exchange on London. This entrance on the Scottish field was by no means relished by the native bankers ; but it is probable that the public profited by it. This will be understood when it is remembered that the usual par of exchange was 40 to 50 days ; whereas Maberly commenced with 20 days, and latterly reduced the period to 10 days. The result showed that the intrusionists overreached themselves in adopting a scale which was only in later years naturally attained to ; but there can be little doubt that their opponents had erred on the side of their own interest. After a career of fourteen years as bankers, Maberly & Co. succumbed in 1832 ; but it does not appear whether their failure is to be attributed to the banking or to the manufacturing business. The liquidation was conducted under an English fiat of bankruptcy, the debts in both departments of the business amounting to £149,082, on which a dividend of 4s. 5d. per pound was paid. As the assets are stated to have realised £76,669, it would seem that the expenses of liquidation were very heavy.

The second bank to which we have referred was the

firm of Hay & Ogilvie, who commenced business in
Lerwick in 1821, under the designation of the Shetland
Bank. They were also engaged in trade, which part of
their business was, no doubt, previously established.
They appear to have ceased issuing their own notes in
1827 ; but for what reason is not stated. They continued for twenty years, when they made a bad failure.
One of the partners, John Ogilvy (the name is thus
printed in the notice, although differing from the spelling
in the official style of the firm), died in 1829 ; and the
failure, according to one authority,[1] occurred in 1830,
with debts, both as merchants and bankers, amounting
to £60,000, on which a dividend of 6s. per £ was paid.
The date is otherwise given [2] as 1842, the liabilities as
£140,000, and the dividend in sequestration as 5s. per
pound, with the prospect of a little more. Perhaps they
resumed business, after a composition, in 1830. From
this time to the closing year of the period, bank extension
consisted entirely in the opening of branches throughout
the country. The Commercial Bank and the British
Linen Company displayed the greatest amount of activity
in this respect.

A marked feature of this period was the disappearance
of a considerable number of banks—the exits being
pretty well spread over the ten years. In 1816, the
Falkirk Union Bank, with liabilities to the amount of
£60,000, was sequestrated. The number of partners was
only eight. Malachi Malagrowther states that they met
their engagements without much loss to their creditors ;
but it is probable he had not asked the latter for their
opinion, seeing the total dividend did not exceed
10s. per £. However, it was a small concern.[3] In 1820
a little - known establishment, called the Glasgow Commercial Bank, withdrew from business. Towards the

---

[1] Boase, 2nd ed., p. 364.   [2] Somers, p. 107.
[3] Perhaps they paid something more, as a dividend was announced
to be paid in November 1818, and another in February 1822. But
these may be included in the 10s.

close of the next year the firm of Sir William Douglas, Bart., & Co., carrying on business at Castle-Douglas, under the style of the Galloway Banking Company, was also wound up. It had existed for fifteen years. It may be presumed that its liabilities were met in full. At this time, also, the Kilmarnock Banking Company, who started early in the century, merged their business in that of Hunters & Co., Ayr (October 1821).

In the following year (1822) a very unfortunate failure occurred. The East Lothian Banking Company had been formed at Dunbar in 1810, with a capital of £80,000, in 400 shares, held by twenty-seven partners. It would seem that the bank never did well. This was principally owing to the disreputable conduct of the cashier (or manager), William Borthwick, who, after involving the bank in much bad business, particularly advances to concerns he was privately interested in, absconded with £21,000, on 10th April 1822. Messrs. Forbes & Co., of Edinburgh, advanced £100,000 to assist the liquidation, pending the realisation of the assets and a call of £250 per share. The liabilities amounted to £129,000, and the assets to £63,000; but the partners paid in full. In connection with this affair there is a rather mythical-looking account of a design on the part of Borthwick to kidnap one of the directors and the law agent—who were probably of too inquiring a disposition for his taste —in order to further his private designs. According to Borthwick's written directions, which were found among his papers, they were to be inveigled to a specified place, seized, gagged, and put into empty puncheons with air-holes. They were then to be taken to Dunbar and shipped (presumably as Scotch ale) on board a vessel belonging to Borthwick's brother, which was about to sail for Dantzic. Thereafter they were to be conducted to a desolate part of Prussia and confined eight or nine months " without change of clothes or shaving materials." The conspirator concludes (what was, doubtless, a day-

dream with which he gratified his spleen) thus : " I will
venture to affirm that at the expiry of that time they
will have repented most sincerely of their conduct." [1]
In 1824 the Edinburgh firm of John Wardrop & Co.
disappeared from the list of bankers.

The year 1825 is notable for the establishment of four
new banks, all of which were successful. One of these
was the Aberdeen Town and County Banking Company,
which is one of only three provincial banks surviving at
the end of the century, from the multitude which had
been started. Let us hope that no amount of charming
on the part of the large banks will induce these establishments to forgo their independence. The roll of banks
in Scotland is small enough ; it can hardly be for the
public advantage to have competition further narrowed ;
and the advantage to the shareholders, so long as their
business is prosperous, of amalgamation, is probably
not sufficient to counterbalance the chances they would
forgo of development into national banks.[2] The Aberdeen Town and County Bank (subsequently the Town
and County Bank, Limited, and now conjoined with the
North of Scotland Bank) started with a subscribed capital
of £150,000, held by 470 partners. In 1825 the capital
was £750,000, and was increased in 1836 to £1,000,000
in £100 shares with £15 paid.

Another bank established in this year was the Arbroath
Banking Company, with a capital of £100,000 subscribed,
and of £40,000 paid. It amalgamated with the Commercial Bank of Scotland in 1844, at 15th July of which
year its capital was £60,000, circulation £13,787, and
deposits £133,279. A third was the Dundee Commercial
Bank (the second of that name), with a capital of £50,000.
It retired in 1838, in favour of a newly-organised company
—the Eastern Bank of Scotland—which was designed

[1] *Banking in Glasgow.*
[2] This hope has not been fulfilled, but, on account of the sentiment,
the passage is allowed to stand in revision.

to carry on a more extended business. Thus euphemistically ; but one who was well able to speak on the subject thus describes the event : " The mystery of this proceeding was revealed in the course of winding up the affairs of the former bank, when the partners came to find that not only had its whole capital been lost, but about half as much more, which, less the premium of £20,000 received from the Eastern Bank for the goodwill of the business, they had to liquidate. For this purpose £40 per share was called up ; but £13 : 10s. per share of this was returned subsequently." [1]

The fourth was the now well-known and powerful establishment, the National Bank of Scotland. From the outset, it appears to have been designed on a large scale. Indeed, it was the result of the combination of no fewer than three distinct banking companies projected in 1824. The first of these seems to have been the Scottish Union Commercial Banking Company ; but it was speedily followed by the Scottish Union Banking Company, and the National Bank of Scotland, the prospectuses of all three being before the public at the same time. The advertisements of all of them state that the subscriptions were rapidly filling up ; but it seems to have become evident, even to the enthusiastic promoters, that such an accession to the number of Edinburgh banks was unadvisable. The Scottish Union and the National made what they termed " a treaty of union," whereby they were to unite their interests and divide the prospective appointments to their mutual advantage, under the designation of the Scottish National Banking Company. They then held out the olive branch to the Scottish Union Commercial ; but their advances were not reciprocated.

However, the united companies were not to be so easily baffled in their design of preventing rivalry. Finding they could not win the promoters to their side, they

[1] Boase.

made a seductive attempt on the subscribers. On 1st
January 1825, the united companies published a long
advertisement, in which they reflected warmly on the
" insidious " conduct of their rivals, and threatened that,
if the Union Commercial Company would not join them,
they would advertise their readiness to receive individual
subscribers to that company into their concern. Whether
as the result of this threat, or from the prevalence of
reasonable counsels, the two parties came to an agreement
within a few days, and announced the " union of all of
the new banking companies of Edinburgh " as the Scottish
National Banking Company. As the subscription lists
were closed on 8th January, there seems to have been no
difficulty in completing them. Further delays occurred,
however, and it was not until 21st March that the company
got finally started as the National Bank of Scotland.
The nominal capital was £5,000,000 (now fully subscribed)
in £10 shares. At first only £500,000 of the capital was
issued.

The bank seems to have at once commenced a branch
system, by the establishment of offices in nine towns,
seemingly rather selected from their geographical positions
as embracing the whole country, than from their business
importance. In 1833 they had 24 branches ; and a
continual increase has now brought the number up to
124. In 1831 the company obtained a Royal charter of
incorporation, granted under the pernicious principle of
unlimited liability, which at that time commended itself
to statesmen as superior to the ancient principle of
limitation, which is now again held, under the light of
terrible experience, to be the proper constitution of
corporations.

Towards the end of 1825, another attempt was made
in Edinburgh to organise a new bank.[1] It was to be on
a different footing from the National Bank, as it was not
intended to extend its operations outside the metropolis,

[1] *Scotsman* newspaper, 26th November 1825.

but to conduct it as the Glasgow and other local banks were then managed.   But the events of the closing months of the year put an end to the project.

The earlier part of 1825 witnessed the climax of the speculating spirit which had been working with ever-increasing excitement since 1820.   The opening of the Spanish South-American Colonies, by the achievement of their independence, to British enterprise, had stimulated industry, and had occasioned a mania for loans to the new States.   These loans are estimated at fifteen millions.   At the same time, bubble companies were rampant, and gambling in their shares was excessive. The economic heresy, called the mercantile system—which proceeded on the assumption that the wealth of a nation was co-ordinate with its command of the precious metals—exercised an evil influence at this time.   It was thought that the boundless natural stores of gold and silver in the Spanish colonies had only to be tapped by British commerce to secure the wealth of the fortunate adventurers.

Lord Lauderdale stated that the schemes subscribed for amounted to two hundred million pounds.   From a statement made at the time, it would seem that " the accumulation of capital which has been progressively going on, since the conclusion of the last peace, and the difficulty of now investing money to advantage, has given rise within these few months to the formation of numerous trading companies throughout the country, with capitals of from £25,000 to half-a-million.   In Edinburgh we have a new Banking Company, a new Insurance Company, a Wine Company, a Porter Brewery Company, an Equitable Loan Company, a Whale-fishing Company, Glass and Iron Manufacturing Companies, Cotton-Spinning Companies, and a variety of others which it would be tedious to enumerate.   No sooner was the prospectus of a new scheme laid before the public than capitalists and speculatists ran eagerly and filled up the shares ;

and it was no uncommon thing to see these shares, in the course of a day or two, selling at a high premium. Much money was lost and won upon this kind of lottery." [1] Of course, in London speculation was on a still greater scale. " It is estimated that the different new schemes on foot in London amount to 114, and the capitals to be more than £105,000,000."

These are enumerated as follows, viz. :—

20 Railroads, with capitals amounting to	.	.	. £23,950,000 [2]
22 Banking, Loan Investment, etc., ,,	.	.	. 36,760,000
11 Gas Companies, ,,	.	.	. 8,000,000
8 British and Irish Mines, ,,	.	.	. 3,600,000
17 Foreign Mines, ,,	.	.	. 11,565,000
9 Shipping and Dock Companies, ,,	.	.	. 10,580,000
27 Miscellaneous, ,,	.	.	. 11,070,000

114 in all.   £105,525,000

The turn of the tide took place in the month of April. Prices of stocks and shares began to decline, calls were made on shareholders, the Bank of England bullion was ebbing away, and want of confidence began to manifest itself. In the three months, April, May, and June, nearly £3,000,000 of bullion were exported, mostly to the Continent, and it was estimated that the demands for exportation had reduced the stock of bullion in the Bank from £12,000,000, on 1st January 1824, to about £4,000,000 at the beginning of August 1825.[3] It was not, however, until later in the year that palpable evidences of a crisis showed themselves. Some private

[1] *Scots Magazine*, March 1825. The bank alluded to above is, no doubt, the National Bank of Scotland. The insurance company might be the Scottish Union (now Scottish Union and National) Fire and Life, but is, more probably, the Standard Life ; but the Thistle, Equitable, and Commercial Marine were also local insurance projects of the time. The Wine Company of Scotland continued to exist until 1853, when the business was transferred to a private firm ; and the pawnbroking establishment spoken of occupies a respectable place, at the present time, on the local share list. Other companies alluded to are the Edinburgh, Glasgow, and Alloa Glass Company, Shotts Iron Company, Scottish Brewing Company, Scottish Wool Stapling Company, Waterloo Hotel Company, and Caledonian Dairy Company.

[2] This item is given as £13,950,000 in the original, but is, doubtless, a misprint.   [3] *Scotsman* newspaper, 3rd August 1825.

firms succumbed, then a few of the English country bankers suspended payment. Distrust became general ; the panic seized London, and every one sought to save himself. On Saturday, 3rd December, rumours of difficulties in the firm of Pole, Thornton & Co., who, in addition to having an extensive London banking business, were agents for a large number of provincial and Scottish banks, gave point to the excitement. The Bank of England advanced £300,000 to the firm, and the catastrophe was deferred.

But on Monday the 12th, no longer able to stand the strain on their resources, Pole, Thornton & Co. stopped payment. Then the panic rose to a crisis. Stocks were unsaleable, and even Government Securities were not looked at. Every one who had coin hoarded it. For two days—12th and 13th December—the financial and commercial world was in a state of paralysis. On the 14th, the Bank of England came to the front. The directors gave assistance right and left to all who produced fair security. The crisis passed, and business men breathed more freely. The dread of universal ruin was past, and they began to estimate the resources of their neighbours with some degree of calmness. £1 notes of the Bank of England were sent into the country, to supply the want of specie ; and affairs gradually assumed a quieter phase. The results of the crisis had, however, been very serious. Many bankruptcies had occurred, including some London and many provincial banks. It would appear, however, from the estimates of liabilities and assets, that the English provincial banks who failed had not been in so bad a condition as might have been expected. Subsequent investigation showed, moreover, that wherever the error lay, the note-issues had comparatively little to do with their position.

In Scotland, as usual, the crisis had comparatively little immediate effect, although the subsequent depression was severe and lasting, as was strikingly indicated by the large amount of heritable property which was thrown on the market within a few months after the crisis. For the most part, business went on as before. The Edinburgh banks seem to have experienced no discomfort. An exception must, however, be made in regard to Glasgow and the West of Scotland. There, if panic did not actually break out, much uneasiness was felt in commercial circles. Contemporary accounts represent the state of trade and manufactures as very bad. Several of the cotton mills were put on half-time, and others were verging on the same condition ; while the country weavers were in vain seeking employment. The Bank of England sent a commission to Scotland, under which a sum of £300,000 was to be advanced in Glasgow. It was believed at the time, that the applications for assistance from this body were very few ; and the action of the bank was, in some quarters, regarded somewhat ungraciously, with true Glasgow independence. The banks were not affected ; indeed, it is stated that they, and especially the Royal Bank branch, under the management of Mr. J. Thomson, were very efficacious in allaying the threatened danger.

But, although banking in Scotland, as a whole, escaped very easily, it was not unscathed. Three banks succumbed. One of these was the Caithness Banking Company of Wick, whose business was taken over by the Commercial Bank. Another was the Stirling Banking Company, with liabilities exceeding a quarter of a million sterling ; but, although it was sequestrated, its eight partners paid in full. The worst case was that of the Fife Banking Company. It had a capital of £30,000, and might have done well. It was, however, grossly mismanaged, got into difficulties during this crisis, and stopped payment on 15th December 1825. It struggled on, however, under rearrangements, and did not finally close until 21st May 1829. Its affairs were not settled until 1850, owing largely to litigation carried to the

House of Lords. The loss to the shareholders was enormous. Fourteen outstanding shareholders paid £5500 per share beyond the original amount. The liabilities were met in full.

According to a contemporary writer the interest on current accounts at most of the banks was the same as on deposit receipts. Previously, however, it had been usual to allow 1 per cent less on current accounts than on receipts, and still more usual to allow 1 per cent less on such receipts if the money were uplifted within six months of deposit.

An important change in the currency was made in this period. Whereas both gold and silver had formerly been legal tender to any amount, by the Act 56 Geo. III. c. 68 (1816) gold coin is declared to be thereafter the only absolute legal tender; silver being good for not more than forty shillings. Bronze coin is only legal tender to the amount of one shilling.

CHAPTER XVI

IN consequence of the severe financial crisis which darkened the close of the year 1825, the Government resolved on radical alterations in the banking legislation of the United Kingdom. In the King's Speech on the meeting of Parliament on 2nd February 1826, the principal place was occupied by references to the embarrassments which had occurred in the pecuniary transactions of the country since the close of the last session. His Majesty also advised the devising of " such measures as may tend to protect both public and private interests against the like sudden and violent fluctuations, by placing on a more firm foundation the currency and circulating credit of the country." The crisis was almost entirely confined to England ; but the Government contemplated a movement towards the assimilation of the paper currency of the three kingdoms. Their first task was to introduce changes in the banking system of England. An almost insuperable obstacle, however, presented itself in the shape of the special privileges of the Bank of England. As far as the public were concerned, the worst of these privileges was the prohibition of any other company or partnership consisting of more than six persons carrying on the business of banking in England. This provision was enacted by a clause in an Act passed in the reign of Queen Anne, 1708. As then understood, the business of banking involved the issue of notes ; and this was always considered, until 1844, as a distinctive characteristic of bankers. Technically, the prohibition was directed only against the issue of notes payable on demand, or for any time less than six months ; but in the then existing circumstances of banking, it effectually precluded the establishment of joint-stock banks other than the Bank of England. The effect of this had been most pernicious, as it checked the growth of strong banks, and encouraged the formation of a multiplicity of weak ones.

The Government entered into negotiations with the Bank of England for a relaxation of this prohibition, and eventually obtained their reluctant consent to an arrange-ment whereby joint - stock banks, consisting of any number of partners, might be formed, with power to issue notes as bankers outside a radius of sixty-five miles from London. This provision was availed of to some extent ; but it was not until the re-enacting and explanatory Act of 1833 that full advantage was taken of the power granted. The branch system of the Bank of England was also an outcome of the proceedings of this time, special powers having been conferred by Parliament on the bank directors to delegate their powers of management to agents. Another important change effected was the suppression of bank notes under the value of £5. The Government appear to have been convinced that note-issuing was essentially connected with the late crisis. As we have already shown, there was not sufficient reason for this belief.

We do not mean to assert that the provincial note issuers were sufficiently trustworthy ; but it appears from the state of the paper currency at the time, that there had been no over-issue of notes. The Earl of Liverpool, indeed, on behalf of the Government, stated that, as estimated by the returns of stamps used, the issues had been increasing to a great extent ; but the statistics compiled of the actual notes in circulation showed a considerable decrease in all the years to which he referred, with the exception of 1825. In that year, however, the amount was but little above the point at which it stood several years before. It was the weakness of the banks, as prescribed by Parliament in favour of the Bank of England, combined with injudicious banking advances, that led to the numerous failures of provincial bankers in England. The enlargement of the powers of banking, without the suppression of small notes, would have been not only sufficient in itself, but would have been more effectual in building up the shattered fabric of the deformed system of banking with which Parliament had afflicted the English nation ; for banks would have been enabled to extend their operations into quarters where, without the use of small notes, banking would be unprofitable.

The Government, however, decreed the abolition of bank notes under £5. Before the English Act—limiting, and, after a certain time, prohibiting, such issues—was actually passed, Lord Liverpool announced that it was intended to introduce a similar measure with regard to Scotland and Ireland. In this, however, the Government were reckoning without their host. When the intelligence reached Scotland, the *Nemo me impune lacessit* spirit was at once aroused. The proposal was almost universally denounced as an infringement of the rights of the nation, and as injurious to its interests. Sir Walter Scott's magic pen was enlisted in the cause. His celebrated letters, under the *nom de plume* of " Malachi Malagrowther," although taking too roseate a view of Scottish banking experience, gave point to the national excitement, and undoubtedly tended greatly to focus the opposition. At the same time, they excited the most extraordinary criticism in Parliament and elsewhere, as calculated to foster rebellion. The agitation was carried on warmly at county meetings, where speeches in favour of the bank-note issues were made, and resolutions unanimously passed disapproving of the proposed change.

As showing the thoroughly convertible nature of the notes, Mr. Gibson-Craig stated, at a meeting of the

county of Edinburgh, that "It was only the other day
that Mr. Maberly's house here had collected £30,000 of
Edinburgh bank-notes, and presented them for payment,
when gold was tendered in exchange. He said this was
not what he wanted, but bills on London ; but he was
told that the promise on the face of their notes was to
pay gold, which they would pay, and nothing else."[1]
He also referred to the bank failures which had occurred,
and showed that the note-issues were in no way connected
therewith, and that the country had suffered no loss.
The position of the Scottish banks was also warmly
defended in a number of pamphlets which appeared at
the time of this attack on one of their most vital characteristics. Indeed, the excitement produced by the well-
meant but misdirected attentions of the Government was
the means of producing in Scotland, for the first time,
anything which could be called financial literature. The
Scottish newspaper press, with a few exceptions, strongly
advocated the retention of the small-note issues. The
Scotch and Irish members strenuously opposed the
intended legislation, and successfully insisted on the
appointment of a committee of each House of Parliament
to inquire into the utility of small notes in Scotland and
Ireland. The committees examined a number of witnesses, and reported against the proposed change. On
the 8th of May, the Government confessed that they had
been convinced of the advisability of leaving the note-
issues of Scotland and Ireland on their present footing.

In looking back on this episode, while one may smile
at the intensity of the excitement, and especially at its
peculiarly Scottish national character, as seeing, in an
honest endeavour of the Government to improve the
currency system, an instance of Southern treachery, one
cannot but recognise the fact that the people were right,
and that it was well for Scotland that the intended change
was prevented. The paper currency of Scotland had been

[1] *Edinburgh Magazine*, March 1826.

of the greatest service in furthering the industries of the country. The total amount of loss by the note-issues of defaulting banks had been surprisingly small. In point of fact, the banking system of Scotland had worked remarkably well, and there was positively no occasion to make any legislative alteration in it, as far as the nation itself was concerned. At least, any changes which might have been advantageously introduced had no connection with the system pursued, or with the state of the paper currency. The object of the proposed measure was to secure uniformity in the currency of the three kingdoms. This was a desirable enough object, if it could have been attained without undue sacrifice. The price the Scotch and Irish people were asked to pay was, however, too much, seeing they were called on to sacrifice an essential portion of their existing system without obtaining any benefit in return.

At the present day the circumstances of the case are somewhat altered. (The legal tender provision of the note-issues is, of course, merely temporary.) Even as late as 1826, the use of a paper currency, which had been originally the great instrument in vitalising the industrial energies of Scotland in its poverty-stricken condition, still conferred some of its old benefits, although the nation had become comparatively wealthy. With still further increase in wealth, and with the restrictions imposed on note-issuing by the Acts of 1844 and 1845, the direct benefits of a bank-note currency have wellnigh vanished. Statesmen appear to be very ignorant on this point ; for, even at the present time, they speak as if the mere fact of retaining an issue of £1 notes would satisfy the necessities of Scotland. It is not the fact that Scotland possesses a paper currency of the denominations of £1 and upward that confers a special benefit on the nation. It is the fact that the *banks are permitted to issue* such a currency that forms the advantage. Without this right, the character of banking in Scotland would be considerably altered ;—the banks

might be forced to contract the extent of their operations; banking facilities would be withdrawn from a
number of localities presently in the enjoyment of them;
and the customers of banks would probably have to pay
increased charges. That, at least, would be the natural
tendency, although expanding economic conditions might
modify its manifestation. The reason of this is that, by
means of their right to issue, the banks can profitably
conduct business at a much cheaper rate than if they had
to use coin of the realm, or—what would be substantially
the same, as far as the present argument is concerned—
Government or Bank of England notes, for which they
would have to give full value.

This is the great point involved at the present time in
the question of Scottish bank-note issues, and it deserves
very full consideration by members of Parliament. But,
in 1826, this indirect advantage was not alone in operation;
the direct benefits conferred on a comparatively poor
country by an efficient paper currency were also active.
So popular were the notes of the Scottish banks—not
only in Scotland, but also in the northern counties of
England—that, during the height of the crisis, large
quantities of them were forwarded to these districts,
where, it is said, " they are equally as valuable as the
paper of the Bank of England." As to Scotland, the
writer adds, " So general is the feeling of security in this
country, that even the most ignorant people have scarcely
ventured to consider it possible that the distress at present existing in the English capital could extend to this
side of the Tweed." [1] It was well, therefore, that the banks
in Scotland were allowed to continue their long-established and well-appreciated custom of issuing £1 notes.

So conspicuously was the superiority of the constitution of the Scottish banking system over that of England

---

[1] *Scots Times* (Glasgow), 24th December 1825. See also Maberly
Phillip's *Banks, Bankers, and Banking*, London, 1894, pp. 100-1,
and Boase.

shown to be by the experience of this crisis, that, as we
have seen, the Government tried, as far as possible, to
extend its principles to the sister kingdom, by encouraging
the formation of large joint-stock banks. The attempt
proved highly successful, despite the difficulties presented
by the consequences of previous banking legislation.
Several banks, which have since become very powerful
institutions, were soon afterwards formed. In this connection, a writer,[1] who was himself a practical and
successful banker, and took an active part in the projection of joint-stock banks in London, very clearly
showed the advantages which were derivable from
adopting Scottish principles, by contrasting the experience
of the systems of banking pursued in Scotland and
England respectively. He further showed, what has
never been fully appreciated by English statesmen, that
paper currency, payable in gold on demand, cannot be
issued at pleasure ; and that the freedom of Scottish
banking, by permitting the growth of a system of large
joint-stock banks, had preserved the northern kingdom
from the disastrous experience which had attended banking in England. On the other hand, he made the curious
statement, that privacy was the cause of the success of
the Edinburgh banks. By this he means that they were
enabled to amass large profits by speculation in the public
funds. This was undoubtedly the case ; but the success
of the system cannot, of course, be used as an argument
against the publicity which is now rightly desiderated.

Another English banker,[2] who, however, is by no
means so complimentary to the Scottish bankers, denounced the past course of banking legislation with much

[1] *Principles and Practice of Banking*, T. Joplin, London, 1826.
The author founded, and was the first secretary of, the Provincial
Bank of Ireland.

[2] *The Scotch Banker*, Thomas Attwood, London, 1828. Mr.
Attwood was a banker in Birmingham. He writes fiercely against
the Scottish banks, styling them " monopolising and engrossing,"
and ascribes their comparative immunity from disaster to their not
being pressed. But why were they not pressed ?

vehemence, but with, perhaps, less discretion. The following quotation, from a more pleasing writer,[1] is interesting as an appreciative contemporary statement of the advantages of a paper currency :—" It has been proved that all the parties who make use of money for purposes of interchange, buyers as well as sellers, share in the great advantages derived from the substitution of paper for metallic money. Consequently, there can be no doubt that, by universal consent, the former will be used in preference to the latter, whenever the security offered for the convertibility of notes on demand is such as to ensure the public confidence. Thus it has been ascertained from experience, that gold and paper money of the same denominations will not circulate together. '*The paper drives out the gold*.' This has been, somewhat absurdly, made a matter of regret by those who fail in perceiving that it only takes place in consequence of the vast benefit which a paper currency confers on all producers, by enabling them to retain and employ that part of their capital which would otherwise be locked up in a metallic currency. So far from being a defect, it is the great merit of a paper currency, without which, indeed, it could neither be introduced into circulation, nor of any service were it introduced."

As the bogey of over-issuing is still raised against the Scottish banks from time to time, it may be well to point out that, under a system in which the notes are payable in legal tender on demand, with regular and frequent exchanges among a plurality of banks, widespread over the country, such as exists in Scotland, over-issuing is practically impossible. Any bank attempting to issue beyond the natural demand of the public, would find its notes coming back on it so rapidly that it would be forced at once to cease such action. The notes would not stay out ; and the other banks would soon bring their erring brother to book.

[1] *Credit Currency*, G. Poulett Scrope, London, 1830.

CHAPTER XVII

A TYPICAL PERIOD—JOINT-STOCK MANIA, AND THE CRISIS OF 1837

THE period which falls to be treated of in the present chapter extends from the crisis of 1825–6 to the death of King William IV. in 1837. It is a well-marked illustration of the theory of cycles in financial and commercial experience. From 1827 to 1832 there was commercial depression, consequent upon the sufferings and losses of the preceding crisis. With 1833 there came a change for the better — activity and enterprise were abundantly manifested, and prosperity shone on the land. Then followed renewed confidence, drifting into speculation, and culminating in the inevitable crisis. In its political aspects, the period is noticeable for the almost profound peace which Britain enjoyed, the only important exception being a short conflict with Turkey in 1827, when the battle of Navarino, fought by the allied squadrons of Britain, France, and Russia, gained the independence of Greece. In the earlier years of the period, much distress prevailed among the working classes, which broke out in riots, among which those at Bristol, in the autumn of 1831, acquired pre-eminence.

The Corn Laws were pressing heavily upon the people by maintaining the price of bread. The sliding scale of duties introduced in 1828 may have mitigated the sufferings ; but the high price of corn was in itself a sufficient affliction. The cholera epidemic of 1831–2 found the country in an unfavourable condition for resisting such a scourge. Meanwhile, however, the spirit of mechanical enterprise, to which we have referred in previous chapters, continued to develop. Following on the establishment of oceanic steam communication, the foundation of the great system of railways was laid on 15th September 1830, by the opening for traffic of the Manchester and Liverpool Railway ; and the application of steam power to various departments of industry was continually on the increase. The final abolition of Colonial slavery, the rapid increase of periodical literature, Parliamentary reform, the manifestation of the power of trade-unionism, and the adjustment of the Poor Laws, were other notable features of the period.

In the department of banking a rapid development took place. This is specially noticeable subsequently to 1833, when the Bank of England Charter Act was passed. By it the formation of joint-stock banks in London and the provinces was greatly facilitated. The Act of 1826, dealing with this matter, does not seem to have been explicit enough, or sufficiently wide in its provisions. Under the powers of the new Act, however, a mania for joint-stock banks sprang up, and this species of investment was greatly overdone. In 1835 and 1836 upwards of one hundred new banks were established in England and Wales alone, and thirteen in Ireland. In 1827 the directors of the Bank of England adopted an important resolution for the conduct of their business. This was, that in future the foreign exchanges, the variations in which had been systematically ignored since 1819, should be deemed a necessary factor in their calculations. Under a provision of the Act of 1833, moreover, they were required to publish a weekly statement of the position of the bank.

Turning to Scotland, which is the main subject of our record, there is much to chronicle. In 1826 there appear to have been about thirty-four individual banks, of which several had numerous branches, and most had some. The total number of offices is stated as 167, or 1 to every 13,000 inhabitants. An evidently very loose estimate of the deposits held by these establishments places the amount at from ten to twenty-five millions sterling; but two estimates which seem to have been thought competent give £20,000,000 and £24,000,000 as the amount. Such calculations are, of course, of little practical use; but they show, at all events, the ideas of magnitude in banking business held at that time. The par of exchange on London was 20 days, to which it had been reduced from 40 or 50 days, by the action of Maberly & Co. Gold and silver were scarce; and it is probable that a permanent issue of 5s. notes would have been very serviceable;[1] but the banks do not seem to have favoured denominations under £1, perhaps because the trouble and expense would have been more than the profit. Of these banks, several passed out of existence during the succeeding ten years. In 1829 the Montrose Bank, which had been established in 1814, was amalgamated with the Dundee Union Bank. The firm of James & Robert Watson failed in 1832. The house had been established in Glasgow in 1763 by David Watson, the later firm dating from 1793. At the time of their failure this firm were agents for a large number of banks; and it would seem that this department of banking constituted the main part of their business; but they are stated to have held the greatest amount of agency business of any bank in Glasgow.

In 1831 their office was robbed by London thieves. The robbery took place " on Sunday, 26th December 1831. The thieves escaped with their booty, but one of them, William Heath, was afterwards captured, tried, and executed. While under sentence of death, this villain confessed that he had nearly committed murder.

[1] It is stated that in Mull and the remoter Hebrides paper tokens or notes for 5s. continued, until about 1835, to have a limited circulation. A note by J. A. Stewart MacKenzie, Stornoway, of 21st January 1823, p. £1 Stg. is in the author's collection.

One Sunday before the robbery, he was in the bank trying the false keys, when one of the gentlemen of the bank came in. The robber had only time to glide behind a door. He saw the gentleman sit down, read a letter, and afterwards go out. The robber had a drawn dagger in his hand, and declared that if the gentleman had discovered him, he would at once have stabbed him to the heart." [1] Whether owing to this disaster, or to unsoundness in their business arrangements, they stopped payment in June of the succeeding year.

The two Edinburgh firms of Thomas Kinnear & Sons, and Donald Smith & Co., amalgamated their business in 1831 as Kinnears, Smith & Co. This arrangement ended, however, three years later by the failure of the new firm, with about £320,000 of liabilities—an event which caused a considerable run on one or two of the other private banks in Edinburgh. [2] In 1832 the exchange and deposit firm of J. Maberly & Co., who were also manufacturers in England, closed their doors after an existence of fourteen years. Their business was an important one on account of the number of offices at which it was conducted, and the active competition they carried on with the Scotch banks proper. The failure disclosed a large deficiency. The Commercial Banking Company of Aberdeen amalgamated with the National Bank of Scotland in 1833. The private firm of Robert Allan & Son, established at Edinburgh in 1776, stopped payment in 1834, with about £108,800 of liabilities. [3] About the same time, the younger firm of James Inglis & Co. (formerly Inglis, Borthwick, Gilchrist & Co.) also failed, their liabilities being stated at £23,000. It is probable that these events were connected with the failure of Kinnears, Smith & Co. just alluded to.

[1] *Banking in Glasgow*, p. 42.
[2] *Tait's Edinburgh Magazine*, September 1834. This firm issued notes of the Bank of Scotland only.
[3] They did not issue their own notes, but used those of the Royal Bank exclusively.

The Thistle Bank Company, established at Glasgow in 1761, amalgamated in 1836 with the Glasgow Union Bank. Another event of that year was the absorption of the Perth Union Banking Company by the National Bank of Scotland. Next year Messrs. Ramsays, Bonars & Co., private bankers in Edinburgh, withdrew from business. It is understood that their business had not, latterly, been of a favourable character; but their retirement was quite voluntary, and the business was wound up by themselves.[1] In November of this same year, the Paisley Banking Company, on the expiry of their contract of copartnership, made over their business, which included branches at Glasgow, Irvine, and Stranraer, to the British Linen Company. An important amalgamation, which took place in the same year, was that of the old Ship Bank and the Glasgow Bank Company, under the designation of the Glasgow and Ship Bank.

It will thus be seen that the period with which we are at present dealing witnessed the extinction of an unusual number of banking companies. It would seem as if those companies who, either from the smallness of their business, or from old-fashioned habits of mind on the part of their managers, were unable to adapt themselves to the altered and continually expanding circumstances of the country, were destroyed or swallowed up by their larger or more vigorous rivals. The doctrine of the survival of the fittest came powerfully into play amid the rapid development of the national industries, fostered by the achievements of mechanical skill. But while old banks disappeared, new ones arose; and the system of branches received a great impetus. The single office system

[1] Mr. Wenley gives the date as 1834; but the circular, stating that the " surviving partners, having determined to retire from business, hereby intimate that they will cease to receive any money on deposit, or to issue notes," is dated 6th February 1837. The business was continued for the convenience of customers, 3 per cent interest being allowed to depositors. Notes were to be retired on presentation either at their own office or at the Bank of Scotland.

appears to have been discarded almost entirely by the older establishments, and all the new banks seem to have considered branches as indispensable to their business. Private banking also was rapidly dying ; and, although a few firms survived this period, their real character was almost always veiled under a local designation. The old system of local, or, at best, district, banks, was rapidly giving way before the modern system of broad-based establishments, partaking to a greater or less extent of a national character. Greater safety and economy in management were thus secured ; but the new system, in its now largely-developed form, while in the main more satisfactory than its predecessor, has not been without its disadvantages to the trading community.

In the earlier years of the period under review, the great depression existing in connection with trade and finance prevented the formation of any new establishments, and very few new branches were opened. In 1830, however, the Ayrshire Banking Company, with a head office at Ayr, and five branches in the county, was established. A still more important movement was the formation of the Glasgow Union Bank, with branches at Edinburgh, Greenock, and Bathgate. Its capital was £350,000, held by 488 partners. By the rapid absorption of a multiplicity of large and small banks throughout the country, this bank fairly justified its name, and fully earned the designation of the Union Bank of Scotland, assumed by it in 1843.

Another great bank was formed in Glasgow in 1832, whose growth was still more rapid than that of the Union, and whose career was destined to secure to it a more unenviable notoriety than any of its predecessors had procured. The Western Bank of Scotland commenced business on 2nd July 1832. At its annual balance on 29th May 1833, the capital is placed at £209,170, held by 430 partners. From the outset it was managed with great activity, and it soon distanced its contemporaries in the growth of its business. But it achieved this result by setting at defiance the soundest principles of good management, in the face of the often-repeated remonstrances of friends and rivals ; until, twenty-five years after its establishment, it became a wreck, such as had never been seen previously in the financial history of Scotland. So innate do vicious principles of management appear to have been to it, that little more than two years after its formation we find that the London house of Jones, Lloyd & Co. declined to honour their drafts, and the Edinburgh banks refused to receive their notes, remonstrating with them in lengthened correspondence as to their action, and particularly as to their omission to maintain a sufficient cash and investment reserve. At length a reluctant consent appears to have been obtained from them. The manager was dismissed ; and it may be presumed some show of amendment was made.

Two years later than the Western Bank, the Central Bank of Scotland, with a capital of £78,125, was established, with its head office in Perth. On 23rd January 1834 they advertised an issue of new stock. The North of Scotland Banking Company was formed in Aberdeen in 1836 with a subscribed capital of £200,000. In 1848, owing to severe losses, their dividend was reduced from 7 per cent to 4 per cent ; but in 1857 it was 10 per cent on £200,000 paid up. In the same year an attempt was made to establish another bank in Glasgow. This was the City Banking Company of Glasgow. The attempt, however, proved abortive, owing, in all probability, to the doubt and hesitation prevailing among business men, as events tended towards the crisis which burst upon the nation soon afterwards.

Among other events deserving record was the passing of the Act 9 Geo. IV. c. 65, in 1828, by which the circulation in England of Scotch or Irish small notes was prohibited. The restriction did not extend to notes of £5 and upward. The Royal Bank of Scotland obtained, at the close of 1829, a new warrant of charter, by which it was empowered to increase its capital to £2,000,000. This power was exercised early in 1831, by appropriating £100,000 of reserved profits, and making a call of £400,000 on the proprietors.[1]   In 1831 the Commercial Bank and the National Bank obtained charters of incorporation. This judicious step was sadly marred by the adoption of the new principle, which had recently been obtaining general acceptance, of attaching unlimited liability to the stock of Corporations.

The amount of branch extension which occurred during the period with which we are at present dealing was extraordinary.   Not only did all the new banks open branches, but the older banks, with the exception of the Royal Bank, which steadily refrained for long after this time from establishing a general branch system, spread their agencies over the land with great rapidity.   About one hundred and ten new offices were opened, of which about 93 were branches of banks existing previously to 1827.   But while the Scottish banks were more or less affected by the prevailing excitement, it may be doubted if the following newspaper paragraph of the time was founded on fact.   It is, however, interesting as a contemporary record :—" Extract from a private letter from London.—' We have heard from good authority, that it is the intention of the Bank of Scotland, as well as the Royal Bank of Scotland, to follow the example of the Dundee Union Bank, and to immediately establish branch banks in London, for the purpose of circulating their notes.' "[2]

As we have already indicated, the turning point of the period was the year 1833.   From that time an active

---

[1] The immediate cause of this movement, which was hardly justified on principles of financial expediency, was (according to office tradition) an impression that the Government contemplated the abolition of the bank-notes issues, and the substitution of a State issue, in which event a large capital might secure special privileges in the conduct of the new system.   [2] *Courant*, 10th July 1834.

spirit of speculation set in, the main subject of which was joint-stock enterprise. In this department railways began to attract the favourable attention of promoters and investors ; but the railway mania proper belongs to a somewhat later date. Of the many forms which speculation assumed, the favourite was joint-stock banks. But numerous other species of companies were promoted. It has been estimated that, in the years 1834–5–6, the new companies projected involved nominal capitals to the extent of two hundred million pounds sterling.[1] But it was not thus alone that the speculative spirit found vent. Owing to the higher rates of interest offered in America, large quantities of United States securities were greedily absorbed in this country. This led to a continuous and heavy drain of gold from the Bank of England, which, despite the efforts of the bank to stem it, reduced the reserve to a low point.

The first actual disturbance began in Ireland in the autumn of 1836, by the suspension of the Agricultural Bank. It appears to have been a badly-managed concern. One or two of the few Irish private banking firms which had survived the crisis of 1820 also gave way. English bankers became alarmed, and their precautions led to a still further reduction of the stock of bullion in the Bank of England. A lull, however, took place ; but, in March of the succeeding year, the storm which had been brewing burst over England and Scotland. Many bankruptcies occurred ; but the recorded number for 1837 is not so much above the general average as might have been supposed, considering the active speculation which had been carried on. Of the failures in England, few appear to have been of bankers. The most notable bank failure

[1] " No fewer than 119 new companies have been started in London during the last year (1835). Of these, 41 are mining companies, 35 for the establishment of railways, and 43 miscellaneous. The nominal capital is—Mines, £2,994,000 ; railways, £34,040,000 ; miscellaneous, £19,811,000 ; total, £56,845,000."—*Edinburgh Chronicle*, 6th February 1836.

was that of the Northern and Central Bank of England. It had only been in existence for about three years. Another case was that of the Norwich and Norfolk Joint-Stock Bank; but it was a comparatively small affair. In neither case do the creditors seem to have lost, and the shareholders did not suffer very severely. We have already detailed the banking events which occurred in Scotland at this time, from which it will be seen that the crisis fell lightly on Scottish banking.

Among minor incidents within this period mention may be made of the loss of a remittance by the Bank of Scotland. On 27th February 1826 the smack *Delight*, on her passage from London to Leith, struck a sunken wreck off the Norfolk coast, and foundered in fifty feet of water. The passengers and crew took to the boats, were picked up and taken into Yarmouth. But a valuable cargo, and specie amounting to £4500 in gold and £500 in silver, going to the Bank of Scotland, were lost. As the remittance seems to have been insured, it is probable that the bank was reimbursed.

In this year (1826) an Act was passed which must have been of considerable service to the unincorporated banks. This was 7 Geo. IV. c. 67 (not c. 46, mentioned previously), to regulate the mode in which certain societies or co-partnerships for banking in Scotland may sue and be sued. It provided that all banks of issue, except the chartered banks, should enter on oath their names, and the name and abode of every partner and manager, in the books at the stamp office in Edinburgh, which were to be open for public inspection; and in the course of the year similar entries were to be made of any change of partners or officers. It also provided that such banks might sue and be sued under the names of their office-bearers. The introduction of the system of closing bank offices earlier on Saturdays, so as to allow the *employés* a weekly half-holiday, seems to have commenced about 1827. It may also be noticed that notes of the Scottish

banks for £1 appear to have circulated freely in the north
of England until 1828, when the Act 9 Geo. IV. c. 65,
prohibiting them, was passed. The issue of them in
England was already illegal, but not their circulation.
The change was not accomplished without opposition,
numerous petitions and other representations in favour
of the practice being presented to Parliament. A modification of the usury laws was made by the Bank of
England Charter Act of 1833, and was extended, and
made permanent, by subsequent Acts in 1836, 1850, and
1856.

Allusion may here be conveniently made to the
system of settling exchange balances. Until 1834 this
was done by the debtor banks giving drafts on London
at ten days' date for the amounts due by them. But in
consequence of the stoppage of a private bank in Edinburgh (presumably Robert Allan & Son, to whom we have
already referred), while many of the other banks held its
drafts, Mr. Blair, treasurer of the Bank of Scotland, proposed that the balances should be settled by exchequer
bills, similarly to the practice of the London Clearing
House. The bills were for £1000 each, the fractional
parts of the balances being paid in Bank of England
notes and specie, and latterly in notes of the three old
Scottish banks. Each bank was to hold an agreed-on
quota of bills. This system was adopted, and continued
in practice for many years. But it was an inconvenient
arrangement, and eventually a return was made to the
older plan, in a modified form. The system was continued
in Dublin, among the banks of issue, until superseded
by settlement of clearings through the Bank of Ireland
by drafts on London given or received by the respective
banks.

CHAPTER XVIII

THE CLOSE OF FREE BANKING

WITH the accession of Queen Victoria to the throne of Great Britain, on 20th June 1837, there commenced a new era in the history of the country. From that date onward there has been a triumphant progress of more remarkable development of industry, science, and social improvement, than history records of any former age. The beginnings of this social revolution have been indicated in previous chapters as concurrent with the century; but it was reserved for the Victorian era to achieve its development. The application of steam to navigation and manufactures had accomplished a mighty work, but the connecting link was wanting so long as inland transit was conducted under the slow and laborious methods of highways and canals. When steam railways became an established system, men's eyes were opened; and from thenceforth they thought and acted with an independence and activity they had never formerly displayed. Improvements in every department of business and social relationship succeeded each other with uninterrupted rapidity.

The general condition of the country, however, at the time with which we are at present dealing, was not yet one of emancipation. Men's eyes were indeed opening to the realisation of brilliant possibilities, but they failed not also to see intolerable evils around them. The achievement of constitutional liberty in 1832 had, as yet, done little beyond making the nation conscious of its power to accomplish its own emancipation. But when that consciousness had been attained, the good work sped apace. Deterrent influences were, however, at work. Wars in China and India—costly and, at times, very disastrous ; Chartist riots and Irish troubles ; industrial and agricultural distress and disturbances, and a high rate of bankruptcies, followed, for a few years, the effects of the crisis of 1837. But the national appreciation of railways was not to be checked in its manifestation. A mania for investment in railway undertakings set in, resulting in a much more rapid expansion of the system than the circumstances of the country warranted. Trade was thus stimulated, both directly and indirectly, to an unusual extent.

The position of banking in Scotland at the close of 1837 was as follows :—There were five chartered banks, with aggregate capitals amounting to £4,600,000, on which dividends averaging 6 per cent were paid. Five other joint-stock banks had capitals amounting to £1,550,000, on which the dividends averaged slightly less than 6 per cent. These ten banks had 213 branches, of which the chartered banks held 158. There were, besides, other seven joint-stock banks, and seven private banks, with 37 branches. This gives a total of twenty-four banks, with 274 offices. The average circulation of these banks does not appear to have much exceeded three millions sterling, the small notes forming about two-thirds of the total amount. The amount of the deposits was estimated at twenty-five millions ; but little weight can be attached to a calculation which, in the absence of official information, must have been largely founded on imagination. The average price of the stocks of the chartered banks was 178 per cent, and such of the shares of the other banks as were quoted stood at high premiums.

In 1838 the affairs of the Western Bank of Scotland again came into prominence. The experience of the recent crisis, combined with the results of injudicious banking in America, and the public attention which was increasingly bestowed on banking, led the Edinburgh banks to consult with the other banks in Scotland as to the advisableness of permanently maintaining large reserves of coin and Government securities, in order to secure the proper conduct of banking in Scotland. It may be presumed that there was a consensus of opinion on this point ; but it was a wise and even necessary step that negotiations on the subject should be held, considering that one powerful establishment had hitherto ignored the principle. This was the Western Bank of Scotland. They had a paid-up capital of £600,000, on which a dividend of 5 per cent was paid, and they had seventeen branches throughout the country. Four years previously they had been remonstrated with on the same matter, on an application by them for assistance. They had then given a reluctant adhesion to the practice, and had obtained large advances to enable them at once to carry it out. But, the immediate necessity past, they appear to have relapsed into their bad habit. When the Edinburgh banks again remonstrated in 1838, they defended themselves on the grounds that investments of a fluctuating character should be avoided, and that the fostering of the trade of the country was their first duty. The banks then intimated that after 21st July they would decline to take Western Bank notes, unless their wishes were complied with. After further negotiations the Western Bank again undertook to conform to the practice of investing in Government stocks, and the Edinburgh banks withdrew their resolution. Later in the same year the Western Bank applied to the Crown for a charter of incorporation ; but, on representations by the Edinburgh banks, based on the tenor of the correspondence referred to, the application was refused.

During the year 1838, six new joint-stock banks were established in Scotland. Of these, the most important,

as viewed from the present time, was the Clydesdale
Banking Company in Glasgow, with a paid-up capital
of £375,000, in £20 shares with £10 paid.   Three years
later its paid-up capital was £500,000, and the shares sold
at £12 : 17s.   At first its only branch office was in Edinburgh.   The only other bank started in this year, which
survived to the close of the nineteenth century, was the
Caledonian Banking Company in Inverness.   It began
with a capital of £125,000, one quarter of which was paid
up.   It would appear that its projection met with serious
opposition in some quarters, but that, nevertheless, its
shares were popular with the public.   In 1841 the paid-
up capital was £75,000, and the £2 : 10s. shares sold at
£3.   The Caledonian Bank was taken over by the Bank
of Scotland in August 1907.   The Eastern Bank of
Scotland was a hurriedly-organised concern, destined for
a special purpose.   That purpose was to take over the
business of the Dundee Commercial Bank, whose affairs
had got into a hopeless condition, before the state of the
latter bank should become public.   This object was
successfully accomplished, and the Eastern Bank of
Scotland commenced business in July 1838, with a paid-
up capital of £112,510.   The chief office was in Dundee,
but there was also a nominal head office in Edinburgh.

A still more important establishment was the Edinburgh and Leith Bank.   It is stated to have been designed
for the benefit of the " industrious middle class," and it
at once sprang into popularity.   A contemporary writer
says of it : " A great deal of speculation took place in
the stock of the Edinburgh and Leith Bank.   The shares
went to 5s. premium as soon as they were in the market,
and 2000 or 3000 shares have been known to change hands
in the course of a single day.   It is now (1841) one of the
most popular banks in Edinburgh, and sells at a high
premium." [1]   Its capital was £500,000 in £5 shares fully

[1] *Manual of the Scottish Stocks and British Funds*, p. 22, by John
Reid.   Second edition.   Edinburgh, 1841.

paid. It had six branches. In 1844 it was re-organised as the Edinburgh and Glasgow Bank, at which time the Glasgow Joint-Stock Bank joined it, with a paid-up capital of £1,000,000. No bank had better chances of a long and prosperous career than this one. Starting with popularity, it rapidly obtained a large deposit business. Its authorised circulation under the Act of 1845 was £136,657, which was much in excess of that of any other bank of its own age. But antagonistic management between the western and eastern offices, and incompetent direction under the two boards, which the Edinburgh directors were too feeble and ignorant of financial business to control, occasioned the losing of the golden opportunity. Heavy losses were incurred; the bank's credit was affected during the crisis of 1857, and next year its valuable business, together with the large authorised issue, passed into the hands of the Clydesdale Bank by amalgamation, in which the shareholders gained nothing except relief from a responsibility which never emerged.

The Paisley Commercial Bank was also formed in 1838. Its capital was £200,000 in £20 shares, one half being paid up. After a short career it was merged in the Western Bank. Another venture of this year was the Southern Bank of Scotland, with its head office in Dumfries. Its projection was coldly received, but it would seem that its shares went to a premium very soon. It had a capital of £500,000 in £20 shares, with £5 paid. In 1841 its shares, with a 5 per cent dividend, were at 2s. 6d. premium; but on 31st October next year it was fain to find rest from incompetent management in the bosom of the Edinburgh and Leith Bank. It had seven branches.

Next year (1839) the prospectus of a new bank in Glasgow was issued, in which it was observed: " It is not a little astonishing that, notwithstanding the rapid strides which commercial enterprise has taken in Glasgow (and a correct idea of its extent may be formed by a glance at the shipping arriving at the harbour, the revenue from which, during the last thirty years, has increased from £1000 to nearly £40,000 during that period), only three new banks have been formed in Glasgow, all of which have been eminently successful." This new financial venture, designed to make amends for want of enterprise in former years in accommodating the expanding trade of the great western community, and intended as an addition to the roll of brilliant banking successes, was the now world-known City of Glasgow Bank. It had a capital of £750,000 in £10 shares, of which £656,250 was paid up by the middle of 1841, the price then being £9 : 10s. for £8 : 15s. paid per share. The lamentable manner in which this bank failed to realise its intentions, as expressed by its promoters, is now only too well known. It suspended payment for thirty-three days during the crisis of 1857, having succeeded, during the eighteen years of its existence, in laying the foundation of a style of bank management peculiar to itself. Having tided over its difficulties, it resumed the practical study of those economic theories, the full development of which won for it, twenty-one years later, greater notoriety than had ever previously fallen to the lot of any business establishment.

The Glasgow Joint-Stock Bank and the Greenock Union Bank were formed in 1840. It is stated that the projection of the former bank " met with great encouragement, and the applications for shares were very numerous." In 1841 it had a paid-up capital of £562,500, and its shares stood at a fair premium. As already stated, it joined the Edinburgh and Leith Bank, in 1844, as the Edinburgh and Glasgow Bank. The Greenock Union Bank had a paid-up capital of £125,000. Its shares sold at a discount soon after it commenced business. It joined the Clydesdale Bank in 1844, after a good deal of coquetting with both them and the Western Bank.

The Glasgow Banking Company (the second of similar name) was formed, or at least promoted, towards the close of 1843, but it does not seem to have commenced business until the next year. At all events, it is said not to have issued notes prior to 6th May 1844, and consequently to have been unable to secure the right of note-issuing in terms of the prohibition of the Act of 1844 applied to banks which were not issuing at that date. It may be that the average issue was so small as to be considered practically worthless, no value being placed at that time on the right to issue against coin in reserve. When the Act of 1844 was passed, it amalgamated in July 1844 with the Western Bank.[1] That it was considered of importance is evident from the facts that its shares at once went to a considerable premium, that it was said to have secured 800 shareholders, and to have met with warm support in Glasgow. Moreover, so strong an institution as the National Bank appears to have contemplated its acquisition as their Glasgow office (although they already had a branch there) on favourable terms. The arrangement with the Western Bank was concluded in July 1844, the new bank getting shares of the former on terms which are stated to have yielded them about 7s. 6d. premium on their own shares. Thus practically ended the formation of new banks in Scotland. It must be admitted, however, that, for a population of about $2\frac{1}{2}$ millions, the finish was rather brilliant.

But while so many new banks were entering the list, some veteran firms were retiring. The business of Sir William Forbes & Company ceased to be a private bank

[1] *Banking in Glasgow during the Olden Time,* p. 32. Glasgow, 1862. See also 1884 edition, p. 22, note 2, which is interesting, particularly to people in Glasgow. See also Boase, second edition, p. 425. Logan, second edition, p. 24, states the National Bank Glasgow branch scheme as having been carried out, which is an erroneous anticipation. R. Allan's Share Circular of 30th November 1843 gives details of the scheme.

in 1838, when an amalgamation was effected with the Glasgow Union Bank. In consideration, however, of the extent of business and high reputation of the firm, the old designation continued to be used until the Glasgow Union Bank transformed itself into the Union Bank of Scotland in 1843. The Paisley Union Bank Company also joined the Glasgow Union Bank in 1838. On 2nd May 1843 the Glasgow Union Bank assumed the national designation of the Union Bank of Scotland, at the same time reducing its nominal capital of $2\frac{1}{2}$ millions to 1 million, one half of which was paid up. Soon thereafter (August) it absorbed the old-established house of Hunters & Co., the Ayr Bank. It made a still more important arrangement a few months later, whereby a junction with the Glasgow and Ship Bank took place as of 1st December. In connection with this event, the paid-up capital was raised to £1,000,000.[1]

In November the Western Bank absorbed the Greenock Banking Company, paying the partners a large premium, an event which is usually considered as the extinction of private banking in Scotland. About this time also the Greenock Union Bank arranged to join with the Clydesdale Bank, an event which appears to have taken place at the close of the year.[2] It is said there was considerable competition between the banks in both Edinburgh and Glasgow to get the business. In 1844, in addition to the Edinburgh and Leith and Glasgow Joint-Stock union just referred to, the Paisley Commercial Bank and the Dundee Union Bank joined the Western Bank (31st March), and the Arbroath Banking Company joined the Commercial Bank.

At this time, moreover, the City of Glasgow Bank

[1] The terms of purchase are stated to have been, that for each £10,000 share of the latter bank (valued at £18,000), 200 shares of the former (market quotation, £90) were given, together with a bonus of about £1000 a share in lieu of dividend.

[2] The equation in this case was one Clydesdale £20 share (£10 paid) at £12 : 10s. for every two Greenock Union, £5 paid, at par ; the new holder to pay the difference of £2 : 10s. in cash.

acquired the Edinburgh establishment of the Eastern Bank, which included a local board of directors. There is also a statement that they took up " the Commercial of Aberdeen " ; but, although they did open a branch there in 1844, the reference is not easily understood, as the Commercial Banking Company of Aberdeen was absorbed by the National Bank in 1833. The acquisition of the new Glasgow Bank by the Western (already referred to) closed this great series of amalgamations. But it was not only by the honourable means of amalgamation that the roll of banks was being reduced. Insolvency, also, was thinning the ranks. In 1842 there were three failures, but none of them was of great magnitude. These were the Leith Banking Company (25th April), the Renfrewshire Banking Company (1st April), and Hay & Ogilvie (the Shetland Bank), all of whom were sequestrated with considerable loss to their creditors. The liabilities of the Leith Bank were £123,582, on which dividends of 13s. 4½d. per pound in all were paid. The circulation was small—about £10,000. They were exceptional in issuing notes of a £2 denomination. There were six branches in Scotland, and, from 1835–37, one in Carlisle, which was registered as an English bank.[1] The Renfrewshire Bank had debts to the amount of £226,545, and paid about 9s. per pound ; but holders of receipts or notes dated prior to 1840 were paid in full by Mr. Dunlop of Keppoch, a former partner. They had five branches. The Shetland Bank's debts were about £140,000, and the dividend 6s. per pound.

A somewhat exceptional action was taken by the Eastern Bank in 1844 (1st November), in repaying one-third of their capital to the shareholders, thus reducing it to £400,000, while at the same time they retained £2 a share to clear off bad debts. The movement seems to have favourably affected the market price of their shares. As curiosity became excited, towards 1843, as to the

[1] See Appendix G.

intentions of the Government in regard to banking and currency, private banks rapidly disappeared by amalgamation with their joint-stock rivals, until, in 1844, all had disappeared with the doubtful exception of Alexander Allan & Co. in Edinburgh.

CHAPTER XIX

THE REVOLUTION SETTLEMENT

THE year 1844 marks a distinct revolution in the constitution of banking in the United Kingdom. Owing to the pernicious effects of special legislation in favour of the Bank of England, the natural development of banking in England had been greatly hampered. The Bank of England would neither themselves supply the necessities of the provinces (indeed, they could not have done so to more than a small extent), nor would they allow any other powerful establishment to minister to them. The consequence was that English provincial banking was perforce conducted by small private partnerships, whose responsibility was, as far as the public was concerned, a matter entirely of faith or conjecture. Until 1826 not more than six persons were permitted to associate themselves for the purpose of carrying on the business of banking. Thus for a period of one hundred and thirty-two years from the formation of the Bank of England, every encouragement was given to weak bankers; strong banks (with one exception) were absolutely prohibited; and the one powerful establishment, for whose special benefit the public interests were ignored, was not required, nor did it spontaneously endeavour, to supply the vacuum.

From this state of matters it very naturally followed that every financial crisis produced a long list of bank failures, and that, periodically, an outcry was made about the insecurity of bank notes. That the results were not worse than they actually proved, must be attributed to the general respectability of the persons with whom the public entrusted their financial affairs, and not to any beneficial element in banking legislation. That was tinkered from time to time, each operation encroaching slightly on the monopoly of the Bank of England ; but the monopoly itself, the real element of weakness, was ever regarded as too sacred an institution to be absolutely removed. No Government would face such a daring operation, nor is it probable that any actually recognised it as the proper remedy. In 1826, as we have already seen, the nearest approach to this course was taken ; but the operation was only half accomplished.

Sir Robert Peel's powerful and practical mind recognised the necessity of putting banking legislation on a proper footing. He saw the weaknesses of the existing system, and wisely determined to remove them. His diagnosis of the case was, however, in one essential particular, very deficient, and his treatment was hampered by preconceived ideas. He certainly did good—he succeeded in establishing the convertibility of bank notes, or, at least, in minimising the danger of their proving inconvertible. But he accomplished this by creating a most cumbrous and artificial system to supersede a simple but pernicious one, in place of sweeping away all monopolies and permitting a healthy and natural development. He failed to study exhaustively the history of the case. He saw correctly enough the existing condition ; he saw that banks were weak, and that notes were sometimes not convertible either on demand or at any subsequent period. He therefore came to the conclusion that the system of private issues was bad, and should be discouraged. He appears entirely to have overlooked the vast public benefits derivable from such issues ; the danger attaching to them was too close to his mind's eye to allow him an unbiassed judgment.

All that he really contended for—that is, the convertibility of the note—might have been effectually secured without paralysing the provincial issues. He might have absolutely abolished issues without security, provided the right of issue had been preserved, and the public interests would not have been injured; but by drawing a hard and fast line, beyond which issues could not go, he prevented bankers from ministering to the wants of the public in as great a measure as they might have done. He seized the idea that note-issuing and banking were essentially distinct; that the former was the prerogative of the State, and that the latter should be conducted without connection with the former. He refused to recognise the danger of entrusting Governments with the power of paper issues, and he failed to appreciate the great public benefit of the association of issuing with general banking. He therefore devised a measure which should so far conciliate existing interests, but tend to the abolition of private issues, and leave the trade of banking absolutely free. As we will see, he succeeded in establishing a new monopoly, and in restricting the freedom of banking.

On 7th May 1844, he introduced a bill, which, on 19th July following, became the Act 7 and 8 Vict. c. 32, " to regulate the issue of bank notes, and for giving the Governor and Company of the Bank of England certain privileges for a limited period." We cannot do better than quote the words of a contemporary writer in describing the Act : " The Bank's charter was renewed by the Act 7 and 8 Vict. cap. 32, 19th July 1844. Its chief points were as follows :—1. After 31st August 1844, the issue of notes to be by the Bank, acting by a committee of directors, under the name of ' The Issue Department of the Bank of England.' 2. Securities of £14,000,000 to be set apart for this, and gold to be held for amount of

notes beyond this.   3. If any bank of issue ceases issuing
notes, the Crown in Council may authorise the Bank's
Issue Department to hold securities for two-thirds the
amount of that bank's issues, and increase the £14,000,000
of notes against securities to that extent. [This has
since been done to the extent of £4,450,000.]   4. Weekly
accounts of the bank's position to be published in the
Gazette.   5. Bank to pay £60,000 more than the £120,000
settled in 1833 for their privileges, and all profits on
notes beyond £14,000,000 to accrue to the public.   6.
No new banks of issue to be permitted after 6th May
1844.   7. Any bank ceasing to issue notes not to be
allowed to resume issues.   8. All banks of issue to be
allowed to issue an amount equal to their average circulation for twelve weeks preceding 27th April 1844.   9.
Bank of England to be allowed to compound with private
banks of issue to withdraw their notes, and get a commission not exceeding one per cent, till 1st August 1856.
10. Privileges of the Bank to continue till twelve months'
notice after August 1855." [1]

Of these provisions, the only one directly affecting
banking in Scotland is the 6th. By it the formation
of new banks of issue, which had hitherto been freely
exercised, was prohibited. There were nineteen banks
of issue in Scotland on 6th May 1844. Their total
average circulation was ascertained to be £3,087,209,
which amount consequently became their authorised
issue of bank notes. Since then, by the failure of two
banks, the absorption of eight banks, and the conjunction
of the North of Scotland and Town and County Banks,
the number of banks of issue has been reduced to eight,
and the authorised issues to £2,676,350. The present
average circulation of all the banks is close on £17,000,000.

Further legislation was deferred until next year,
when the cases of Ireland and Scotland were dealt with
specially. The Irish Act, 8 and 9 Vict. c. 37, 21st July

[1] Boase, second edition, p. 428.

1845, rectified one great evil which had resulted from the establishment of the Bank of Ireland on principles of special privilege, as in the case of the Bank of England. Hitherto no partnership or company consisting of more than six persons, other than the Bank of Ireland, had been permitted to conduct banking business in Dublin, or within fifty miles of it. This prohibition was abolished by the 1st section of the Act, from and after 6th December ensuing. Provision was made for the repayment of sums advanced by the Bank of Ireland for the public service, and for the dissolution of the bank if determined on. Bank of England notes were not to be a legal tender in Ireland ; banks might surrender their right of issue in favour of the Bank of Ireland ; and notes for less than 20s. were prohibited. With the exception of a special provision referring to an agreement between the Bank of Ireland and the Tipperary Joint-Stock Bank (which had been established by John Sadlier in 1839, and failed in 1856, with great loss to creditors through the fraud and forgery of its founder), under which the latter only issued notes of the former, the other enactments of the Irish Act are similar to those of the Scotch Act, to which we must now refer.

On the 21st July 1845 there received the Royal assent " an Act to regulate the Issue of Bank Notes in Scotland," 8 and 9 Vict. c. 38. This is the Act under which the note circulation of Scotland has since been conducted. As no special privileges existed among the Scottish banks (the matter of incorporation was entirely within the power of the Crown), legislation was comparatively simple. Sir Robert Peel was convinced that he could not extirpate either the small or the large notes, as the people strongly believed (in what he doubtless considered their ignorance) that their bank-note system had been an efficient agent in advancing the prosperity of the country. That the public of Scotland were correct in their view of this matter, will, it may be hoped, be evident from the former chapters of this history. At the same time it may be conceded in favour of Sir Robert Peel's theories, that the usefulness of the notes was not in 1845 what it had been in former times. The paper currency, formerly indispensable to the commerce of a country which was too poor to indulge in the precious metals, was no longer absolutely necessary under the happier circumstances to which the country had attained ; but the people liked the notes, and continued to regard their existence as of as much necessity as formerly.

It does not appear from contemporary writings that the true value of bank-note issues in modern times was actually appreciated. The defenders of the *status quo* always drew their arguments from past experience, which, as we have seen, was every year losing, to some extent, its applicability. The great use of bank notes in relation to banking at the present time, from a public point of view, is their function of enabling banks to extend banking facilities into all parts of a country—thinly-populated and poor districts as well as dense centres and wealthy provinces. The saving in wear and tear of coin is another important benefit. Not only is there much less loss in this way, but such as there is practically falls on bankers.

Sir Robert Peel, however, was determined to restrict to some extent the rights of issue in Scotland, although he was forced to confer freer powers of action than he had accorded to English bankers. The 1st section of the Act re-enacts the prohibition of new issuing banks contained in the English Act, and made arrangements for ascertaining the average circulation of each existing bank, so that the amount of their authorised issues might be fixed. Sections 2, 3, and 4 provided that uniting banks might retain the full powers of issue enjoyed by them separately. Section 5 prohibits notes for fractional parts of £1. This was no new provision, as it had existed since 1765. Section 6 permits banks to issue to the extent of their

14

authorised issues, *plus* the average amount of gold and silver coin held at their head offices during every successive period of four weeks. Section 7 provides for the rendering to the Commissioners of Stamps and Taxes of weekly accounts relating to note-issues. Section 8 defines bank notes in circulation as those which had left bank offices and had not been returned thereto. Section 9 enjoins Commissioners of Stamps and Taxes to publish monthly returns of the state of the bank issues. Section 10 regulates the mode of ascertaining the average amount of notes in circulation. Section 11 enacts that silver coin shall only count as against the note-issues to the extent of one-fourth of the gold so held. Section 12 empowers the commissioners to inspect bankers' books for the purpose of ascertaining the accuracy of returns. This power has never been exercised. Section 13 orders all bankers (except the three limited banks) to render a yearly return of the names of all partners. Section 14 prescribes that the penalty on excess of issues, beyond the authorised circulation and the metallic reserve, shall be forfeiture of the excess. Section 15 provides that Bank of England notes shall not be legal tender in Scotland. This was merely a specific enactment of the existing law. Section 16 makes notes under 20s. not negotiable. Section 17 prescribes the form of notes for amounts from 20s. to £5. Sections 18 and 19 prescribe penalties for the non-observance of provisions of the Act. Section 20 exempts cheques from inclusion under the provisions of this Act. Section 21 refers to the mode of recovering penalties ; and Section 22 (the last) interprets the words used in the Act.

Although this Act does not square in all respects with economic principles, there can be little doubt that its main provisions have proved salutary to the public interest. The needless formation of new banks at once ceased, much to the public benefit. Now that the note-issues exceed the authorised circulation, a bullion reserve on the part of every bank is secured. No doubt a well-regulated bank would hold such a reserve without being forced to do so ; but then all banks are not well regulated. The provisions in favour of amalgamating banks have tended to the elimination of small and weak banks. A system of large and widespread banks was encouraged. All these benefits, however, are more incidental to the operation of the Act than actually designed by it. The convertibility of the notes, and the prevention of over-issues, were the great objects of Sir Robert Peel's measure. But it did not secure, although it perhaps strengthened, the convertibility of the notes ; and over-issues were already impossible under the long-established system of exchanges subsisting among the banks.

Some positive disadvantages, moreover, attach to the Act. A monopoly of banking, although not directly established, has been a practical outcome of its provisions, for it is believed to be impossible to successfully conduct a non-issuing bank in competition with the banks of issue. The relative proportions of the authorised issues also, although accurate at the time they were fixed, are now out of keeping with the actual circulations of the various banks. It must also be borne in mind that the elimination of local banks and bankers has not been an unmitigated benefit to the country. These were in much more direct contact with their clients than great centralised institutions can be, and could thus recognise more intimately individual circumstances. No doubt agents have this knowledge ; but the restrictions on their discretion tend to become more stringent from the operation of the necessarily stereotyped principles of distant head-office control. Had that system prevailed from the outset, there would have been fewer cases of individual progress from zero to fortune during the earlier period of Scottish banking than have been actually witnessed. But, whether the Act has fully answered the real intentions of its framer or not, it has not interfered with the public interest in retaining a widespread system of banking, and it has tended to the solidification of the banking institutions of the country.   Had England been blessed with as good an Act, it would have been spared many grievous banking questions, which have disturbed the equanimity of economists and statesmen.

CHAPTER XX

IN last chapter an account was given of the revolution
in banking legislation effected by the three Acts passed
under the auspices of Sir Robert Peel, for the three
kingdoms respectively. To complete the survey of banking in Scotland to the close of the year 1845, only a few
further particulars require to be specified. In 1844 the
National Bank of Scotland increased its paid-up capital
from £500,000 to £1,000,000. The new shares were
allotted to the existing proprietors. As it does not appear
that any premium was required, and as the market price
was about 50 per cent premium, this would constitute a
large bonus. The shares were at the same time converted
into stock. The Commercial Bank of Scotland absorbed,
in the middle of the same year, the Arbroath Banking
Company, a small joint-stock bank, which seems, like
Dogberry, to have had losses, of which, however, it was
not so proud as to resist the temptation of security under
the *ægis* of the brilliant metropolitan establishment which
had so rapidly and surely won success in the banking field.

Early in 1845 there seems to have been an attempt
to form a new bank in Glasgow, which, however, was
unsuccessful. But that it assumed concrete form is
indicated by a remark in a contemporary stockbroker's
circular : " Clydesdale is also better, in consequence of
an arrangement they have entered into with a second
establishment recently formed under the title of the

' Glasgow ' Bank, which has not succeeded." [1] The Western Bank increased their capital at this time, by £300,000, making it £1,300,000, which enabled them to add £120,000 to the reserve fund. They also bought the business of the Ayrshire Banking Company, giving them a premium of £60,000. The Ayrshire had existed for seventeen years, and had nine well-placed branches.

In this same year some excitement was occasioned by the removal from office of Mr. John Thomson, cashier of the Royal Bank of Scotland. This unusual incident was occasioned by Mr. Thomson's refusal to retire gracefully by resignation, when the interests of the establishment seemed to the directors to require a change of management. Mr. Thomson angrily addressed the proprietors on the subject, but the nature of his defence only served to justify the action of the board. He subsequently became manager of the Edinburgh and Glasgow Bank, and in that capacity he did not disprove the wisdom of the Royal Bank board in relieving him of his duties.

During November 1845, a sharp stock exchange panic occurred, as the result of long-continued and excessive speculation in railway scrip. The effects were very acute while it lasted, and heavy losses were sustained by private persons ; but the banks only benefited by an increased demand for advances and improved interest rates. The market quotations of their stocks, however, were materially lowered by forced sales on the part of embarrassed holders.

It will be proper to refer here to a species of company which, about this time, was the subject of a speculative mania, and whose operations were to some extent allied to banking. Indeed, some of these companies actually styled themselves " banks," although most of them were content with the less pretentious and more appropriately descriptive term of " exchange companies." The occasion

---

[1] R. Allan, 31st January 1845. This was the third company of that name.

of the formation of these companies was the great development of all classes of joint-stock associations, and more
particularly of railway companies, to which reference has
already been made. This extensive joint-stock enterprise was, to a large extent, mere speculation, and
applicants for shares had very often no intention of retaining their allotments longer than was necessary to secure
the premium to which public credulity and the wiles of
promoters usually raised the shares soon after the floating
of the company. In order to carry on these transactions
to the best advantage, speculators sought for advances
on the security of their stocks.

Banks looked on such business as beyond the limits
of their legitimate profit ; but the demand for accommodation produced the necessary means for supply. Exchange
companies sprang into existence, and achieved a rapid
and brilliant success, beyond the expectations of their
projectors. It was in Glasgow that this industry was
originated, and where, also, it was most extensively
carried on. The first of these companies formed in
Scotland appears to have been the Glasgow Commercial
Exchange Company, which commenced business in May
1845. The capital was £1,000,000, of which half was
paid up. Before the close of that year four similar
companies were formed in Glasgow, and other two followed
soon thereafter. In Edinburgh only one exchange
company seems to have been established, although
another (probably the British Exchange Company [1]) was
projected towards the close of 1846 ; but Aberdeen and
Dundee helped to swell the list. The Edinburgh establishment was called the Exchange Bank of Scotland,[2] and
was under the management of Mr. Duncan M'Laren,

[1] First quoted by Allan, 1st December 1846, £10 share, 5s. paid,
price 6s. 3d. ; and last, 1st April 1848, @ 2s. 6d. No dividend is indicated during the interval.
[2] Paid-up capital £350,000, dividend 6 per cent, share £100, £50
paid, price £54 ex. div.—R. Allan, 1st March 1847. In the official
stock list of 3rd August 1846, the shares are stated as £10, £5 paid,
price £5 : 10s.

afterwards well and honourably known in connection with the affairs of the city of Edinburgh.   It obtained a Royal charter in December 1846.

The extent of the operations of these companies may be estimated from the fact that they usually had a full staff of officials, such as manager, secretary, cashier, and accountant, with a staff of clerks to correspond.   Indeed, they aimed at appearing as thoroughly-equipped banking offices.   As, during the height of the speculative mania which followed the brilliant harvests and general prosperity of the years 1842–45, speculators paid from $5\frac{1}{2}$ per cent to 8 per cent for advances, while deposit money could be obtained with a margin of $2\frac{1}{2}$ per cent profit, the operations of these companies were attended with very great success. But, like Sancho Panza's enjoyment of power and luxury, this bliss was of short duration.   The approach of the severe crisis of the autumn and winter of 1847–48 cur-tailed their business, and during the crisis they suffered heavy losses—a contingency which they seem never to have contemplated.   Public confidence in them completely broke down, and in rapid succession they collapsed. Three of them disappeared in 1848, after a brief career of three years' duration.   The British Exchange Company was wound up about the end of April 1848 with a dividend of 3s. $2\frac{1}{2}$d. for the 5s. deposit.[1]   The Exchange Bank sur-vived till 1852, one of the Glasgow companies till 1853, and another maintained for many years a sort of galvanic existence, and a place in the *Banking Almanac*, although even its name is but little known.   This is the North British Bank.   It was established at Glasgow in August 1845, and in 1872 its paid-up capital was stated to be £120,000, held by 155 partners, on which it paid a dividend of 1 per cent.[2]   In later years, however, it seems to have

[1] R. Allan, who somewhat cryptically remarks, " under the cir-cumstances a proper auditing of the accounts would give satisfaction "; but whether to the critics or to the shareholders is not stated.

[2] 1848—Paid-up capital £250,000, no dividend, share £50, £10 paid, price £1 : 17s.   3rd August 1846—price £10.

refrained from paying even that small dividend, and it
has, at the same time, modestly withheld particulars as
to its financial position. Subsequently it conducted a
bonded store business, but was wound up some years ago,
the business being taken over by the Warroch Street
Stores, Ltd.

The theory on which these companies were formed
was by no means an unsound one. Had they been
managed with sufficient caution, and had time been given
them to secure consolidation, they might have weathered
the storms which inevitably disturb the financial world
in well-marked cycles. But they were formed at a time
when the securities in which they dealt were at inflated
prices, and they acted as if the vast extension of financial
activity which brought them into being would prove
perennial. They were guilty, moreover, of grave errors
in business management in regard to the securities they
accepted. They also indulged in reckless competition
with each other, and, strange to say, involved themselves
in each other's liabilities, by taking over exchange
companies' shares as security for advances. The soundness of the business, when properly conducted, is best
evidenced by the fact that, when exchange companies
had paid the forfeit for their bad management, banks
adopted the business of advancing on stocks as one of
their regular departments, and have since conducted it
with much profit. In a pamphlet [1] written in defence
of the companies when they were beginning to get
into difficulties, a complaint was made that the banks
attempted to suppress the companies by the formation
of an association to deal with this business in their own
interest, under the designation of the British Trust
Company.

The interval of about ten years and seven months

[1] *Banks and Exchange Companies.* George Kinnear. Glasgow,
1847. The author was manager of the Glasgow Commercial Exchange
Company. He also issued *A History of the Rise of Exchange Companies in Scotland, and a Defence of their Proper Business.*

which elapsed from the crisis of 1837 to that which we must now refer to, shows the usual rotation of experiences in financial and commercial affairs. The years 1838–42 are marked in the main by quiescence. In exception to this, however, it must be noted that the last great burst of the bank - projecting mania in Scotland took place in 1838. But this would seem to have been more the completion of projects conceived previous to the crisis, and found to be feasible in Scotland (where most of the crises from 1793 to 1857 fell with extraordinarily small effect, so far as banking is concerned), than a new outburst of speculation. The harvests of 1842–3–4 were exceptionally good, and were accompanied with great general prosperity. With this the speculative fever broke out with great intensity. The special form it assumed was the formation of railway lines. No number of railway projects seemed too many to the insatiable public. Every prospectus that appeared was greedily seized on, and shares applied for and gambled with both before and after allotment. Money was borrowed on shares obtained, in order to apply for the next venture. The game reached its maximum in 1846, and by the fourth quarter of the next year it was all over.

In 1847 there was a marked diminution in the railway mania, although the commitments were still on a sufficiently large scale. Speculation was giving way in 1846. This was the second year of the great Irish potato famine, and the famine fever had commenced its ravages. Distress in England, too, was manifest. Next year matters grew worse. Money was scarce and dear. Bankruptcies were numerous. The Bank of England minimum discount rate rose steadily from 3 per cent to 8 per cent during the months from January to October. The change was so impressive that a writer in 1847 asserts, with pardonable exaggeration, that there was a sudden and almost total cessation of commerce, and that mercantile cities appeared as if men were liquidating debts, winding up concerns, and retiring.[1] From the 18th to the 25th of October a state of acute crisis existed. Several joint-stock banks and a number of private banks failed in various parts of England. Assistance could hardly be got by men possessed of the best securities on any terms. On the 25th of October the crisis suddenly ceased. Accommodation could be had with ease, and was comparatively little asked for.

What was the cause of this extraordinary change? How were men's minds suddenly placed at rest, and their strained financial relationships instantaneously relaxed? The patent perpetual self-acting and generally beneficent Bank Charter Act, by which the powers of the Bank of England were restrained for the good of the community, was suspended by an arbitrary and illegal act on the part of the Government. As soon as it was known that the Bank of England would be allowed to set aside the provisions of the Act of 1844, which prohibited the issue of notes by the issue department beyond a fixed amount against securities, *plus* the amount of bullion held by the department, the alarm subsided. Holders of securities, who before were panic-stricken to find that they were cut off from all assistance, were now perfectly satisfied with the knowledge that, should they require accommodation, they could easily get it, and in most cases did not even seek it. Thus, three years after Sir Robert Peel had so elaborately adjusted the basis of the financial system of the country, it came to a dead-lock. The restriction imposed on the Bank of England acted like the sudden jamming of an engine's works—intense friction and heat were produced. When the restriction was removed, the engine worked to the utmost satisfaction.

The effect of this crisis on the banking business of Scotland was not specially noticeable; but one point

[1] *The Crisis and the Currency.* John G. Kinnear. Edinburgh, 1847.

calls for attention. The Western Bank of Scotland, to whose affairs we have already referred, again got into difficulties. It does not appear, however, that the other Scottish banks were aware of this at the time. Pursuing its habitual course, despite remonstrances on the part of the other banks, and reluctantly-granted promises of amendment, the Western Bank had been lending out all its funds, re-discounting its bills, and neglecting to provide a reserve of convertible securities. In order to meet its engagements in London, it applied to the Bank of England, and got the loan of £300,000. This it repaid soon afterwards, owing, doubtless, to its growing popularity in Scotland replenishing its coffers. At the same time, the past-due bills account was running up to an alarming extent. Nothing could avert the fate in store for this establishment, its directors and manager being the complacent subjects of an infatuation that is almost incredible.

For it must be remembered that, up to the time of which we speak, it would have been an easy matter for the bank to reverse the policy which precept and experience had both condemned, and at the same time to have permanently established one of the best banking businesses in Scotland. The capital was nearly, if not entirely, intact. The bank enjoyed the utmost credit with the public, if not with the other banks. Losses might have been gradually made up from the large profits earned, and before the next crisis came, the bank might have been in a thoroughly strong and healthy state. But all the experience of bankers in the past, all the reason and wisdom of those of the present, were contemptuously thrown aside by men who were mere tyros in the business. Carried away by the brilliance of the success they had achieved by their active and daring policy, they did not pause to secure the conquest they had made. When they had again to encounter trial, they found it ruin.

It remains only to notice a few other points in this period.   Prior to the middle of the year 1845 silver three-penny pieces, except as Maundy money, appear not to have been issued by the mint, although their circulation was lawful under proclamation of 5th July 1838.[1]   An Act was passed 26th August 1846 (9 & 10 Vict. c. 75) to regulate joint-stock banks in Scotland and Ireland, which applied certain provisions of the English Act of 5th September 1844 (7 & 8 Vict. c. 113) and made specific regulations.   This was amended by an Act (17 & 18 Vict. c. 73) passed 31st July 1854, which relates chiefly to selling shares under lien.   The stamp duty of 1d. on cheques was introduced about this time, at first with exemptions, such as on personally negotiated debits and demand orders within a fifteen miles radius, which seem to have been withdrawn by an Act of 21st May 1858 (21 & 22 Vict. c. 20), making all demand drafts liable to the duty.   The validity of purporting endorsements of demand orders was also affirmed by the Stamp Act, No. 1 of 1853.

---

[1] See *Letters of Queen Victoria*, vol. ii. p. 44.

CHAPTER XXI

IN its political aspects the period from 1847 to 1857—of which we must now treat—was marked by stirring events. During the first six years Britain was at peace with all the world; but the state of the nation at home was, for part of that time, very unfavourable. The country was suffering from the effects of the great crisis of 1847–48; cholera was manifesting itself again; the French Revolution of 1848 disturbed men's minds; conflicts between labour and capital were very bitter; and agitation for parliamentary and financial reform added to the disturbed state of the public mind. The late Dr. Norman Macleod described the year 1848 as a time of " famine, pestilence, riots, and rebellion." By 1850 matters appear to have improved, for the people seem to have been so far freed from material cares as to be able to join heartily in national excitement over the aggression of the Church of Rome in re-establishing the Papal hierarchy in England.

The circumstances of the nation continued to improve. Unpopular taxes were successfully contended against; international communication was improved by the laying of ocean telegraph cables; and although in 1853 there were strikes and riots in connection with a general agitation for an advance of wages, these seem to have been the outcome of the increased volume and profitableness of trade. In 1854 the usury laws were abrogated. In the same year the peace which had hitherto blessed the nation was broken by the declaration (28th March) of war with Russia. The Crimean war, undertaken by Britain and France on behalf of Turkey, lasted more than a year, and is estimated to have cost this country between £80,000,000 and £90,000,000, and an immense number of lives. Hardly had it been successfully concluded when hostilities with China broke out in 1856. Next year the last of the period under review, was burdened with the horrible Indian Mutiny (May to December). The close of the same year witnessed a great commercial and financial convulsion.

In the preceding period the ruling feature of financial affairs was railway enterprise. The period from 1847 to 1857 was, on the other hand, marked specially by general commercial activity, which seemed to pervade all nations. Railway commitments, although steadily engaged in, were not on anything approaching their former scale ; and the formation of joint-stock companies seems rather to have followed in the wake of advancing commercial prosperity than to have been the special subject of speculative attention, as was the case from 1825 to 1836.

As regards banking in Scotland, the period up to the crisis with which it closed is almost destitute of important features, other than those evidencing a quiet but rapid development of the banking system within the limits laid down by the Legislature. In 1849 the British Linen Company obtained a new charter from the Crown, authorising them to increase their capital, which stood at £500,000, by £1,000,000. Next year this power was availed of to the extent of £500,000, making their total capital £1,000,000. In July 1849 the old-established Banking Company in Aberdeen was merged in the Union Bank of Scotland ; but it continued to retain its local designation for four or five years. The terms of purchase were that one Union £100 share with £50 paid, valued at £81 : 15s., was given for 36⅓ of the

Aberdeen shares with £5 paid up, or a discount of 55 per cent. During the earlier years of its existence this bank experienced quite extraordinary success ; but, seemingly, its star had set.

The last surviving private banking firm in Edinburgh, Messrs. Alex. Allan & Co., disappeared about this time. They had, it may be presumed, long ceased to do any active business as bankers, but the designation was kept up to the last. Their business as insurance agents and stockbrokers continued under another firm. A more important concern, the Perth Banking Company, was, on 1st August 1857, amalgamated with the Union Bank of Scotland. Although the roll of bankers was practically closed by the Act of 1844, the banking system continued to develop. During the first half of the period the increase in bank offices was under 30 ; but in the second half no fewer than 240 new branches were opened. The Royal Bank commenced in 1855 an active extension of their branch system ; but the banks which figured most prominently in this respect were the Western Bank and the City of Glasgow Bank.

The whole course of the year 1857 was one of tension in commercial and financial circles. It began with the Bank of England minimum discount rate at 6 per cent, which rose in April to $6\frac{1}{2}$ per cent. The rate subsequently dropped to $5\frac{1}{2}$ per cent in July ; but the average rate for the first half of the year was nearly $6\frac{1}{4}$ per cent, the average for the whole year being £6 : 13 : 3. The foreign trade of the country had been extended during the immediately preceding years in a formerly-unknown ratio. The enormous dimensions which it had reached by 1857 were quite beyond the legitimate bounds of the world's requirements. Thus naturally arose a reaction which produced the crisis of the autumn of this year. Other causes, such as the great development of banking facilities, and some loose methods on the part of merchants giving credit to foreign correspondents, have also been ascribed as contributing causes. But these can only be considered as subsidiary, for they were merely the natural accompaniment of the inflated sanguineness with which traders were imbued. The banks, as a whole, cannot be burdened with much blame for the troubles which arose ; for it is evident from the final outcome that the great bulk of their advances had been well secured. Some of them, doubtless, did err to a culpable extent, and paid the forfeit with their existence ; but for the others, it was not to be expected that they should refrain from transacting sound business, as judged from their own standpoint, merely because they thought that trade was being overdone. That was the merchants' business. It is thus evident that the real cause of the crisis of 1857 was over-trading by the merchants of the world. It might, perhaps, be still further limited by specifying the merchants of Britain and the United States.

The first serious trouble came from the latter quarter. Bankruptcies in America became numerous early in the year, and increased as it progressed. The banks there became embarrassed, and in September adopted a general suspension of specie payments. This course seems to have worked satisfactorily, without putting a stop to business. But, although the Americans could get on pretty well in that way, the consequences on this side of the Atlantic were very different. Failure of remittances from the United States forced British mercantile houses to stop payment. Undoubtedly solvent firms were obliged, for the time being, to succumb ; and, of course, their weaker brethren were at once crushed hopelessly. The Bank of England discount rate, which had fallen to 5½ per cent on 16th July, rose on 8th October to 6 per cent. Four days later it was advanced to 7 per cent, and next week to 8 per cent. The banking reserve had been steadily and largely falling, and on 24th October reached the low point of £3,485,840. On 27th October the Borough Bank of Liverpool failed, after a hopeless

15

appeal to the Bank of England for assistance. The Northumberland and Durham District Bank also applied for assistance ; but, after examination, aid was refused, and it had to succumb. Two large bill-broking houses in London, and a long list of minor houses, also failed. On 5th November the bank rate was raised to 9 per cent, and excitement reached a high pitch. The banking reserve had fallen to £2,155,315.

It was seen that the bank's ability to render assistance was, under the fetters of the Act of 1844, rapidly falling to zero. The directors made every effort in their power, by the forced sale of consols, to replenish their reserve ; but the drain was beyond their power to supply. On the 9th November the Western Bank of Scotland suspended payment, and the panic became excessive. On the 11th the banking reserve was only £1,462,000. Day after day the bank was forcing consols on the market to replenish the reserve. The applications for assistance were far beyond its power to meet. On the 12th affairs looked hopelessly dark. Suddenly there was a ray of light. It was whispered that the Government were about to sanction the breaking of the law. On the 13th the panic vanished, as by the virtue of a magic wand. The Lords of the Treasury wrote to the directors of the Bank of England, authorising them to disregard the enactment of Parliament restricting their power to issue notes. As in 1847, so now ; when people knew that there was no limit to the note-issue of the Bank of England, and that therefore they could get assistance when they required, they no longer sought it.

It is probable that this crisis would have been comparatively slight in Scotland, had it not been for the rottenness of the Western Bank of Scotland. As it was, the crisis was intense in Glasgow and Edinburgh, and disastrously affected the whole country. What gave peculiar sharpness to the panic was the unexpectedness of its immediate cause. The Scottish public have always displayed an amount of confidence in the banking institutions of their country, which at first sight seems somewhat out of keeping with their hereditary canniness. In point of fact, however, their reliance on the soundness of the banks was by no means unnatural. Experience had shown that the public loss through bank failures in Scotland was quite exceptional, and never serious. The total loss sustained up to the present time is quite insignificant. Thus a habit of unsuspicious confidence had grown up which could not easily be disturbed. Had it not been for this, the Western Bank would not have enjoyed the great popularity which distinguished it from all its rivals. It was supposed to embody the solidity of the old banks with the broad-mindedness of modern principles. It is not to be wondered at, that the sudden shock of its failure should have, for the moment, driven the public to an opposite extreme of distrust. The distrust, however, was of very short duration ; for it soon became evident that, whoever might suffer, the creditors would not. It was noticeable, also, notwithstanding the great stress laid by statesmen and economists on the dangers of private note-issues, that the note-issues of the Scotch banks did not contribute in the slightest degree to the causes of the crisis, and were not particularly the subjects of the panic which ensued.

The Western Bank of Scotland had a fully paid-up capital of £1,500,000, which was one half larger than the capital of any other bank in Scotland, except the Royal Bank. The shares were of £50 each, and sold in 1841 at £71, while shortly before the stoppage they stood at £84 : 5s. The bank had 101 branches, which was more than any of the other banks had established. Its note circulation, although declining, was among the highest, and testifies to the great extent of its business. Its deposits, although reduced by rising distrust in Glasgow, amounted at the time of failure to £5,306,569 (a very large sum for those days), of which £4,402,973 was held by the branches. It would seem that of the total deposits less than one-tenth consisted of sums under £50.

As we have seen from time to time, the system of management of the Western Bank was not only directly opposed, in some essential points, to the principles adopted by the other banks, but had actually led it into grave embarrassment on more than one occasion. Assistance had been given to it on promises of amendment, but no sooner was the immediate danger past than the old system was resumed. The great point which not only the Edinburgh banks, but also the Western Bank's correspondents in London, had urged on the bank's attention, was the danger of dispensing with a large reserve of high-class convertible securities. To a certain extent the advice, backed as it was by intimation that continued disregard of it would lead to exclusion from the banking concert, was acted on. But it is evident that the adoption of the principle was little more than nominal. A still more serious evil was meanwhile undermining the foundations of the bank. Neglect to provide proper reserves endangered the bank as a going concern ; but the reckless manner in which the directors were lending their money on a few large risks was courting ruin. One of their wildest schemes was establishing a discount agency in New York, which eventually occasioned a loss of £185,250.

Owing to their close connection with New York business, the troubles in America, which reached a height in September, occasioned great embarrassment to the Western Bank. On the 15th October, Mr. John Taylor, the manager, resigned office, and was succeeded by Mr. J. S. Fleming, who was then law secretary of the bank, and in 1871 became cashier and general manager of the Royal Bank of Scotland. For a week, negotiations were conducted with the Edinburgh banks, with the object of obtaining assistance ; but this was refused, pending the result of application to the Bank of England. That being unsuccessful, the Edinburgh banks at length advanced £510,000 in consols. This was on 29th October. The crisis in London increased, and the want of confidence in the Western Bank became serious. Further aid was asked from the Edinburgh banks, but was refused. The failure of Dennistoun & Co., of London and Glasgow, with liabilities of over £2,000,000, on 7th November, brought the crisis in Scotland to a focus. (The firm were only temporarily embarrassed by want of remittances from America.) The note exchanges continuing to run heavily against the Western Bank, the directors intimated to the Bank of Scotland their probable inability to meet the settlement of 9th inst. At two o'clock on that day the doors of the bank were shut, and the branches were directed not to reopen next morning. The total liabilities of the bank at the stoppage were £8,911,932, exclusive of capital and rest, amounting together to £1,726,777.

After some attempts at reconstruction, the bank went into voluntary liquidation. Two calls, amounting together to £125 per share, or 250 per cent on the capital, were made on the contributories. These produced a total sum of over £2,000,000, of which, however, more than £800,000 was subsequently returned.[1] The net loss to shareholders exclusive of premiums on purchases of shares, including capital at par and reserve fund, was £2,816,354.

On the failure of the Western Bank, the other banks hesitated to accept their notes. This increased the public panic, and a run on the banks took place. On the 11th, however, the banks resolved to take Western notes in course of business, and influential statements of confidence in the ability of the Western Bank to meet all its engagements having been made, the excitement rapidly subsided.

On the 10th November, the City of Glasgow Bank suspended payment, with liabilities to the extent of

[1] See Appendix H.

£5,107,142. It reopened on the 14th December. The capital at this time was £745,410. In 1859 the liabilities were £4,651,053 : 3 : 6, and the assets were valued at £4,579,464 : 18 : 2, showing a deficiency of £71,588 : 5 : 4. That loss had been carried to a " contingent account " with the intention of writing it off by yearly instalments of £20,000 out of profits. Doubts of the legality of such a proceeding (more probably doubts of the legality of paying a dividend—3 per cent was paid in 1859—under the circumstances) caused the directors to recommend that the capital be written down. Accordingly we find the capital stated in 1860 as £670,869—a reduction of £74,541. Evidently the former estimate had erred on the side of modesty !

The only minor point claiming notice here is a provision of the Stamp Act, No. 2 of 1853 (Clause 7), by which the Treasury were authorised to compound with all the Scottish banks, both for the stamp duties on their notes and for those on their bills, under such security and forms as the Treasury might require. This arrangement was carried out on the 4th November, the rate being fixed at 8s. 4d. per cent. A calculation made by the Dundee Bank showed that, during twenty-four years, they had actually paid an average of about 6s. 8d. per cent per annum on their note circulation.

CHAPTER XXII

CONSOLIDATION OF SCOTTISH BANKING—THE CRISIS OF 1866

THE political experience of Great Britain from 1857 to 1866 was one mainly of peace ; but in other quarters of the globe several severe wars occurred which sometimes endangered its neutrality.   Indeed, throughout this period it may be said that Britain's condition was rather one of armed neutrality than of perfect concord with the other Powers.   In 1859 France and Sardinia conducted a successful campaign against Austria, which was the commencement of the formation of the kingdom of Italy. In the middle of the same year Britain went to war with China, one incident of which was the repulse of our fleet off the Peiho.   This war was continued almost throughout the succeeding year, during which Garibaldi commenced his career as the great liberator of Italy, at Marsala, in Sicily.   The most important event in the world's history for the year 1860 was, however, the secession, on 19th December, of the State of South Carolina from the great American Union—an action which was speedily followed by the secession of the other Southern States of the Union.   Early in 1861 the seceding States numbered eleven, united as an independent political organisation, under the designation of the Confederated States of America.   The civil war which ensued assumed enormous proportions : it was protracted and bloody, involving vast expenditure ; and its direct and indirect effects on the trade and financial conditions of the world were very great.

At one time, moreover, Britain was on the eve of a rupture with the Federal States, owing to the violation (8th November 1861) of the neutrality of one of her mail steamers by the American warship *San Jacinto*,—an incident popularly known as the *Trent* affair—two commissioners from the Confederated States being forcibly taken from the British vessel while on their voyage from Havana to Southampton. Before the close of the year, however, reparation having been made by the Federal Government, all danger of war had passed away. A small war with the natives of New Zealand broke out at the close of 1863, and another with Japan in the succeeding year, in which the French, Dutch, and United States fleets were allied with the British. In January 1864 Britain was nearly involved in war with Prussia and Austria, in defence of Denmark ; but, at some sacrifice to her prestige, she refrained from an interference which must have been attended with very serious results. The close of the American civil war was signalised by the assassination (14th April 1865) of President Lincoln. Prussia and Italy were at war with Austria in 1866, but in that conflict Britain had no direct interest.

Meanwhile the arts of peace had been progressing satisfactorily. No great inventions or discoveries revolutionised the conditions of trade or society, but existing facilities were developed and availed of to a great extent. An important step in ocean navigation was taken in the building of the *Great Eastern* steamship, which was launched on the Thames on 31st January 1858. Unfortunately this great project was beyond the knowledge of its designers and the requirements of the time ; and it proved an almost total financial failure. The *Great Eastern* was practically useless until the comparatively small value to which it fell permitted it, in after years, to be successfully employed in the laying of ocean telegraph cables. It was eventually sold to be broken up. This department of business was developed very widely during the period of which we are treating. On 5th August 1858 the first Atlantic cable was successfully laid, and congratulatory messages were interchanged between Britain and the United States. This was speedily followed, however, by the grievous disappointment of a total cessation of communication, through some flaw which the electricians of that time were unable to deal with. At a later time the location of the flaw was ascertained and the cable repaired. In other quarters of the world telegraph cables were laid with more success.

From an economic point of view, the period extending from 1857 to 1866 displays the usual features of depression, activity, speculation, and collapse ; but, probably owing to the greater complications consequent on advancing civilisation, and to the disturbing influence of the striking political events to which we have referred, these characteristic transitions are not so clearly marked as in some previous periods. One noticeable point is that the period of depression following the crisis of 1857 was of unusually short duration. Within two years a marked advance of prosperity had occurred ; and the *Times* was able to record that, with the exception of the shipping interest, " every branch of industry is flourishing as abundantly as at any former period, and the England of 1860 is richer, stronger, and better contented than the wealthy and prosperous England which in 1850 commanded the respect and envy of the world." Increasing commercial activity reached the phase of speculation in 1862 and 1863, when bubble companies—principally banking and trading—became numerous, and foreign loans formed the subject of a monetary mania.

In the former year, however, a serious counteracting influence came into play. This was the so-called " cotton famine," consequent on the blockading of the ports of the Confederate States of America. By this event the cotton industry of Lancashire was paralysed, and large numbers of operatives were thrown out of employment. The nation came nobly forward to avert the danger of starvation which threatened the working classes of the district ; and, although great loss occurred by the cessation of this industry, the nation was able to bear the strain with surprising ease.   The money market, however, became much affected towards the close of 1863, and during almost the whole course of the next year the value of money was very high.   Indeed, it may be said that, at this time, there occurred one of those semi-crises sometimes observable during the course of a decennial period. This speedily passed away, and the nation resumed its career of prosperity unchecked, until inflated credit and over speculation brought about their invariable sequel. It is probable that joint-stock enterprise received a great stimulus by the passing of the Companies Act of 1864, under which the formation and incorporation of all kinds of companies was much simplified.

The record of banking in Scotland during this period is marked in the main by increasing prosperity, development, and consolidation.   Only one instance of adverse experience occurred ; and it belongs properly to the immediately preceding period.   The Edinburgh and Glasgow Bank—whose career we have already sketched—got into a condition of embarrassment in the middle of 1858.   Half of the capital (£500,000) had been written off on 4th February, but the bank found the attempt to recover from the discredit into which it had fallen during the recent crisis hopeless ; and it was fain to seek repose by amalgamation with the Clydesdale Banking Company.   This operation conferred no benefit on the shareholders of the Edinburgh and Glasgow Bank, for they received no consideration for the goodwill of their business.   They were indeed freed from danger of calls ; but they lost their whole right of property in the bank.   Had they shown sufficient courage in facing their difficulties, they might have come out of the struggle in a much more satisfactory manner.[1] As it was, the new connections secured by the Clydesdale Bank through this amalgamation, obtained practically without any outlay, had a material effect in improving their business. The number of their branches was increased by more than twenty offices of the Edinburgh and Glasgow Bank, many of which were believed to be very profitable concerns.

Another amalgamation secured by the Clydesdale Bank was that of the Eastern Bank, in January 1863. In this case a very handsome price was paid for the business, principally in stock of the former bank. By these two purchases the authorised circulation of the Clydesdale Bank was extended by £170,293.[2] Next year (20th February 1864) the Dundee Banking Company was amalgamated with the Royal Bank of Scotland— the transaction being accomplished by a transference of stock of the latter bank to the Dundee Bank shareholders. The Royal Bank thus acquired six new branches, and an increase of authorised circulation to the extent of £33,451, raising it to £216,451. The Dundee Bank had a paid-up capital of £100,000, held by 74 partners, selling at 60 per cent premium, with a dividend of 10 per cent. About the middle of 1864, the City of Glasgow Bank increased its capital from £670,869 to £850,000 by the issue of new stock to the shareholders at a premium of 30 per cent.[3]

The Commercial Bank of Scotland added £400,000 to its

[1] It is said of one of the directors that, after the board meetings, he used to call on a stockbroker of his acquaintance to discuss the situation. The clerks, with youthful intelligence, were quite alive to their opportunity ; and, when the director was closeted with their principal, used to make a pretext for entering the room, so as to be able to leave the door open. They thus heard the conversation, and were kept *au courant* of the state of affairs at the bank. They were not likely to be more reticent than the director himself. The story was told in later years by one of the clerks.

[2] Previously the authorised circulation of the Clydesdale was £104,028 ; that of the Edinburgh and Glasgow, £136,657 ; and that of the Eastern, £33,636, making £274,321 in all.

[3] *Courant*, 2nd June 1864.

capital by two allocations of stock, by way of bonus, to its proprietors, each to the amount of £200,000—the first being made in 1859, and the second in 1864. This was accomplished by a transference from the reserved profits of previous years, and occasioned much adverse criticism on the part of previous shareholders who had sold out in ignorance of the existence of so large an accumulation of profits. The paid-up capital thus became £1,000,000. This proceeding was quite in accordance with traditional usage, the old banks having repeatedly acted in this way. But the more open system of accounting to shareholders, adopted by the Scottish banks shortly after this time, and since established as a yearly practice in the publication of balance sheets, makes one now regard such a transaction as a relic of a bygone age ; as, indeed, it has become otherwise, through the practical impossibility now of making such special profits as were then obtainable.

On 6th February 1863, the Scottish banks conjointly took an important step, which had probably been forced upon them by the largely-increased extent of their branch systems. This was a general instruction to their branches to follow at once changes made by the Bank of England in the minimum rate of discount. The effect of this was to bring the banking system of Scotland into more immediate sympathy with the monetary system of the world than had formerly been the case. It was also an evidence of the increasing importance of Scottish banking as part of that system.

One phase of the Western Bank liquidation which came prominently forward at this time has more than special interest ; that is the endeavour made to secure some value for the right of note-issuing, the exercise of which had been lost to the shareholders by the failure of the bank. This was no small question, for not only did the authorised issue amount to £337,938, but, under existing conditions, the right to issue practically conveyed

the power to carry on the business of banking. So early
as April 1858 application was made to Mr. Disraeli as
Chancellor of the Exchequer to give whatever legislative
sanction might be required to enable the bank to dispose
of the privilege of issue to one or more of the other banks
of issue in Scotland. But the application was refused.
The hope of making something out of this lapsed right
was, however, maintained for some years ; and on 11th
February 1864 a bill was introduced into Parliament to
divide the authorised circulation among the other Scottish
banks in proportion to their existing authorised issues.
In his report presented in February 1864, the liquidator,
Robert Lumsden, referred to the question and stated
that a deputation had waited on the Chancellor of the
Exchequer (Gladstone). He had, however, refused to
recognise the right as a matter of law, but expressed
his willingness to consider the application on other
grounds.[1]

Later in the year, a provisional committee, which had
been formed for the resuscitation of the bank, applied
for a free grant of the lapsed right of issue ; but this
the Treasury declined to accede to. As is well known,
all the efforts made in this direction came to nothing.
Indeed, in face of the 12th section of the Act of 1844, it
is difficult to understand how the negotiations went as
far as they did. Doubtless the warm feeling of sympathy
for the injured shareholders which existed, must have
prompted the desire to afford them every chance of
obtaining this mitigation of their losses.

An effort at legislation in connection with Scottish
banking (in its currency aspects) was made in 1864, by
the introduction of a bill by Sir John Hay, with the object
of making Bank of England notes a legal tender in Scotland. The Chancellor of the Exchequer discouraged
the attempt, and when Mr. Adam Black, one of the

[1] *Courant*, 26th February 1864. *Bankers' Magazine*, 1864, pp.
310, 366, and 475.

members for Edinburgh, seconded by Mr. Dalgleish, moved its rejection, the bill was withdrawn.[1]

The activity manifested in the formation of banking companies, to which we have referred, affected Scotland to a slight extent. No new native bank was proposed ; but two or three companies were formed in England whose object was, more or less, to do business in Scotland. Probably the first of these was the Scottish and Universal Finance Bank, Limited. It does not, however, concern us much, for notwithstanding its designation, it appears to have been more anxious for a name than for a local habitation that was Scottish. It was really a finance company, not a bank. In 1865 it is referred to as bankrupt. Another was the Mercantile and Exchange Bank, Limited, established in Liverpool early in 1863. It opened a branch in Glasgow which it withdrew eighteen months later. In the same year the London Bank of Scotland, Limited, was formed, which had branches in Edinburgh and Glasgow. Proceedings for the amalgamation of these two by merging the London Bank in the Mercantile were proceeding, and the former was actually put into liquidation with that object, when the suicide of the manager of the Mercantile Bank caused delay for investigation.[2]

The proceedings were resumed, however, when an arrangement was made that some of the branches of the London Bank (including the Edinburgh Office at No. 17 Princes Street) should be taken up by a specially formed company, the London and Scottish Bank, Limited. Within about six months, being pressed for payment of £2000, this new venture applied for, and obtained, a winding-up order. The Mercantile and Exchange Bank was in difficulties in 1864, which, however, it overcame. The character of its business may be gauged by the fact that in 1866 its directors congratulated the shareholders

[1] *Memoirs of Adam Black*, Nicolson, Edinburgh, 1885.
[2] *Courant*, December 1864.

that their losses did not exceed £131,337 : 10 : 2. The London Bank acknowledged losses to the extent of £65,554. The extent of these banks' business in Scotland is not revealed ; but it was not supposed to be much. On the other hand, the aggregate business as shown by a balance-sheet of 1866 was considerable for a two years' career ; and there is reason to think that the want of success, in England at least, was due to ignorant management. This English invasion of Scotland was followed by a return visit on the part of the Scots which will form the subject of a subsequent chapter.

The year 1866 is described in contemporary history as " gloomy, eventful, and ominous." In its financial aspect it was one of great disturbance in the money market, of bankruptcies of merchants and of bankers. The year opened with the bank minimum rate of discount at 7 per cent, from which it was soon raised to 8 per cent. It thereafter gradually fell to 6 per cent until May. It then rose with great rapidity. On 3rd May the rate was placed at 7 per cent, on the 8th at 8 per cent, on the 11th at 9 per cent, and on the 12th at 10 per cent. At that point it stood until 16th August, when it fell to 8 per cent, and thereafter gradually diminished to $3\frac{1}{2}$ per cent at the close of the year. Symptoms of the approach of a state of crisis seem to have become apparent towards the close of 1865 ; but it was not before the commencement of the new year that anything of a marked character occurred. Then one or two English country banks failed. Subsequently uneasiness began to exist in London. The Joint-Stock Discount Company, Limited, suspended payment on 7th March, with liabilities amounting to £3,657,229, and other bankruptcies took place.

But the phase of crisis was not reached until 10th May, when Overend, Gurney & Co., Limited, failed, with liabilities to the extent of £18,727,915. This was a crushing blow, for not only was the amount involved enormous, but this discount house was relied on as a strong establishment. The shock to credit was almost unprecedented, and general panic ensued. The Agra and Masterman's Bank, Limited, and the Consolidated Bank, Limited, were forced to suspend for the time being ; and the Bank of London and other establishments went into liquidation, while even the strongest were doubted. The credit system was thrown into a state of paralysis. But this was not long continued. The Government, taught by experience, at once authorised the Bank of England to exceed the limits of their circulation fixed by the Act of 1844, on condition of the minimum rate of discount being raised to 10 per cent. This was done on 12th May, and the panic was at an end when men knew that accommodation could be procured. Thus, for the third time, the great banking Act of 1844 was infringed, under the responsibility of the Government, for the salvation of the business of the nation.

The crisis did not affect banking in Scotland to any serious extent. No panic occurred, nor did any distrust in the banks manifest itself. Indeed, the banks rather gained than lost by it ; for while they benefited by the high rate of interest, their credit was improved by the steady way in which they came through this time of trial. Shortly before this the National Bank of Scotland had been tempted to essay an inroad on the London field, which was successfully carried out ; and it is understood that, as a result of this crisis, their business there was established on an extensive basis. It was the commencement of an invasion which was continued by others of the Scottish banks in later years, and which led to complications, involving a good deal of heated controversy on the part of English bankers which has now happily cooled down.

CHAPTER XXIII

THE INSTITUTE OF BANKERS IN SCOTLAND

It will be proper, at this point, to devote some consideration to the establishment of an institution which has exercised an important influence on the banking world of Scotland during the forty-two years of its existence, and which, if prudently conducted, is calculated to materially benefit future generations of bank officers, and to elevate banking to a position partaking somewhat of the nature of a scientific profession.

Up to the time of the formation of the Institute of Bankers in Scotland, the education of bankers in the theory and practice of their profession—nay, even the ascertainment of their most ordinary educational acquirements—was of the most haphazard description. Not the smallest attempt was made either to encourage, or to provide means for, the study of the theory of banking. It may be thought that the practice, at all events, would be learnt in the discharge of daily duties ; and to some extent this was necessarily the case. But no effort was made to induce young bankers to acquire any but a mechanical knowledge of details ; and from the thorough way in which their interests were neglected by their superiors, there was instilled into their minds a conviction of the uselessness of efforts at self-improvement. Their directors and managers virtually — sometimes actually—told them that they need not hope for promotion. The more active-minded of the young men, who would think and study in spite of all discouragements, were either snubbed or left to cool their ardour in the shade of neglect.

It was the practical experience of this state of matters which led the present author to write an article, which appeared in the *Money Market Review* of 2nd May 1874, advocating a more systematic consideration of the interests of young bankers, as at once advisable from motives of justice and of policy. Among other suggestions it was proposed that a system of examinations should be established, in connection with which certificates would be issued to the more proficient candidates. It is highly probable that these suggestions would not have produced any practical result, had not the idea been taken up by a gentleman possessing the influence and energy necessary for conducting it to a successful issue. To Mr. John Gifford, late cashier of the National Bank of Scotland, belongs the credit of inaugurating and effectively conducting the desired reformation. Mr. Gifford addressed a letter to a literary society of bankers, of which he had at one time been president, urging them to consider the advisableness of establishing a system of classes, courses of lectures, and examinations, and the provision of libraries, bursaries, and all necessary accessories for the acquirement of financial and general knowledge. The society took the matter up warmly, and referred it to a committee to consider and report as to the feasibility of such a scheme. In the capacity of secretary to that committee, it devolved on the present writer to lay some practical scheme before the members. He accordingly proposed that the society should not attempt to undertake such responsible duties, but should promote the institution of a new association, which would be representative of the profession as a whole, in all its grades, throughout the country, and therefore, commanding an amount of authority and influence sufficient to give confidence in its diplomas, and to secure general interest in its proceedings.

On this basis a scheme was drafted, which secured the approval of the society. It provided for the formation of a provisional committee, partly appointed by the banks and partly by the society. After some untoward hesitation on the part of some of the banks, which required all Mr. Gifford's tact and good management to overcome, that committee was eventually constituted. The practical designing of the edifice was a laborious work ; but the members of the committee were earnest for its completion, and spared no effort to secure its accomplishment. Mr. Hamilton A. Hotson, subsequently manager of the British Linen Bank, undertook the duty of preparing the constitution of the new association (whose name was until almost the last moment a matter of uncertainty) ; and it speaks well for his foresight and discretion that, with the modifications made by the committee, forty-two years' experience has only produced a single alteration on it, and that not an admitted improvement.

The movement, which at first was confined to Edinburgh, received a great accession of vitality when Mr. James A. Wenley, then manager of the Bank of Scotland in Glasgow, began to identify himself with it. He organised a Committee in Glasgow, in correspondence with that in Edinburgh, and was the means of creating and directing a widespread enthusiasm in the West of Scotland in favour of the scheme. But it was not alone in the West that his influence was felt. To a very great extent the scope and action of the Institute were thenceforth moulded by him. No important step was taken in the movement which was not either suggested by him, or first received his approval. He threw himself into the work with an amount of ardour and personal exertion which must have occasioned him much self-sacrifice, but which at the same time enabled the new vessel to be launched with much *éclat*. He was also instrumental in procuring from the banks promises of recognition and material support.

A meeting of those gentlemen who had formally intimated their adhesion to the proposed association was held in the Bank of Scotland, Edinburgh, on the evening of the 6th July 1875, when the Institute of Bankers in Scotland was constituted, with a membership of about 200. Mr. David Davidson, at that time treasurer of the Bank of Scotland, who had warmly espoused the cause, was elected president. Three vice-presidents, among whom Mr. Gifford naturally found a place, and other office-bearers, were elected at the same time. The Council, consisting in all of twenty-one members, embraced representatives from all the banks in Edinburgh and Glasgow. Nearly all of these held official position in the banks, so that the Institute at once secured an influential position.

In spite of the numerous difficulties which invariably beset new schemes, the success of the Institute was both rapid and marked. The membership, beginning, as we have said, with 200, was reported to the first annual meeting as 582. Two years later (1878) it stood at 925. Owing in great measure to the untoward effects of the crisis of that year, involving the failure of the City of Glasgow Bank, which itself contributed 107 names, the roll subsequently dropped to 759. The last report states the number as 2801. That number is in itself satisfactory proof of the continued interest of the profession in the proceedings of the Institute. For it must be borne in mind that, since 1878, it has become almost impossible to gain admission except through examination. The examinations have been attended with much success. March 1914 was the record year, 1160 candidates presenting themselves at the various centres. Even in the third year of the war, with its abnormal military demands, in 1917 there were 650 entrants for the examinations. The chief centres of the Institute's operations have from the first been at Edinburgh and Glasgow, but subsequently, through the influence of the managers of the

North of Scotland, Town and County, and Caledonian Banks, centres were established at several provincial towns. Besides the annual examinations, there have been regular courses of lectures on banking, financial and literary subjects, political economy, banking law, etc. The other operations of the Institute have included annual essay competitions, and the establishment of libraries and reading-rooms for the use of all members of the profession.

It cannot be doubted that the Institute has been instrumental in fostering, to a large extent, the spirit of self-improvement among the younger members of the banking profession ; and, in a less degree, it has tended to advance the scientific study of banking and economic subjects. It has also been the means of enabling energetic young bankers to obtain lucrative situations in English and Colonial banks, by the use of its examination certificates. That it has not accomplished more is hardly its fault. It is often said that it does not improve young men's chances of promotion in their own banks ; and it must be admitted that, while the banks have acted handsomely in regard to pecuniary aid, they have not given the still more desirable assistance of recognising its certificates in a practical manner. Too little allowance, however, is made for the great difficulties in the way of an immediate adoption of such action. Old officers cannot be overlooked in favour of young ones, however brilliant their qualifications ; and, besides, the mere possession of certificates of knowledge does not prove suitability for office.

Although the Institute of Bankers in Scotland was the first association of its kind which was successfully established, an important attempt of a somewhat similar nature had been made previously. More than half a century ago, the late Mr. W. H. Logan, banker, Berwick-on-Tweed, previously and subsequently resident in Edinburgh, projected an Incorporation of Bankers, which seems actually to have been formed, so far as the enrolment of members is concerned, although it never came into active existence. The preliminary meeting was held at the London Tavern (a well-known meeting-place, subsequently purchased by the Royal Bank of Scotland as a site for an office in London), on 22nd October 1851, when about 300 gentlemen connected with banking attended. A proposal submitted to form a Banking Institute was approved of, and a committee or " Council " appointed. But, for some unexplained reason, the project seems to have been dropped. The scheme was revived by a correspondence in the *Bankers' Magazine* during 1870 ; but, although Mr. Logan again gave a detailed account of its objects, it was not proceeded with. On the establishment of the Institute in Scotland, the idea was warmly taken up in Ireland ; but the state of that country prevented a successful issue until a later date. The bankers of London were more fortunate in efforts which they made in the same direction, and the well-known Institute of Bankers was founded under influential auspices. Their Journal has rendered excellent service to the profession, both in the way of giving information to young bankers and in ventilating questions of interest ; and their examinations and other operations must have been productive of good results, similar to those accomplished in Scotland.

CHAPTER XXIV

THE RAID ON ENGLAND

THE period with which we have now to deal, namely, that extending from the great crisis of 1866 to the (in some respects) even more disastrous convulsion of 1878, is full of stirring incidents in the political, commercial, and financial world. Early in 1867, Fenianism developed itself to such an extent as considerably to retard trade (especially that of British manufacturers with Ireland), and seriously to alarm the public mind. Towards the close of that year the first of those dastardly conspiracies, which subsequently became so common in pursuance of the so-called " policy of dynamite," was manifested in a fatal explosion at the Clerkenwell House of Detention in London. Wars, in which Britain was either directly engaged, or seriously interested, succeeded each other with but little intermission. The French troubles in Mexico in 1867, although the sequel to British action in connection with France, did not compromise this country ; but, in the succeeding year, Britain was forced to undertake a military expedition to Abyssinia, which, under the direction of General Napier, fortunately proved a great success. The cost was, however, very serious.

Next year the Eastern question again became troublesome ; and in 1870–71 the great struggle between France and Germany, with its attendant disorganisation of commerce and finance, took place. This was immediately followed by the outbreak of hitherto suppressed villainy in Paris, which manifested itself in the temporary establishment of the Commune. In 1873–74 Britain was engaged in war against the Ashantees in Africa. Soon afterwards the Eastern question assumed a very grave aspect ; and, to aid Egypt and to protect her Indian interests, Britain effected the purchase, in 1876, of the Khedive's Suez Canal shares at a cost of about £4,000,000. Next year hostilities broke out between Russia and Turkey, and ended, in 1878, by the submission of the latter State. In the readjustment of matters Britain took a leading part ; but the warlike policy of this country, though necessary, was very costly. In the closing months of the latter year, India was engaged in an expedition to Afghanistan, which was successfully conducted under General Roberts.

Meanwhile the arts of peace had not been neglected. There was a great Exhibition of the products of all the world in Paris in 1867, at which this country was well represented. Several great industrial works were accomplished, such as the Union Pacific Railway in the United States, and the navigable canal from the Mediterranean to the Red Sea, both of which, but especially the latter, were destined to greatly influence the commerce of Britain. They were both opened in 1869. In Scotland, a great engineering feat was accomplished by the opening of a railway viaduct across the river Tay at Dundee. But, unlike all other great engineering projects carried out in Britain, the sequel was destined to make this bridge more a type of inferior workmanship than a monument of national enterprise.

The crisis of 1866 was mainly financial in character. Trade, both home and foreign, was good at the time when it occurred. A change, however, speedily followed on the distrust engendered by the financial disasters which took place. This was increased by a railway crisis which occurred in the middle of 1867, and by the pressure of calls in connection with joint-stock companies formed in great numbers previous to the crisis. It is noticeable, however, that the trade of Scotland did not so readily lose its vitality. The crisis had not affected it to a serious extent ; but eventually it suffered in sympathy with the trade of England. Depression lasted until the middle of 1870, four years after the crisis, and then a decided revival occurred. The Franco-German war had a bad influence ; and in the next year there was much disturbance on account of the payment of the indemnity and the loans negotiated in connection therewith. But no sooner had matters been fairly settled, than trade at home and abroad expanded, almost suddenly, to unparalleled proportions. For fully a year this high-pressure trade was continued. But the harvest of 1872 was deficient, and there was a turn in the tide of prosperity. It soon became evident that there had been great inflation. The last five years of the period marked increasing depression. By the month of June 1875, the bad state of Indian trade manifested itself conspicuously in the collapse of the great house of Alexander Collie & Co. Following, as it did, a series of heavy failures in the iron trade, this disaster produced a semi-crisis, in the course of which a considerable number of other firms came down. Heavy losses were entailed on bankers, one or two Scotch banks suffering severely.

For some time after the crisis of 1866 the state of banking was, as might naturally be expected, very unsatisfactory. There was a prevalence of low rates, and much difficulty in profitably employing capital. But this state of matters gradually wore off, and banking in Scotland entered on a new phase of extension. So early in the period as 1869 about a hundred additional branches had been opened, many of them being sub-offices in Edinburgh and Glasgow. During the height of commercial prosperity, the number of bank offices rose to nearly nine hundred, or an increase of nearly three hundred in seven years. But the process was not checked by the cessation of prosperity, for year by year the number rose until, in 1878, there were fully nine hundred and fifty bank offices.

In view of the rampant speculation in bank shares which had been manifested prior to 1866, an Act (popularly known as Leeman's Act) was passed in 1867, prohibiting the purchase and sale of bank stock, unless the specific stock to be transferred was definitely indicated, and misrepresentation was made a misdemeanour. Although the intention of the Legislature in this matter was highly laudable, the Act has not proved a success. It does not appear that it is unworkable, or even unsuitable to the requirements of investors, but it is so uncongenial to speculators that they systematically evade it. This they can do very easily, as there is no one whose special interest or duty it is to question their actions. There is reason, however, to believe that, in a passive way, the Act has had a beneficial tendency; for, although speculation in bank shares is still carried on, there is a prevailing feeling against it. The comparative neglect of bank shares by speculators may be due in great part to the greater attractions of other securities; but undoubtedly the spirit of the directions of the Legislature is often followed in the business world when the letter seems to be directly violated.

In 1868, the beginning of the end of the liquidation of the Western Bank of Scotland came into view. In that year there were two payments, the one of £7 : 10s. and the other of £3 per share, made to the solvent shareholders by way of return of surplus funds. This completed eight returns, amounting in all to £68 per share, on which £175 in all had been called, including the original sum of £50. In other words, £250 per cent had been called for the purposes of the liquidation; and of this £136 per cent had been returned. In 1870, the outstanding liabilities were assumed by the National Bank of Scotland in consideration of a payment of

£8448 : 1 : 4. The final completion of the liquidation was, however, delayed for other three years by the dependence of litigation with wealthy ex-directors.[1]

The extension of Scottish Banking, to which we have already referred, was not wholly confined to Scotland. The National Bank of Scotland had opened an office in London in 1864. This step having seemingly been attended with much success, the Bank of Scotland imitated the example set a few years later. The Royal Bank of Scotland, in 1874, also opened an office in London, having obtained a special Act of Parliament, authorising them to do so, in the previous year. These successive movements were by no means relished by the London bankers, and they were also jealously objected to by English provincial bankers, who felt themselves aggrieved by the permission given to Scottish issuing-banks to establish themselves in London, while retaining their powers of note-issuing elsewhere—a privilege which was denied to English bankers.

The heat of opposition was, however, gradually expending itself, when the Clydesdale Banking Company made a sudden raid on the English preserves by planting three branches in Cumberland, nominally for the convenience of their customers in the South of Scotland. This was the signal for the renewal of the contest on a grand scale. The battle became general all along the line. London bankers, London and provincial bankers, and English provincial bankers, joined in protecting their common interest. The conflict was carried into Parliament, where Mr. Goschen introduced (1875) a bill, the object of which was to drive the Scottish banks back to their own country. His efforts, however, although strongly supported, ended in the temporary compromise of a select committee " to consider and report upon the restrictions imposed and privileges conferred by law on bankers authorised to make and issue notes in England,

[1] For details of repayments to shareholders see Appendix H.

Scotland, and Ireland respectively." After arduous labours, and the accumulation of a large mass of more or less valuable information, the committee reported to the House without making any recommendation other than their reappointment next session. This suggestion was not, however, acted on ; and very soon all the other large Scottish banks, except the Commercial Bank of Scotland, opened offices in London without more opposition than that conveyed in indignant growls and threats of future vengeance. The Commercial Bank opened in London in July 1883.

Much interest was excited, towards the close of 1866, by the discovery of a forgery of the £1 notes of the Union Bank. The perpetrators were John Henry Greatrex, a photographer in Glasgow, Sewell Grimshaw, an engraver, and Thomas Grimshaw, who financed the adventure. The manufacture was carried on in Greatrex's premises ; and several months were spent in the process. Photography was first tried, but discarded in favour of engraving on a copperplate and transferring to a stone for printing. Lithography seems thus to have been the finally approved system, with the numbers type printed, and the signatures written. It is stated that nearly 1400 notes were prepared ; but the evidence of witnesses indicates a much larger number. It does not appear, however, that many were actually passed before the forgery was discovered. Greatrex, who had gone to Aberdeen in happy confidence of having achieved success, was greatly surprised at the early detection ; and, leaving his wife and child, fled to New York. He was accompanied by one of the women in his employment, Jane Weir, whom he had taken into his unholy confidence. The police followed him to New York, but lost his trail. A bogus advertisement for a first-class photographer, however, lured him from his den. He walked into the trap, and was brought back to Scotland, where his confederates had already been arrested in the act of uttering the spurious notes. The trio were tried in the High Court, Edinburgh, on 9th to 11th May 1867, and were sentenced,—Greatrex to 20 years' and the others to 15 years' penal servitude.

A few minor banking incidents fall to be recorded. The Bank of Scotland opened an office in London on 15th April 1867 ; and they purchased, in 1868, the business of the Central Bank of Scotland, whose head office was in Perth. This bank had ten years previously a paid-up capital of £78,125, on which a dividend of 8 per cent was paid ; and about the time of the amalgamation the capital was £100,000 in £40 shares which sold at £111. The dividend in 1867 was 12½ per cent. The bank had nine branches. In 1873, the Bank of Scotland obtained a seventh Act of Parliament, increasing its authorised capital from £1,500,000 to £4,500,000. The extra powers thus given were availed of to the extent of £375,000, of which £250,000 was called up. This issue of stock was made in April 1876, and, as it was placed at a premium of £375,000, the bank was enabled to raise its reserve fund to £750,000, and also to write off the balance of the price paid for the Central Bank business.

During the currency of this period, the volume of Scottish banking business had largely increased. In 1865, the total liabilities were about 77 millions. Seven years later they were 96½ millions. In 1877, they reached their highest point, namely, 108¾ millions. Next year they dropped to 106 millions, even including the balance sheets of the City of Glasgow and Caledonian Banks. This reduction, however, was more probably owing to withdrawals from certain banks who balanced after the crisis of 1878 than to any general decrease in the liabilities of the bank during the year.

CHAPTER XXV

THE CITY OF GLASGOW BANK

THE first three-quarters of the year 1878 are noticeable for little except a continuance of depression in the national industries and commerce. Heritable property, which is always last in being affected by alterations of prosperity and adversity, began to show symptoms of depreciation ; but prices were maintained to an extent which seemed to justify hopefulness of the future, and proved that there was little pressure on holders. Indeed, the nation did not show signs of impoverishment from the long-continued experience of bad trade. The Scottish banks seemed to be in a satisfactory state ; if money was accumulating in their hands from the want of proper channels for its profitable employment, they were at least able to maintain their dividends at the former rates. There was nothing in their reports to indicate the imminence of untoward events. People were rather looking and longing for a return of prosperity, than groaning under the experience of adversity.

In these circumstances, rumours, which first received utterance in the London correspondence columns of the *Glasgow News*, towards the end of September, regarding difficulties on the part of one of the banks in Scotland, were received with incredulity. In banking circles only one opinion as to which bank was referred to received any support. It was freely said that if any of the Scottish banks was in a weak condition, it was the City of Glasgow

Bank. But there was no alarm, for it was confidently believed that the report would prove to be a Stock Exchange *canard*. So little effect had it, that the prices of Scottish bank stocks were not materially affected ; and in a very few days it almost ceased to be spoken of. There was, however, a general pressure of sales of pledged railway and other stocks, indicative of impending disturbance ; but this circumstance did not attract general notice. Notwithstanding this extraordinary public confidence, negotiations were all the time being carried on by the City of Glasgow Bank and the Edinburgh banks, through the Bank of Scotland, with the object of obtaining assistance.

As far as its business in Scotland was concerned, the City of Glasgow Bank was not in the slightest degree inconvenienced. The depositors were sleeping as soundly as if their money had been invested in Government securities, and noteholders would not have accepted sovereigns in exchange. The London money market, however, had begun to feel that it had absorbed a sufficiency of City Bank paper. Unable longer to retire maturing bills with new paper, the bank had the greatest difficulty in taking them up, and saw that in a very short time its available resources would be exhausted. In these circumstances it sought an advance from the other banks, to enable it to tide over its difficulties. It would seem that, in consequence of the prevalence of rumours about the position of the bank, the Bank of Scotland had, on 11th September, urged the City Bank to retire a large amount of their acceptances ; whereupon the latter bank asked if they might rely on assistance from the other banks to the extent of £200,000 or £300,000—an estimate of requirements which they subsequently extended to £500,000. Further negotiations having revealed the fact that the bank was involved with a few firms to the extent of some millions sterling, on the 28th September an examination of the books by an Edinburgh accountant was decided upon. After receiving his report, the banks declined to give any assistance ; and, on the 1st October, the doors of the City of Glasgow Bank were closed at the usual hour, never more to be reopened for business.

The announcement of the suspension of the City of Glasgow Bank, which appeared in the newspapers of the 2nd October, had a paralysing effect throughout the business community, and feelings of alarm and distrust arose among the general public. The City Bank, although never in the enjoyment of the thorough confidence of the other banks, was known to have a large proprietary whose liability was unlimited, and had therefore been always trusted as much as any of the others. In the eyes of the general public it obtained a full share of credit. Although the youngest of the existing Scottish banks, it had, by a constant policy of branch extension, built up a deposit business of over £8,000,000 ; and, as its reports were always framed so as to show steady progress, it was in many quarters regarded as the most active and pro- spectively prosperous bank in Scotland. Its customers and shareholders would sometimes taunt the officials of the older banks with being " old-wifish " and slow of movement. Its stock, moreover, commanded a good price in the market. It afterwards appeared that there was actually a considerable pressure of sellers, and that the price was maintained only by continual purchases on account of the bank itself ; but these facts were unknown to the general public, who naturally estimated the position of the bank to a great extent by the Stock Exchange quotations. The revulsion of feeling from confidence to distrust was naturally very strong. People had believed so thoroughly in the banking system, that the failure of one member of the circle tempted them to lose belief in all. But it must be said that the public acted with wonder- ful prudence and self-control. The action of the other banks greatly tended to this result ; for they at once announced that, with a view to lessen the inconvenience of the stoppage to the public, they would receive, in the ordinary course of business, the notes of the City Bank which were in circulation.

From the first no hopes of resuscitation were held out by those conversant with the bank's affairs ; and, although for several days no details of the extent of the disaster were forthcoming, fears of a very grave state of matters were steadily increased. These were augmented by the failure of some London and East Indian houses, and rumours of further suspensions. On the 5th October, Dr. M'Grigor and Mr. Anderson, who had been asked to examine into the state of the bank, reported that it would be advisable to wind up the business ; and a meeting of the proprietors was summoned for the 22nd of the same month. Meanwhile the banks were actively engaged in making arrangements for accommodating City Bank depositors who might require the use of their money, and for taking up branch offices of the bank.

Until the 19th inst. almost nothing transpired regarding the position of the bank ; but failures in various parts of the country were daily announced, some of them being for heavy amounts. Nevertheless, a somewhat easier feeling prevailed throughout the community. It was, therefore, with feelings of surprise, indignation, and dismay that the public read the report of the investigators, which was issued late on the evening of the 18th. The *Scotsman* of 19th October records that " the report of Dr. M'Grigor and Mr. Anderson brings out a state of matters which far exceeds the anticipations of the most despondent shareholder. The actual loss amounts to the almost fabulous sum of £6,190,983 : 11 : 3, which, deducting the capital of £1,000,000, leaves £5,190,983 : 11 : 3 of a deficiency to be made good by the shareholders. This estimate takes no account of the reserve fund of £450,000. Amongst other startling disclosures, the investigators say that the shareholders had been led to believe the bank had lent upon credits less

17

than was the fact by £1,126,764 ; that the bank had good securities belonging to themselves absolutely more than was the fact by £926,764 ; and that there was more reserve gold in the bank than was really the case by £200,000. The total amount represented by bad debts, estimated at £7,345,357 : 15 : 6, the bank had been in the habit of treating in the balance-sheet as an available asset. Four debtors under this head owe the bank £5,792,394, while the securities held show a deficit of £4,269,957. The investigators add that ' it is by no means improbable that our own estimate is beyond the mark, as the bank's title to much of what we have entered as good is of a very imperfect description.' "

Such, in abstract, was the frightful statement presented to the shareholders and the public as the first official account of the position of the bank's affairs. It is no exaggeration to say that people were stupefied by the astounding disclosure. No such failure had ever previously been known. As was naturally to be expected, public and private comment was of the fiercest description. Yet the attitude of the shareholders and of the public was that of dignified self-restraint. Righteous indignation was hurled at the offenders ; but there was little tendency to confound the innocent with the guilty. One or two of the banks suffered for a short time from diminished confidence on the part of the public ; but the satisfactory manner in which they met their engagements speedily restored their credit. Most of the banks were not exposed to any actual trial ; and the older banks reaped a rich harvest of business from the suspension.

Immediately after the publication of the report of the investigators as to the affairs of the City of Glasgow Bank, the directors, manager, and secretary of the bank were arrested on a charge of fraud—the latter, however, being subsequently accepted as a witness. This action of the authorities met with the unanimous approval of the public. Indeed, considerable excitement was created by an apparent probability that the state of the law would necessitate the prisoners' liberation on bail for £300 being tendered. But to the charge of fraud, that of theft was added, and only one of their number was permitted to avail himself of the privilege. The trial commenced before the High Court of Justiciary, at Edinburgh, on 20th January 1879, and lasted for eleven days. The jury found the prisoners guilty of fraud, and next day, 1st February, the Court sentenced two of them to eighteen and the others to eight months' imprisonment.

The first meeting of the shareholders, after the stoppage, took place in Glasgow, on 22nd October 1878. It passed off with remarkable quietness, due in great measure to the absence of the imprisoned directors, but also, doubtless, to the utter futility of remonstrance. It was resolved unanimously to liquidate the affairs of the bank voluntarily. (Subsequently, 27th November, the liquidation was put under the supervision of the Court of Session, the First Division of which was for a long time entirely occupied therewith, and with cases relative thereto.) Four liquidators were appointed, and a committee of shareholders were nominated to consult with them. A few days afterwards a call of £500 per cent on the capital stock was announced, payable in two instalments, on 22nd December and 24th February following. This step naturally elicited much comment, some persons expressing surprise at the largeness of the call, others considering that it should have been much larger. For the most part, however, the action of the liquidators was viewed as a prudent preliminary step ; it being thought that a smaller sum would have been quite inadequate, and that one materially greater would have seemed harsh as a first measure.

A number of failures followed immediately on the stoppage of the bank. Of these, several very large ones were those of firms in direct connection with the bank, and through whose operations the disaster had been chiefly produced. The most important of these firms was James Morton & Co., whose liabilities amounted to about £2,500,000. Others were Smith, Fleming & Co., with £1,600,000 ; Matthew Buchanan & Co., £1,310,000 ; John Innes Wright & Co., £750,000 ; Glen, Walker & Co., £445,000 ; and Potter, Wilson & Co., whose affairs, including the private estate of the senior partner, showed a surplus of about £70,000. From day to day numerous other failures occurred—notably that of Heugh, Balfour & Co., with liabilities to the amount of £400,000, and trifling assets. Although technically a distinct suspension, that of the Bank of Mona was practically part of the failure of the City of Glasgow Bank, with which it was amalgamated, while retaining its corporate identity. Another bank failure was that of J. & J. Fenton & Sons, at Rochdale, who, while nominally private bankers, were actually stockjobbers. Subsequently (9th December), a more important English bank, the West of England and South Wales District Bank, was forced into liquidation ; but it was afterwards resuscitated as the Bristol and West of England Bank, Limited.

One of the most painful consequences of the disaster —the more painful from having been perfectly un-necessary—was the suspension of the Caledonian Banking Company. It most unfortunately happened that that bank had taken over from a customer £400 of City Bank stock, in security for an advance, and had thus become liable as a shareholder. The excitement of the time exaggerated the extent of probable liability of wealthy shareholders, the opinion being expressed that even the total estates of all the shareholders, including the Caledonian Bank, might be insufficient to meet the require-ments. This, of course, was an erroneous supposition ; but allowance must be made for the heated imagination of people who were dealing with a crisis without precedent, and for the fact that the question of the personal liability of trustees holding stock was in suspense. In the event of trustees having been absolved from liability, the pressure upon ordinary shareholders would have been greatly increased. The shareholders of the Caledonian Bank were seized with panic, and threw their shares into the market, glad to be rid of them on any terms. Dreading the contingency of the shares of the bank getting into the hands of men of straw, who would not be good for possible calls, the liquidators of the City of Glasgow Bank demanded that the register of proprietors should be closed. This, the directors intimated, they had no power to do. The liquidators replied by threatening to apply to the Court for the liquidation of the bank's affairs.

Meanwhile, or rather previous to this point in the proceedings, negotiations were carried on with the Bank of Scotland with a view to the business of the Caledonian Bank being acquired by that establishment. The entanglements into which the north country bank had got its affairs would seem, however, to have been too ravelled to admit of this solution of the difficulty. They were aggravated, moreover, by a pressure which set in on the part of depositors, who were naturally unwilling complacently to rely on the responsibility of a bank which was seemingly doubted by people who might be supposed most capable of judging of its contingent liabilities. The little bank fought nobly for existence ; but, baffled in its attempts to shake off liability, and refused credit for its ability to meet it, it had to succumb. On 5th December it closed its doors, and an application was made to the Court of Session for liquidation of its affairs. Eventually it was discovered that the full liability in connection with the failure of the City of Glasgow Bank would be met by a sum of £11,000—an amount equal to one half-year's profits. A guarantee fund of £150,000 was raised by the shareholders and their friends ; the final decision of the question of the liability of trustees, by fixing the responsibility of the full list of contributories to the City Bank liquidation, relieved the ordinary shareholders of a large share of their problematical liability; and further occasion for proceedings against the Caledonian Bank ceased. By arrangement, the liquidation order was cancelled, and the bank resumed business in August 1879, after about seven months' interval.

A large amount of litigation followed the suspension of the City of Glasgow Bank. Indeed, for a long time one of the divisions of the Court of Session devoted itself entirely to City Bank cases. But, if the number of cases was notable, the admirable manner in which the Court disposed of them was equally so. Celerity and sound judgment went hand in hand, so that, in a surprisingly short space of time, the causes were satisfactorily disposed of. The great majority of the cases were for rectification of the register of shareholders; and in several cases shareholders were fortunate enough to get their names erased. But attention was centred on the great question of the liability of trustees. Only the great interests involved could have made this question worth raising. The House of Lords had unmistakably given its decision at the time of the Western Bank liquidation—a decision by which the law of Scotland was practically assimilated to that of England. Very probably that assimilation was not warranted; but it had all the force of a legislative assimilation, as far as future cases were concerned. For there was no reason to hope that the House would stultify itself, by applying an English rule on one occasion and establishing an opposite Scotch one on another. The test case was that of *William Muir and Others for Rectification of the List of Contributories of the City of Glasgow Bank*, in which four trustees sought to evade liability on the ground that they had not agreed to become individually members of the bank. On 20th December 1878 the Court of Session refused the petition. The case was carried to the House of Lords, but the judgment of the Court below was affirmed.

The liquidation of the City of Glasgow Bank was completed on 1st October 1882, when the unrealised assets were acquired by the Assets Company, Limited, which had been formed for the purpose. This was in the interests of the outstanding shareholders, who were thus enabled to nurse properties and claims which could not be dealt with immediately to advantage. These rights consisted of large blocks of preference and ordinary stock of the New Zealand and Australian Land Company, Limited ; estates in Lanarkshire, New South Wales, and New Zealand ; interests in Indian gold mines, etc. On the other hand, the new company undertook responsibility for unclaimed deposits, unpresented notes, and other liabilities of the bank, to the extent of £37,832. The Assets Company has justified the expectations of its projectors.

This was the third of three great banking disasters in Scotland, which it is interesting to contrast. The Ayr Bank was a high-class concern, founded on the landed interest. Although it was doubtless taken advantage of by self-interested people, there was more of ignorance and folly than of actual iniquity about it. The Western Bank, while not having aristocratic connection, was of good commercial standing ; and, although its infatuation was culpable to a degree almost requiring the plea of insanity to excuse it, yet it did not descend to criminality. The City of Glasgow Bank was never highly esteemed outside the circle of its dupes, and seems to have been a long-continued fraud. It traded on the respectability of its neighbours and the unlimited liability of its shareholders. Blessed would it have been if, when it temporarily ceased the issue of notes in 1857, it had been held to have forfeited its right to issue. This would have practically terminated its evil career at a comparatively early stage.

CHAPTER XXVI

LIMITATION OF LIABILITY

THE effect on the public mind of the revelations of sufferings entailed on the shareholders of the City of Glasgow Bank, by the necessity of providing for the enormous deficit discovered in the accounts of the bank, was very strong. There was an almost wild desire to take the burden from their shoulders, or at least to ease the strain to as great an extent as possible. It was in this spirit that an association was formed with the object of promoting a great lottery to raise money, which, after payment of prizes and expenses, should be applied in meeting the bank's debts. The proposal met with a good deal of public approval ; and there can be little doubt that, so far as the adhesion of supporters was concerned, it might have been carried out with considerable success. Led away by the hope of achieving a grand result in the mitigation of misery, many persons forgot that even charity must be founded on high principle. Even the Government authorities hesitated to suppress a movement which had so much good for its object, although it could with difficulty be regarded as legitimate. A little consideration, however, convinced people that to cure the City Bank troubles by imitating the action which had caused them, and to pay gambling debts by further gambling, even although the sufferers were innocent parties, would be a violation of the national honour, and an establishment of a precedent prejudicial to commercial morality. The Crown authorities then intimated that the scheme seemed to violate the law ; and, after some reasonable negotiation, the proposal was withdrawn (January 1879).

It then became evident that the shareholders must face their difficulties unaided. They had a duty to do, and it must be said that they did it nobly. They could not escape their responsibilities, but the spirit in which they met them was admirable. But, while the public saw that there could be no interposition between the debtors and their creditors, they were not the less resolved to stand close by and help those who fell. A relief fund subscription was opened for the benefit of those who were deprived of their means of support by the calamity. This at once met with great success. People of all classes felt relief in the opportunity of affording material assistance to, and substantially testifying their sympathy with, the hundreds of innocent sufferers whose case had engrossed their attention for months previously. The various committees throughout the country obtained subscriptions for about £400,000 within a few months. Of that very large sum only a small fraction was not eventually paid up by the subscribers, and all but about £20,000 was raised in Scotland. This result was one of which Scotland may well be proud ; the more so as it was accomplished at a time when, irrespective of the direct consequences of the disaster which had occasioned it, the nation was sadly straitened by dull trade, bad harvests, and lessened incomes.

The great question which was evolved, as the main economic principle, from the experience of the crisis, was the advisableness of continuing the system of unlimited liability of shareholders in banks. While other business establishments had, as a rule, availed themselves of the provisions of the Companies Acts permitting limitation of liability, the Scottish banks, like most of the larger English banks, had not thought it expedient to do so.

Those which had not been specially incorporated were
registered under the Acts as unlimited companies. The
fact of any of the banks being in the enjoyment of a
limitation of liability was questioned by many writers ;
but, after a fierce discussion, this argument came to
nothing. It was evident to candid minds that the
doctrine of limitation of liability by virtue of incorporation under special Acts of Parliament or Royal
Charters was as old as the law of the land. In point of
fact, the raising of the question was the result of the
conflict of interests between the unlimited banks and
the three old chartered banks, and not the discovery of
any legal principle which had been overlooked by lawyers
and statesmen for hundreds of years.

An exception should be made, however, in the case of
one writer among those who doubted the sufficiency of
the charters to cover liability of the stockholders of the
banks in question. Mr. William Mitchell,[1] waiving the
untenable position of those who doubted that Acts of
Parliament and Crown Charters conferred limitation
unless the contrary was stated, founded his argument
on special provisions in the constitutions of the banks
themselves, whereby powers were conferred on the banks
to make calls on their proprietors to a limited extent. It
was shown, however, by the other side, that these provisions were of a purely optional character, had been
inserted for a specific purpose, and afterwards dropped.
But, even admitting that these powers are still available,
the fact of their insertion is an argument in favour of
the doctrine of limitation by incorporation. The proportions callable are, moreover, distinctly specified, and
small in amount.

There was a general cry for legislation, but great
difference of opinion existed as to what form it should
take. Early in January 1879, Mr. John M'Laren, M.P.
(afterwards Lord M'Laren), introduced a bill providing

[1] *Our Scotch Banks*, Edinburgh, 1879, p. 84 *et seq.*

for the auditing of the books and accounts of the banks in Scotland, but it was talked out. Later in the session, the Government took up the question on a broader basis, and introduced a bill, which, after great modifications, became the " Companies Act, 1879." It was not a measure of which its framers had much reason to be proud, but it had the effect of removing all legal difficulties which seemed to stand in the way of the adoption by some of the banks of the principle of limited liability.[1] It also established a new system of reserve liability. The leading London banks at once adopted its provisions, and their example was largely followed by other English banks.

The Scottish banks, however, refrained from recognising it as suitable for their needs. The three old banks held that it had no applicability to them, and the unlimited banks were fearful of appending the depreciatory word " limited " to their names. Again and again they were attacked in the public press for their hesitation. In letters to newspapers the old banks were abused for harbouring every species of evil spirit which words could define or imagination depict, as applicable to business establishments, and the other banks were taunted with weakness and cowardice. The criticism of responsible editors was, of course, more dignified, but generally not less adverse. But the banks would take no hurried action.

At last, however, the three old banks made a movement which was a surprise to every one. In November 1880 they individually gave notice of application to Parliament for power to increase their capitals, alter their existing capitals, and provide a large margin of responsibility of stockholders as additional security to creditors. This resolution met with little or no opposition from the proprietors of the banks, and the directors'

[1] The inexpediency of unlimited liability had been discussed as early as 1839 by John Fairfull Smith, W.S., in a letter to the Chancellor of the Exchequer published by Bell and Bradfute, Edinburgh.

proposals were formally confirmed by them in each case.
In the public press, however, the new movement was
not so favourably received, and in several cases it was
denounced with more severity than accuracy of criticism ;
indeed, a large amount of ignorance was manifested
regarding the matter. The bills were duly introduced,
but met with considerable opposition in Parliament.
The Government expressed objection to proceeding in
such matters by private legislation, but intimated their
willingness to introduce a public measure, giving the
powers asked, provided the banks would agree to certain
conditions, including the adoption of the term " limited "
as part of their titles.

In a few very able letters addressed to the Treasury,
the banks showed the impossibility of their agreeing to
the views of the Government ; and in April 1881 they
finally closed the negotiations, and intimated that they
would not proceed with their bills. This conclusion to
the movement was a very happy one for the three old
banks. The alterations proposed would have spoilt their
constitutions, and, as experience has since shown, were not
necessary for maintaining public confidence. The action
of the banks, however, had a good effect in showing that
they were sincerely anxious to study public sentiment
in the matter of providing enlarged security for their
liabilities. There can be little doubt that, in their
correspondence with the Treasury, they greatly strengthened their position in the public view, and swept away
the ignorant criticism to which they had been subjected
in the public press.

Shortly after the abandonment of the scheme of the
old banks, the unlimited banks took into favourable
consideration the propriety of adopting the provisions of
the Act of 1879. The result was a mutual resolution to
become limited, on the basis of having subscribed capitals
five times as large as their existing paid-up capitals. In
the case of the National Bank, no alteration of capital

was necessary, as it stood at the required proportion ; but each of the other banks had to enlarge its subscribed capital. As there was no issue of new stock, as had generally been made by the English banks adopting the Act, there was no opportunity of immediate pecuniary benefit to the shareholders. But general satisfaction was felt that limitation of liability had been accomplished, and it does not appear that this action was followed by any prejudicial effect to the business of the banks.

Another question evolved, or rather brought prominently forward, by the disaster was the propriety of the appointment of neutral auditors to report on the statements of accounts issued by the banks. Hitherto most of the banks had considered the practice as unsuited to the nature of banking business. Even when vehemently (sometimes not over politely) urged to adopt the system, there was a good deal of hesitation. But, as one after another gave in to the public demand, within three years after the City Bank's failure, all had permanently adopted the principle of appointing two independent professional accountants to examine the accounts and cash balances, and certify as to the accuracy of the published annual balance-sheets and profit and loss statements. This result was certainly in the general interest, even if the security thus attained was less absolute than the confidence sometimes reposed in professional audits.

CHAPTER XXVII

HAVING traced the progress of Scottish banking from its modest commencement in 1695, through trials, failures, and brilliant successes, to the time of its greatest trial, we may appropriately add to our sketch a review of the position of the surviving banks, as exhibited in their published balance-sheets for 1883, and by a contrast of that position with the statistical condition of banking in Scotland eighteen years previously—the date at which the banks first generally adopted the practice of making a public disclosure of their financial state ; for, until 1865, almost absolute secrecy shrouded their affairs. Except the amount of their capitals, and the rates of dividends they paid, but little was known regarding them which could serve as a guide to intending purchasers of bank stock. Customers had to exercise blind faith as to the solidity of the establishments they dealt with, and economists had to trust pretty much to imagination in estimating the position of banking and its relations to the progress of the nation.

Since 1865 we have had an unbroken series of yearly statistics, portraying, with nearly complete accuracy, the position of the several banking establishments.[1] The elements vitiating the accuracy of the portraiture are not numerous, nor do they materially affect the general

[1] See *Scottish Banking during the Period of Published Accounts* (by the present author), Effingham Wilson, London, 1898.

result. The *dénouement* of the City of Glasgow Bank
showed that its official reports were not worthy of implicit
belief ; but it is impossible to dispense with them.
Another result of the same catastrophe was the ascertainment of the fact that the actual capital devoted to banking
had not been so great as had been supposed, many of the
banks having held large portions of their capitals in their
own names. Stock so held, while nominally still in
existence, and capable of being transferred without formal
re-creation, was practically non-existent, as it in no way
exercised any power, or was capable of meeting any
responsibility.[1]   These holdings having now been disposed
of, there has really been a greater increase in proprietors'
funds than the official statements would lead one to
believe. Again, although a system of publicity is, in the
main, very superior to that of secrecy, it has some dangers
special to itself. There is an increased tendency to what
may be called " racing," with the resulting danger of
over-exertion, the banks vying with each other, con-
sciously or unconsciously, as to the creditableness of their
annual statements.

As we have already seen, it was an old habit of Scotch
bankers to pile up their profits from year to year, and
make a grand stroke when the accumulation had reached
a considerable point. While this practice, to the extent
to which it was carried, is inconsistent with the
interests of proprietors who may not hold long enough
to participate in the distribution, there can be no doubt
that it sometimes saved the banks from the effects of
large losses which would otherwise have been difficult to
deal with. A system of publicity tends to prevent such
a course of action, and, in order to put on as good an

[1] This view of the question is controverted by some bankers, on
the ground that, the capital having been actually created, taken up
by subscribers, and not lost by the bank, it must still exist, although
purchased by the bank. The case of the City of Glasgow Bank, however, supplies practical proof that this is a purely technical or book-
keeping view of the matter.

appearance as for the time being they are entitled to, the banks are apt, from time to time, to lessen the extent of the hidden strength which, in times past, had secured their steady progress. Thus, the reserved fund shown in the balance-sheet—drafts on which have always a serious effect in public estimation—tends to become the only source from which extraordinary losses can be met. Such losses no amount of prudence and foresight can avert—they can only provide for them. Competing openly in the eyes of the public, each bank, urged on by its shareholders, seeks to pay as high a dividend as its profits will allow. When reverses come, a sharp reduction follows, producing unreasonable disappointment on the part of investors, who seem to think they should be able both to eat their cake and have it. Of course, the main point is that provision should be made for extraordinary reverses of fortune, and, if this be done to a sufficient extent by public additions to reserve funds, the result may be the same in the long run ; but the system of hidden reserves has a steadying effect on the progress of an establishment.

The progress during the eighteen years which elapsed between the points of comparison is marvellous, and much beyond the ratio of the increase in population. The population of Scotland in 1865 was probably about 3,074,000, and an official estimate for 1883 places it at 3,825,744. The increase would thus be 751,744, or nearly 24½ per cent. But the deposits held by the banks rose 45 per cent during the same period ; indeed they had reached that point much earlier—viz. in 1877—although they subsequently fell, as a result of the crisis of 1878. It is probable that the improvement thus shown is actually representative of a much greater advance of the nation in material prosperity, for the competition of investment companies of all kinds had, in an intensified degree, tended to lessen the natural inflow of deposits. But, without reference to such matters, it is a striking fact that while, in 1865, the twelve banks then existing held deposit money equal to £18 : 12s. per head of the population, the ten banks existing in 1883 held deposits equal to £21 : 14 : 1 per head of the population.

The aggregate liabilities of the banks increased in a slightly lower proportion than the deposits. This was owing to the comparatively small increase in the circulation of notes, and to a small decrease in the amount of paid-up capital. The reduction of capital was due to the absorption of the Central Bank and the failure of the City of Glasgow Bank. If allowance be made, however, for the portions of capital held by the banks in their own hands, and subsequently issued to the public, as already referred to, it is probable that there had been no actual decrease in the total capitals. The amount of circulation given by the reports of the banks is not reliable as a basis of calculation, as the individual amounts are merely those of the particular days on which the balances were struck. The average yearly issues showed an increase of 34 per cent. Grouping the banks for comparison, as Edinburgh, Glasgow, and country, according to the location of their head offices, the distribution of the total liabilities was, in 1865—Edinburgh, 62 per cent ; Glasgow, 30 per cent ; country, 8 per cent. By 1883 the first group seems to have gained at the expense of both the others, for the proportions in 1883 were—Edinburgh, 70 per cent ; Glasgow, 23 per cent ; country, 7 per cent. The failure of the City of Glasgow Bank was, doubtless, the cause of this change, which was, indeed, natural, as it could not be expected that two Glasgow and three provincial banks would secure as much of the lapsed bank's business as the five large Edinburgh banks.

A striking feature of the increase in liabilities is supplied by the acceptances. (The drafts current, although conjoined in the tables with the acceptances, as they were not usually separated in the earlier reports, do not materially affect this comparison.) The increase in this department of banking was much more marked than that of any other, amounting to 85 per cent. It would seem, however, that this is due mainly to that exceptionally good department of acceptance business supplied by the colonial banks drawing on London, and not so much to mercantile acceptances. The acceptances of some banks actually decreased in amount.

While the public liabilities of the banks were thus extended, the banks did much towards supporting the proportion of proprietors' funds to them. Although, as we have seen, there was a decrease to the extent of 4 per cent in the amount of total capital, owing to the withdrawal of two banks, the amount added to reserved funds was no less than 91 per cent, or twice the proportion of increase in deposits. But the relative proportion of the proprietors' funds to public liabilities was not quite so great as in 1865, the proportions being 19 per cent in the earlier year against 16 per cent in 1883. But, if recent issues of stock be allowed for, it is probable that that apparent falling off is deceptive.

Turning now to the assets of the banks, some interesting features are manifested. The banking advances, which might naturally have been expected to increase in somewhat similar ratio with the deposits, had actually advanced at not very much more than half the rate. This would seem to indicate that the demand for banking accommodation had not progressed to the same extent as the increase in wealth of the nation. There may have been a determinate policy on the part of the banks to strengthen the banking reserves, but it is not probable that they desired so large an increase as had actually taken place—viz. 80 per cent. The outstanding expenditure on bank buildings also shows a large increase. As there were 218 more bank offices than existed in 1865, a considerable increase is natural. But the banks studied appearances as well; for, while the average cost of the buildings was formerly about £1600, the later amount is £1943.

Considering the great extension of the banking business which had taken place, a large increase in net profits might have been expected. But, on the contrary, the improvement was very small. The ten existing banks declared, in 1883, profits only 3 per cent in excess of those declared by the twelve banks carrying on business in 1865. This comparison is, of course, quite fair, as the Central Bank and City Bank businesses are enjoyed by the surviving banks. It is thus evident that banking in Scotland was not, in 1883, nearly so profitable as it was eighteen years previously. To a large extent this is due, doubtless, to the smaller proportion of funds employed in banking advances, the reserve securities not yielding so high a return. But other causes probably contribute to the result. Perhaps allowance should be made for the fact that 1865 was a year of high pressure in commercial activity, the price of money ruling high during the greater portion of it, while 1883 was mainly one of low rates. But this will not entirely account for the disproportion of profits. The average rates of dividend and prices of stock are in accordance with the rate of increase in profits.

CHAPTER XXVIII

A CRITICAL PERIOD

Between the close of 1878 and the crisis of 1890, the public history of the nation records many important incidents, but few of outstanding magnitude. With quite a crop of small wars, and continuous Boer and Irish troubles, the country crept along ever without the moral courage to pluck safety from the nettle danger. Nations seem, like individuals, to have alternating periods of nerve experiences. At any rate, an imperialistic-ascendency condition ended with the Berlin settlement of 1878, securing " peace with honour " ; and thereafter set in an opportunist spirit which had its manifestations in the Majuba capitulation treaty, tinkered Boer conventions, the sacrifice of General Gordon, dangerous vacillation in Irish policy eventuating in the almost fatal Home Rule weakness ; until, tired of perpetually yielding to everybody only to be bothered for something more, the nation closed its teeth.

The twelve years which elapsed from the crisis of 1890 to 1902 were full of the makings of history. The great battle for the maintenance of the Union—the most momentous, probably, of the last century—was fought and won ; *laissez faire* policy in South Africa, the first overt act of which had been the recall of Sir Bartle Frere on 1st July 1880, was followed by both parties in a weak-kneed manner, until, nineteen years thereafter, the Boers, taught that pressure only was necessary to obtain con-

cessions from the British, launched their insolent ulti-
matum, and started to sweep the rooineks into the sea.
Then the nation paid in blood and treasure for the false
peace it had indulged in. The economic error had been
dreadful, but, probably, under psychological conditions
it was inevitable. At the same time, the results of the
costly remedy which the nation calmly, and great-
mindedly, unhesitatingly resorted to probably formed an
experience necessary for the wellbeing of the body politic,
and were eminently beneficial to the higher life and
aspirations of the race. And the units of the Empire were
welded together as only such titanic force could effect.

Notwithstanding widespread agricultural depression,
and Irish and anarchist plots, the domestic state of the
nation was fairly good, if not so prosperous as it had
sometimes been. There was much complaint of bad
trade until later years, but the bulk of the people seem
to have thriven on the low prices ruling for commodities.
Strikes, however, were a pronounced feature, both from
their number and their magnitude ; but, although they
entailed losses and privations out of proportion to the
results obtained by either party, they tended to teach
labour that it was not invincible, and to adjust the
relationships to capital. As the century drew towards
its close there was a continuous improvement in the
state of the nation, until 1896 could be styled " a wonderful year of prosperity." That, however, was the zenith,
since when wars and heavy taxation weighed on the
weary citizens, with the close of the Victorian era.

Arts and sciences progressed if they did not achieve
brilliant results ; and industry produced the Severn
Tunnel, the second Tay Bridge, the stupendous Forth
Bridge, and the Manchester Ship Canal,—all works of
the first rank in engineering. In fiscal matters, Mr.
Goschen's consols conversion scheme, whereby a large
saving of interest payable on the national debt was
secured, was perhaps the only outstanding favourable

incident ; while the large issues of war stock and consols in connection with the Boer War are conspicuous on the other hand. But revenue collection experience, and the statistics of foreign trade (apart from prices), showed fairly healthy features ; and, all things considered, the condition of the people was better than similarly disturbing influences produced in former times, evidencing an increase of inherent strength.

The crisis of 1890 is associated mainly with the failure, and liquidation under exceptional circumstances, of the firm of Baring Brothers & Co., by the Bank of England, supported by the leading banks and bankers of the kingdom. It is an instance of a suppressed crisis, the results manifesting themselves in a long continuance of unfavourable conditions in business. The Scottish banks were largely interested in this liquidation, and supported the action of the Bank of England : the seven banks in Edinburgh and Glasgow subscribed £300,000 each to the guarantee fund. Again, the crisis which might have been expected about the year 1901 appears to have been a disguised one. The exceptional circumstances of the war in South Africa may have acted as a counter-irritant, dispersing the ordinary course of events. There were, however, large liquidations which may well represent the wreckage of a joint-stock crisis.

The history of banking in Scotland during the eighteen years 1884–1902 may be epitomised by a paraphrase— Happy is that banking system that hath no annals. While it cannot be absolutely affirmed that all the companies in all respects improved their positions, there is but slight exception to the rule. In the main there was extraordinarily healthy growth during the period, with an absence of unfavourable circumstances of a serious character. There was an absence of sensational circumstances which, while giving interest and colour to a narrative, indicate trouble and disease among the *dramatis personæ.*

The period treated of in last chapter, and that now falling to be dealt with, are of nearly similar duration, viz. about eighteen to nineteen years. In both there is shown a great and healthy growth ; but the latter period does not show increases so great, either in bulk or by percentage, as the former period. The only departments in which the cash increase is greater are those of the banking reserves and capital paid up ; and it is only in the case of the note circulation that the percentage increase is greater than formerly. Perhaps the same rates of expansion were hardly to be expected, considering the great increase of financial business competing more or less with the banks. On the other hand, when we turn from the balance-sheets to the profit and loss statements, it is gratifying to find that the remunerativeness of the business considerably improved.

Having in a previous chapter treated of the progress of banking in Scotland from 1865 to 1883, we propose now to examine the changes which occurred during the almost similar period which elapsed from the latter date to 1901.[1] So far as amounts go, the changes in the two periods bear some striking resemblances. Thus the total assets increased by 30 millions, as against rather more than $31\frac{1}{4}$ millions formerly. The reserved funds, $2\frac{1}{2}$ against $2\frac{3}{4}$ millions. Deposits, $24\frac{1}{4}$ compared with $25\frac{3}{4}$ millions. In other words, the sum of increases in these important items appears to have averaged much the same per annum during the two periods. But, of course, the percentage increases were much less than formerly. On the other hand, other items show a widely different experience. Thus there was no such effort during the latter eighteen as in the former eighteen years towards strengthening the capital accounts. The solitary instance of extension of capital is supplied by the British Linen

[1] The present review is not in as full detail as the previous one, as the writer has elaborated this matter in his *Scottish Banking during the Period of Published Accounts*.

Bank in 1892, which issued £250,000 of new stock at a premium of 200 per cent. Again, the amount of acceptances and drafts hardly moved, the half million increase shown being possibly accidental. The note circulation, however, expanded to a marvellous extent, reaching two millions, or 36 per cent, greater than in 1883, against an increase of less than 1 million, or 18 per cent, in the former period. This great advance was, of course, solely an effort to meet the public convenience, and was a pecuniary loss to the banks owing to the increased expense of maintaining the issues without any counterbalancing profit. Advocates of the abolition of note-issues may console themselves with a calculation of the saving to the State of the wear and tear of metallic currency which would have accrued on this great increase of the circulating medium.

Among the asset groups, the experience of the two periods was widely different. A trifling increase of $5\frac{1}{2}$ millions, or 8 per cent, occurred in the banking advances, as compared with $13\frac{3}{4}$ millions, or 25 per cent, formerly. The amount of expenditure outstanding under the heading of bank buildings showed a very moderate increase—less than half of the increase of the preceding period. To some extent this result may be due to more generous appropriation of profits to writing down the cost of buildings. As there was so small an outlet for the increasing resources of the banks, the banking reserves rose 24 millions, or 63 per cent, contrasted with 17 millions, or 80 per cent. They thus show the extraordinarily high proportion of 45 per cent to the total liabilities ; equal to more than one half of the liabilities to the public.

A continuous expansion in the matter of branches was shown ; but the rate of increase only equalled about two-thirds of what it was in the former period. The number of offices totalled nearly 1100, of which thirteen were in England. This gives a proportion of one bank office to every 4155 of the then population of Scotland, a very liberal supply of banking facilities.   All the banks participated in this activity in branch extension ; but the most progressive were the Commercial, Clydesdale, British Linen, and Union.   While this policy was accompanied by increased profits, it may be doubted if it contributed in any marked degree to that result.   The National Bank, which showed the second largest increase of profits, was hardly over average in the matter of branch extension.   It is more probable that the improvement in profits was mainly due to the large increase of public liabilities, the abolition of payment of interest on current accounts, and other lessening of burdens on revenue.

The question of special banks for the working classes was considerably discussed in this period.   The idea was borrowed from the continent, where people's banks had been in operation for long, and especially with reference to those of the Schulze-Delitzsch type, which were supposed to be of special efficiency.   As a result the People's Bank, Limited, was established in Edinburgh in January 1889.   According to a statement made at the time " the object of the bank is to furnish banking facilities to those classes whose money transactions are at present generally considered too small to require such services, and who, from this cause, too often fall into usurious hands.   It is registered under the Industrial and Provident Societies Act, 1876.   It will conduct, in the main, the business of an ordinary Scottish bank, though, of course, it does not possess the power to issue its own notes. . . . The accounts of depositors may either be current or deposit accounts.   On the former 1 per cent of interest will be allowed, calculated on the minimum monthly balances, and on the latter $2\frac{1}{2}$ per cent. . . . Loans will be granted, but each borrower must be a shareholder to the extent of at least one share. Advances will be made on such securities as stocks, ground-rents, feus, leases, life policies, building and co-operative society shares, house property and land ; and credits upon cash-accounts current will be granted when the security is considered good, and approved bills will be discounted." The bank appears to have carried on a modest but successful business. The latest report, to 31st December 1916, shows a holding of deposits to the amount of £57,257 and an accumulated reserve fund of £2600 ; with advances to the amount of £31,179. It pays a dividend of 5 per cent per annum.

Shortly afterwards a similar institution was organised in Glasgow which has grown more rapidly than its earlier compeer. It has eight branches and five agencies, £136,039 of deposits, and a reserve fund of £9250. How far it has adhered, however, to its original field of operations, seems uncertain. It changed its name to the Mercantile Bank of Scotland, Limited ; and its latest balance-sheet shows that the bulk of its funds are invested ; less than 30 per cent being advances to customers. Owing to losses, no dividend was paid for the year 1915–16.

It is still too early to decide whether the system of people's banks is likely to be permanent. Probably the result will depend largely on the amount of care bestowed on the business, which, it may be presumed, will involve considerable risks accompanied by narrow margins of profit. There will be a tendency to enlarge the field of operations.

There are still a few events which it will be proper to refer to ere closing this period of our narrative. Owing to the continuance of low profit rates, the banks made important alterations in their deposit interest arrangements. On 1st July 1885, the initial step was taken by the discontinuance of the daily balance rate, all interest allowed on current accounts being thereafter calculated on the minimum monthly balances,—that rate being at the same time reduced from $1\frac{1}{2}$ to 1 per cent. The old minimum of 2 per cent on deposit receipts was also given up, and the rate reduced to $1\frac{1}{2}$ per cent. As an offset, some concessions were made in regard to discount terms. These arrangements held until 1st October 1892, when the continued pressure of low rates necessitated a further change. The old established system of allowing interest on current account creditor balances was entirely abolished, and the deposit receipt minimum rate was reduced to 1 per cent. On the other hand, the overdraft rate was reduced by ½ per cent.

In November 1888 a forgery of a new issue of £1 notes of the Bank of Scotland was discovered. It seemed to be the work of a skilled engraver aided by an expert lithographer. Even the watermark was ingeniously imitated by a special process. About a dozen notes were put in circulation. This bank suffered more seriously, on 16th February 1891, by the robbery from a London branch clerk of his remittance bag, containing £11,580 in bank notes, while he was at the counter of one of the other city banks. The British Linen Company made, in 1892, an issue of new stock to the extent of £250,000 at 300 per cent. This enabled them to secure the place of honour in regard to amount of proprietors' funds. Although matters of but little importance, it may be right to record that, in 1883, an honest but mistaken venture called the Money Order Bank, designed to conduct a so-called improvement on the Post Office remittance system, was started in Edinburgh ; and, in 1894, an English concern calling itself the London and Scottish Banking and Discount Company, Limited, opened an office in Edinburgh. In both cases the inevitable ending was not long deferred, and the close of the latter's career was ignominious.

Investors in Scotland suffered severely by a crisis among the banks of Australia in 1893. The immediate cause was the effects of continuous drought on the pastoral interests, but it was due mainly to an undue extension of advances to squatters and town-builders. Several of the banks failed disastrously, while others reconstructed with heavy writings-down of capital. Depositors, a large proportion of whom were resident in Scotland, had practically no option but to accept terms which involved loss, either permanent or temporary, of considerable portions of their loans, and sometimes the necessity of becoming preferential shareholders. They were presented with the alternative either of accepting the arrangement proposed or of facing immediate heavy loss. The results showed that the choice of approving reconstruction, whereby the banks were allowed time to nurse their assets, was generally best. But there was introduced into company management a practice of reversing the Bible story of the creditor seizing his debtor by the throat and saying, "Pay me that thou owest." The new system was that the debtor grasped the creditor and told him, "Take what I offer or it will be worse for you." But perhaps the depositors, had they foreclosed, might not have been so expert as the banks themselves in managing the derelict estates. The large old-established banks came through the trial with much credit.

An exceptional episode occurred in 1909. This was the trial in the High Court of Justiciary, Edinburgh, of five directors of the Mutual Bank, Limited, whose head office was in Dumbarton Road, Glasgow, on charges of issuing false balance-sheets and misapplication of funds to the extent of £8449. This humble imitator of the City of Glasgow Bank had been registered on 17th August 1895 as a Friendly Society under the name Co-operative Bank of Scotland, Limited, which was altered in April 1896 to Mutual Credit Bank of Scotland, Limited, and again in May 1900 to Mutual Bank, Limited. It opened a branch in Edinburgh. On 15th November 1906 it went into liquidation. Some of the accused appear to have been more or less victims of interested parties, but the evidence indicated that the society had its origin in a design to finance certain firms, the advances to which involved irregularities and entailed bad debts to the amount above stated. One of the prisoners was acquitted, three were sentenced to imprisonment for three months, and one, Alexander Wilson, who had latterly acted as manager and secretary, was sentenced to imprisonment for eighteen months.

A somewhat dangerous forgery was discovered on 18th March 1912. The subject was a £1 note of the Royal Bank dated 5th May 1908. The counterfeits were hand-done on paper thicker and softer than the genuine article ; but the work was so clever that inexpert people were apt to be deceived. A residenter in Kirkcaldy, Matthew Marshall Martin, who had previously been in the employment of large engraving and publishing firms, was tried on 5th November 1912, in the High Court, Edinburgh, on a charge of uttering as genuine thirty-one of these fabricated notes between 1st March and 7th October of that year. The game had been allowed to go on after the forgery was discovered, with the object of making sure of the culprit. Martin was sentenced to six years' penal servitude.

Another forgery case with somewhat extraordinary features was discovered at Peterhead about the middle of September 1913. Counterfeit notes in circulation were traced to the local convict prison, and it was presumed that the manufacture was carried on there ; but this was not publicly ascertained. There seems to have been one note at least of £5 denomination, but the bulk of the forgeries were of £1. They were hand-drawn with a fine sharp pencil by a clever draughtsman " working with crude materials," and not calculated to deceive any person of experience. They were generally treated as mere curiosities and commanded, as such, it is stated, almost their face value. Both the North of Scotland Bank and the Union Bank notes were the subjects of this criminal *jeu d'esprit*. One of the former representing the old issue with a picture of King's College, Aberdeen, finely done, but incorrect, was challenged on presentation at the Bank's Harbour Branch. After investigation and, presumably, suppression of the issue, the case seems to have been dropped.

An incursion of small, recently formed London banks offering comparatively high rates for deposit money took place early in the present century. The Charing Cross Bank, Limited, opened an office in Edinburgh about 1905, and Farrow's Bank, Limited, also established a branch there about the same time. The former made a bad failure in 1910, but during the few years of its existence the local branch seems to have attracted a considerable number of customers.

An increase of capital was made by the Bank of Scotland in August 1907, to carry out amalgamation arrangements with the Caledonian Bank, as described in next chapter. The amount issued was £112,500, with £75,000 paid up, making the total capital £1,987,500 subscribed, and £1,325,000 called.

It should, perhaps, be recorded that the Union Bank of Scotland, Limited, at a special general meeting of shareholders held in Glasgow on 25th April 1917, adopted a Memorandum and Articles of Association in modern statutory form (under the provisions of the Companies Act, 1908) in place of the original contract of co-partnership of 1830, as amended from time to time. This was confirmed by the Court of Session on 31st October 1917, with the exception of the clause in the Memorandum empowering the company to sell or dispose of the whole or any part of the undertaking or assets of the company, and with a slight modification of the clause authorising the company to amalgamate with other companies having similar objects.

In June last an announcement was made that the London City and Midland Bank, Limited, had purchased premises in Glasgow with intention to open an office there. They have also made arrangements for extending their activities to Ireland.

See Appendix I, page 320.

CHAPTER XXIX

THE DECADE PRECEDING THE WAR

THE opening years of the twentieth century witnessed an event of considerable interest in the history of Scottish banking, namely, the amalgamation of the Caledonian Banking Company, Limited, with the Bank of Scotland. Since the absorption of the Central Bank in 1868 no fresh fusions had taken place among the existing institutions —ten in number in 1906. The South African War (1899–1902) and the United States troubles in the year which we have now reached in our narrative had led to a persistent and serious depreciation in British Government securities, and consols, which stood at 113⅛ in 1898, had fallen to 80¾ by the August of 1907. The Caledonian Bank, struggling on the barren soil of the north, had felt the depreciation keenly. It held about £135,000 in consols, and although it maintained a dividend of 6 per cent its Reserve Fund had shrunk in 1906 to £43,000. It was felt that if the Caledonian Bank was to survive at all, it must be as an integral part of a larger concern. After a full review of the whole position the directors opened negotiations with the Bank of Scotland, who had all along acted as their correspondents and London agents, and an arrangement for amalgamation approved by the shareholders of both banks was carried into practical effect on 19th August 1907.

The agreement between the two banks provided for an undertaking by the Bank of Scotland to meet the whole liabilities of the Caledonian Bank, on the latter making over its whole assets of every description, including the right of note-issue and business good-will. The shareholders of the Caledonian Bank were treated with considerable magnanimity, receiving £1 : 5s. of Bank of Scotland stock for each share of £2 : 10s. or an optional cash payment of £5. The directors of the smaller bank were continued as an Advisory Board for a period not exceeding ten years—demitting office on 29th June 1917—and the general staff joined the service of the Bank of Scotland on existing emoluments. The Bank of Scotland undertook the payment of all expenses connected with the amalgamation and winding up of the Caledonian Bank.

The immediate amalgamation benefits were, of course, practically all on the side of the smaller concern. The Caledonian Bank shares, which at the time of the amalgamation were marketable at only £3, were now worth £5 for a cash transaction. To the Bank of Scotland there came additional capital to the extent of £75,000, and an extension of the authorised note-issue amounting to the sum of £53,434, while it gained in deposits over a million and a quarter sterling. The thirty-four branch offices added to the senior bank gave it a distinct lead among Scottish banking institutions. It is interesting to note that in only four of the Caledonian Bank districts had the Bank of Scotland already been a competitor. In amalgamating with its younger colleague the Bank of Scotland of course saddled itself with many small offices, from whose future development little or nothing could be expected, and the supervision of which from Edinburgh would naturally be much more expensive than from Inverness ; but in any case the amalgamation extended the field of the Bank of Scotland from the Tweed to Ultima Thule, and its action saved a situation already assuming a species of gravity in the north which later developments would probably have rendered critical.

Within a year of the amalgamation which we have just noticed, another important banking union was consummated in the north. This was the amalgamation of the Town and County Bank, Limited, with the North of Scotland Bank, Limited. The possibility of an amalgamation between the two banks had been long in view, and the death of Mr. Thomas Cochrane, the manager of the Town and County Bank, led to negotiations being opened.

The head offices of both banks were in Aberdeen, and both had an extensive sphere of operations radiating from the old city of *Bon Accord*. The two banks had each a branch in the same town at thirty-one places (exclusive of the city of Aberdeen). It was felt that the fusion would consolidate and extend the valuable connection in districts where both had hitherto operated, and that the united bank would be in a stronger and more favourable position to open up connections in other parts of the country, a policy which for some years previous had, in the case of the North of Scotland Bank, been attended with considerable success.

Under the Contract of Co-Partnery of the North of Scotland Bank there was no power to amalgamate with any other bank, and accordingly the agreement provided that in order to give effect to the amalgamation the bank would *inter alia* take steps for having alterations made on the Co-Partnery Contract, a resolution being passed and confirmed by the shareholders, those of the Town and County Bank also approving of the Provisional Agreement. These preliminaries being mutually adjusted, the Court granted sanction to the alteration under the *Companies* (Memorandum of Association) Act 1890. The Town and County Bank, as in the case of the Caledonian Bank on its amalgamation with the Bank of Scotland, then went into voluntary liquidation, and appropriate steps were taken to carry out the agreement with all possible speed.

Although the amalgamation was carried through by

the North of Scotland Bank, the shareholders of both banks assumed an equal footing. Those of the Town and County Bank received one and three-fourths ordinary shares of £20 per share (£4 per share paid) of the united bank for each share of the Town and County Bank, Limited, such shares of the united bank ranking equally with the shares held by the shareholders of the North of Scotland Bank, Limited, and carrying dividend from 31st January 1908, fractional parts being paid in cash at the rate of £16 : 17 : 6 per share, with interest at 5 per cent from 31st January 1908. Alternatively at the option of the shareholder a cash payment was made of £16 : 17 : 6, with interest from the same date. The Town and County Bank shareholders also received a sum in lieu of dividend for the period to 31st January 1908 of 8s. 9d. per share free of income tax.

The Directorates of both banks were combined for a period of two years from the date of the amalgamation, the chairman and deputy chairman being elected from the Board of the North of Scotland Bank. Mr. James Hutcheon, the General Manager of the North of Scotland Bank, was appointed General Manager of the combined undertaking, and the officials and general staff of the Town and County Bank were taken over by the united bank at existing salaries and remuneration.

The policy of the North of Scotland Bank had in later years been to develop its sphere of operations southwards, and the amalgamated bank has steadily persisted in the same course. Under the somewhat cumbersome title of The North of Scotland and Town and County Bank, Limited, it has now large offices in both Edinburgh and Glasgow, and its agencies are found in Fife, Stirling, Perth, Ayr, Dumfries, and Lanark. So far the bank has no London office. Meantime the North Bank is the only one of the Scottish institutions without an office in the city.

The serious depreciation in securities, to which we have

already made reference, led several of the Scottish banks to extend their powers of investment about this time. In 1907 the British Linen Bank obtained a supplementary Charter which among other provisions enabled it to drop the word " Company " from its title, and to alter the close of its financial year from 15th April to 15th January.

In a former chapter we reviewed the rise and progress of the Institute of Bankers in Scotland, now in the pre-war years of our narrative numerically and financially prosperous beyond the highest hopes of its founders in 1875. The year 1908 witnessed an important extension of its activities in the resolution to inaugurate a Magazine in the April of the succeeding year. Hitherto the Scottish Institute had felt that they were somewhat behind their contemporaries in this direction, all or most of whom had already formed a sort of national adhesion through the medium of a Journal devoted to banking interests. During the presidency of the late Mr. Alexander Bogie the project of an Institute Magazine was again revived and cordially approved by the Council. The Journal which now appears each successive quarter has amply justified its existence by the high standard of its articles and the educational facilities which it affords to younger members of the profession, while through its medium country bankers are kept in close touch with important developments occurring from time to time.

Another important adjunct to the educational facilities of Scottish banking was created at this time through the generous gift of £5000 made to the University of Edinburgh by Mr. Charles Bruce for the purpose of endowing a Lectureship in banking to be associated with his name. Mr. Bruce, who was himself educated at the University which he now sought to benefit, was for over forty years Agent at the important New Town Office of the Bank of Scotland, and in the evening of his days made known his intention of making possible an academic consideration of the principles and practice of the profession with which he had himself been so long connected. After some time spent in adjusting the preliminaries, the lectureship was inaugurated in October 1910, and shortly thereafter the founder was honoured by receiving the LL.D. degree in recognition of his services in the interests of Scottish banking. The proposed Degree in Commerce, a prominent feature in the younger universities and now formally approved by the Edinburgh University Court, will give the banking lectureship a new and enhanced importance.

The year 1910, at which we have now arrived, witnessed two important Centenaries. The first of these was that of Savings Banks, and the second the hundredth anniversary of the Commercial Bank of Scotland, Limited. The Savings Bank Centenary was made the occasion of extensive celebrations in Edinburgh, when delegates from all parts of the world assembled to mark the occasion and worship under the sturdy oak which had sprung from the acorn planted by Duncan of Ruthwell a century before. We have already traced the origin and growth of Savings Banks in a former chapter. The International Thrift Conference, held in Edinburgh under the presidency of Sir Albert. K. Rollit on 10th June 1910, was one of the most important gatherings of its kind ever held in the Scottish capital. At this time it was calculated that the Trustee Savings Banks of the United Kingdom held deposits to the extent of £54,000,000, while the Post Office Savings Banks, an extension of the older Trustee system, dating from 1861, held no less a sum than £184,000,000 at the credit of their clients. Dominie Sampson would have cried " Prodigious " in 1910, and still " Prodigious " a few years later, but a shrill whistle could alone have greeted the ear in a survey of the millions which lie scattered throughout the pages which form our next chapter.

CHAPTER XXX

ARMAGEDDON

OUR new chapter is by no means an easy one to write, for it deserves rather a new volume than an incidental page by way of continuance to our present narrative, and just as Napoleon failed to realise the vastness of the Pyramids until he saw the tiny tents of his soldiers pitched at their base, so in like manner the cataclysms of the past seem but petty whirlings in the stream of time when contrasted with the earthquakes and tornadoes which have convulsed the world since the fateful July of 1914.

It is unnecessary for our present purpose to enter upon the political events which led up to the inferno now raging in Europe. The story is already too familiar. For a number of years there had existed in well-informed quarters a feeling of apprehension and mistrust, a premonition which amounted latterly to almost a certainty, that all was not right among the nations; armaments were being piled up to a suspicious extent, and sinister rumours wafted across the North Sea. In home politics, Irish affairs were assuming a condition of menace, and civil war was regarded as by no means improbable. The strained relations on the Continent between Austria and Serbia had already combined to stiffen money rates in the weeks which immediately preceded the Great War. On 30th July 1914 the Bank of England rate again rose, and by Saturday, 1st August, it had reached 10 per cent.

War had now been declared between Great Britain and
Germany, and by Royal Proclamation the Bank Holiday
was extended until the following Thursday inclusive.
A Moratorium was proclaimed under which the obligation
by the banks to pay their depositors was temporarily
suspended, and the notes of the Scottish banks were
declared legal tender throughout the branches in Scotland.
In anticipation of the re-opening of the banks the following poster appeared at all the offices :

NOTICE

1. Customers of the Bank are reminded that only small sums
of cash are actually required for ordinary purposes. Cheques
should therefore be used for making payments to the utmost
extent possible.

2. This is a

GREAT NATIONAL EMERGENCY.

The Banks are not in any way responsible for the financial
situation which has arisen, but they have made arrangements
which will be amply sufficient for meeting all reasonable needs.

3. Depositors are assured that their interests are absolutely
protected. Under the Moratorium the obligation of the Banks
to pay Deposits ceases for the time, but they are anxious that
their customers should be put in a position to meet all payments
for necessary requirements.

4. The notes of the Scotch Banks are now legal tender throughout their branches in Scotland, the wish of the Government as
expressed by the Chancellor of the Exchequer being that gold
should not be parted with merely to be hoarded. Patriotism,
therefore, demands that all should join in strengthening the
hands of the Banks at this time of national trial.

Friday, 7th August, was awaited with no small
anxiety. The crisis was acute. All through the week
the leading newspapers had been instant in season
schooling the public as to the calm and reasonable
attitude which a national patriotism demanded. The
banks re-opened at the customary hour, and it speaks
well for the good sense of the public that demands
were limited to strict requirements. Although the effect
of the Moratorium was practically a freezing up of the
assets on the creditor side of every balance-sheet, the

banks were in every instance more than able to meet all
demands, and advances for all legitimate trade purposes
were cheerfully granted. Repayment of bills and loans
was of course temporarily suspended.

At the close of a busy day many banks were able to
report lodgments largely in excess of withdrawals, and
cases were not infrequent where gold was patriotically
exchanged for notes. Heavy clearings were expeditiously
handled at the exchanges, and by Saturday evening
the normal conditions of the Monday were anticipated.
It was a triumph for the one-pound note. Never before
in Scottish history had its utility been so markedly
vindicated as in the opening days of the Great War.
The circulation of the banks for the four weeks ending
15th August 1914 showed as follows :

Bank.	Authorised Circulation.	Actual Circulation.
	£	£
Bank of Scotland	396,852	1,376,325
Royal	216,451	1,111,587
British Linen	438,024	893,580
Commercial	374,880	1,091,377
National	297,024	918,716
Union	454,346	1,042,983
Clydesdale	274,321	858,108
North of Scotland and Town and County	224,452	833,562
	2,676,350	8,126,238

Three months passed. By 7th November 1914, the
circulation, steadily on the increase, had reached a total
of £9,449,000. Under the Currency and Bank Notes
Act 1914, Treasury Notes of £1 and 10s. denominations
had already been issued by the Government, and these
were placed at the disposal of the Joint-Stock Banks
throughout the kingdom to the extent of 20 per cent of
their deposits, a charge being made for the accommodation
thus provided at the rate of 5 per cent per annum. Under
a subsequent Treasury Minute it was also provided that
a certificate as to a holding of Treasury notes earmarked

as against excess circulation would be deemed equivalent to coin held at the Head Office or principal place of issue. Postal orders were also declared legal tender, but this sub-section was revoked by Royal Proclamation on 3rd February 1915. The Bank of England also undertook on behalf of the Government to discount bills accepted by the accepting houses and bills accepted by foreign banks domiciled in London, which could not be met owing to the exigencies of war.

The conflict of the nations had now assumed a magnitude which presaged a conflict of some years' duration, and in the closing days of November 1914, the Chancellor of the Exchequer budgeted the first War Loan. The gold at the Bank of England had increased from 26 millions in August to 85½ millions in November. A loan of £350,000,000 at 3½ per cent was offered at 95, and in a few days was over applied for. Hitherto this was the largest loan in history. The banks of the United Kingdom made themselves responsible for something like £100,000,000. It speaks volumes for the stability of the banks that they were able to respond to such an extent, for not only were the Stock Exchanges still closed, but private dealings in high-class securities were only possible for " cash," and at fixed minimum prices.

Mr. Lloyd George was then Chancellor of the Exchequer, and he took occasion, when introducing his first War Loan, to review the part played by the Government in hypothecating public credit and the State credit with regard to pre-moratorium bills. By this time the total discounted on Government guarantee amounted to £120,000,000, and the unimpeachable character of the British bill of exchange was fully maintained. Mr. Lloyd George's speech on this occasion will go down in history as one of the great rhetorical efforts connected with the crisis, doubly interesting to a historian of Scottish banking : " The Scottish banks showed great courage right through. . . . Confidence has been completely restored, and at present we do not hear of any complaints from traders from any part of the United Kingdom."

The second War Loan, a 4½ per cent loan at par, was announced by prospectus dated 21st June 1915. No limit was fixed on this occasion, but the conversion options which it provided for as regards Consols and Annuity Stock augured well for a new financial record. The extraordinary sum of £600,000,000 was on this occasion raised by 10th July. Towards these two loans the banks of the United Kingdom had subscribed close on £300,000,000.

We have now arrived at a stage when we may profitably review the position of Scottish banking after a year of conflict. From balance-sheets published during 1915, deposits show an increase of £10,000,000, and note circulation an advance of £2,561,000 on the previous year, while cash and securities, including War Loan holdings, had increased since 1914 by £21,000,000. Net profits among the eight Scottish banks showed an increase as compared with the previous year of £45,951.

So far as banking is concerned, the most serious effect consequent upon the war has been the heavy provision which has been necessitated through depreciation of securities. In 1915 the sum of £1,285,000 appears in the balance-sheets under this head, and a further sum of £1,265,342 is similarly apportioned in the twelve months succeeding.

The year 1916 closed under practically the same conditions as its predecessor, and perhaps figures may at this time be more eloquent than words in placing on record some details as to banking progress. Balance-sheets published during its course give the following chronicle :

Deposits	£152,822,000
Note Circulation	13,977,000
Banking Advances	78,954,000
Cash and Securities	107,768,000
Reserves	6,753,000

At the June 1916 meeting of the Institute of Bankers in Scotland, the President, Mr. Adam Tait, in the course of his address, said that he calculated that Scottish banking had already contributed something like £60,000,000 sterling to the finances of the war.

The *Statist* of 6th January 1917 estimated the total amount of British debt as at 30th December 1916 at approximately £3,461,852,000, but still more money was demanded for the prosecution of the war. On 12th January 1917 the prospectus of the third War Loan was issued. This was a 5 per cent loan at 95, subject to income tax and redeemable by the Government at par 1929–1947, or optionally a 4 per cent loan at 100 per cent free from all tax and redeemable 1929–1942, also at par. It was felt that this " victory " loan, as it was called, must exceed in volume all its predecessors, and 16th February was announced as the date on which the subscription lists would be closed. In common with other banking institutions throughout the country the Scottish banks were urged by the Chancellor of the Exchequer not only to make their offices available for receiving subscriptions, but also to urge their managers and agents to bring the claims of the nation prominently before their customers. A general circular was accordingly issued on 13th January 1917. As this circular will rank as a historic document in the annals of Scottish Banking, we reprint it. It is as follows :

GENERAL CIRCULAR.

EDINBURGH, 13*th January*, 1917.

To THE AGENT OF

SIR,

NEW WAR LOAN

In common with banking institutions throughout the country, the Scottish Banks have been requested by the Chancellor of the Exchequer not only to make their offices available for receiving subscriptions for the New War Loan, but to urge their Managers and Agents to bring the Loan prominently before their customers. It is of the utmost national importance that the Loan should be well taken up and that every reasonable means should be adopted by you to that end. We have therefore to request that you will immediately proceed to use every effort, by personal communication with customers and others whom you may be in a position to influence, to get subscriptions to the Loan to as large an extent as possible.

Banks, generally, will be prepared to lend reasonable amounts to approved customers for the purpose of assisting them to take up the New War Loan. We shall be prepared to give favourable consideration to proposals of this nature—the sums being fairly within the ability of borrowers to repay over a not-too-protracted period. Whether or not a small margin in security should be required will be a matter for discretion in each case.

Accommodation allowed for this special purpose should appear as a separate overdrawn account, the operations on which would be confined thereafter to debits in respect of instalment payments, and credits in reduction of the indebtedness.

For the present, the rate of interest to be charged will be one per cent under the Bank of England Discount Rate, fluctuating, with a minimum of 5 per cent,—this rate to apply whether the security offered be the 4 per cent or the 5 per cent Loan. In this connection, between the Bank and the borrower, it will be understood that the advance is payable on demand.

In order that the Bank may derive the benefit of the Special Commission allowed on War Loan applications made through their agencies, care should be taken that each application form —excepting those with the stamp of Stockbrokers and Financial Houses—bears on its face the Bank's stamp with the name of the Branch. A memorandum should be made at each office of the amounts applied for—the names of the respective applicants being also preserved for purposes of reference. Applications made on forms cut from press advertisements of the Loan should be pasted on blank application forms, which should bear the Bank's stamp.

Applications must be forwarded to our London office as and when received, and all sums tendered in connection with the New War Loan will be transferred to London *free of charge*.

It is understood that the Authorities have caused a supply of prospectuses to be sent direct to each banking office in the country. When these are received, the application forms should be stamped distinctly with the Bank's stamp bearing the name of the Branch.

The phenomenal success of the 1917 War Loan is well

known. It exceeded the most sanguine anticipations of its promoters, and over £1,000,000,000 was subscribed. The result was all the more remarkable in view of the fact that the banks themselves, by arrangement, made no direct contribution. In reviewing the various figures we find that again Scotland acquitted itself with a characteristic credit. The applications actually made through the Scottish banks amounted to £105,000,000, and it is probably safe to estimate that at least £10,000,000 more was sent by their clients direct to the Bank of England, a total of £115,000,000, which, viewed in relation to gross deposits of, roughly speaking, £160,000,000, shows how Scottish patriotism still burned with its old unquenchable flame.

The business of the historian is to chronicle the past. To assume the prophetic mantle is not his rôle, and it is too soon to speak with anything like a certainty of after-the-war conditions. In the fourth year of worldwide strife Scottish banking still maintains its honoured place secure on the foundations upon which our fathers built it, and with a good hope for days yet to dawn. By the time these sheets issue from the press, nearly 3000 young men drawn from Scottish banking staffs will have joined the forces of the Crown, and of these many have already made the supreme sacrifice on the field of battle. The lady clerk, for the first time in our history, is conspicuous in all the various institutions. Doubtless many strenuous days still lie before us, but these will fall to be dealt with by the historian of a future time.

CHAPTER XXXI

CONCLUSION

THE present sketch of banking in Scotland may be fitly concluded with a short consideration of some of the leading features of the system which has made Scottish banking conspicuous among the banking systems of the world. Perhaps the chief of these is its suitability to the circumstances of the country and the genius of the nation. This may almost seem a truism, in as far as the system was of almost entirely natural growth. But this is in itself a circumstance quite unusual in other countries. Elsewhere the State has been the motive power in calling banking into existence, has moulded its character, and has regulated its action all along. In Scotland the State took little interest in the matter beyond sanctioning the formation of a few of the earliest establishments. The consequence was a naturally-evolved system, moulded by the requirements of the people.

The nation was extremely poor, with a debased and insufficient currency. Even the small amount of capital at first put into the banking business was a great boon to the people, but it was the note-issues, founded on the credit of the banks, that actually gave the impulse to trade. The small amount of actual capital available would, by itself, have given only temporary assistance ; but, by means of the note-issues, the banks were enabled to extend their advances in proportion to the wants of the people. This, it may be thought, would lead to excess of issues ; but it does not appear that such a condition was ever experienced in Scotland. It is doubtful, indeed, if it be actually possible, where notes are not legal tender and are payable on demand. The banks had no desire and little temptation to grant advances which they did not believe to be good, as there was a great field of legitimate requirements before them. The notes so issued would at first not come back to the banks, except as worn, for there was a great vacuum of currency to be filled. Thus the profitableness and safety of early banking in Scotland are fully accounted for. The note-issues fulfilled the functions of capital, the absence of which was crippling the nation, and did so in a cheap and convenient form.

As the nation advanced in wealth, the note-issues began to lose somewhat of their indispensable character. A wealthy country can afford to indulge in a metallic currency. But, even when they might have discarded the notes, the Scottish people continued to use them as much as ever. And it was well that they did so ; for, as the original function of the notes was losing somewhat of its force, a new necessity for the issues was arising. The banks were extending their branches more and more into the rural districts—an operation which could only be performed through the aid of the note-issues ; for it is only in comparatively wealthy centres that a bank office can be successfully conducted on a metallic basis. From a public point of view this is at present the great argument in favour of the retention by the banks of their right of issue ; and it is a very powerful one. The cost to Scotland of the abolition of these issues would be a more expensive currency, lessened banking facilities, and probably, heavier banking charges. If the note-issues had proved defective, this would not, perhaps, be too heavy a price to pay for security ; but it seems too much to pay for the destruction of an institution which has been a vital instrument in producing the prosperity of the nation, which has never been productive of harm, which has always been thoroughly efficient, and which at the present time is a convenience to millions of people.

The utility and power of the Scottish one-pound note was never more clearly demonstrated than in the early days of the great war crisis. Since 1826 the lowest denomination of bank note available in England has been £5, and it was with the greatest difficulty that the Bank-holiday maker could get change for his immediate requirements. It is a known fact that in London restaurants people could hardly procure their requirements because change was not obtainable for a £5 note. On the Friday before Bank Holiday long queues of note-holders waited at the bank to have their notes changed. In Scotland there was all the necessary machinery to tide over the immediate demand. In England it took several days to make the same provision for the convenience of the general public, and in hot haste a stock of paper destined for the manufacture of postage-stamps had to be commandeered for an emergency currency of £1 and 10s. to be ready for the opening of the banks on the Friday. The fact that in Scotland the £1 Treasury note has not entered seriously into competition with the bank-note currency shows conclusively that our note-issue is beneficial and popular alike in peace and war.

The cash credit system is another important feature of Scottish banking, but it is secondary to the note-issues. Cash credit bonds extended the range of good advances, but advances of any kind would have been impossible, except to a small extent, without the note-issues. But, as a part of the system, the cash credit was not only ingenious, but was a potent factor in the commercial progress of the nation. It secured the debt on which the notes were issued, and it enabled clever and industrious men, who had no capital of their own, to supply the requirements of the public, and to lay the foundations of individual and national wealth.   In our modern day the

old cash credit bond has been largely superseded by the
personal letter of guarantee, and by other forms of security,
notable among which may be reckoned the life policy
and the share certificate, but the general principles
governing the relationship of borrower and lender still
remain the same, while the £1 note maintains the even
tenour of its way.

The deposit business was of slower growth than the
departments we have referred to, for the simple reason
that poor people have no money to deposit. But the
Scotch have always been a saving people, and, when once
they began to have a little more cash than was necessary
for current requirements, they naturally availed themselves of the opportunity afforded by the banks of making
it profitable to themselves and useful to others. As the
banks have always given liberal facilities in this department, the spirit of saving was much encouraged, to the
general benefit. At the present moment the deposits of
the Scottish banks stand at record figures. The nation
is wealthier to-day than at any previous era of its history,
as is amply evidenced by the various balance-sheets of
the banks.[1] No doubt the steady rate ruling for a considerable time for deposit money is largely responsible
for the increase being maintained, and the factor has also
to be taken into account that money at call is generally
favoured at a time when national events and future issues
are problematical.

The widespread character of Scottish banking has been
a great source of stability to it. In other countries the
general practice is that banks confine themselves to
particular localities, or even to particular departments of
commerce. Under such a system risks are not sufficiently
spread, and a bank stands or falls according to the fortunes
of a small *clientèle*. In Scotland, also, this system was
general for long, and it is only in comparatively recent
times that it has entirely disappeared. But with the

[1] See Appendix B.

gradual consolidation, which is so marked a feature of its history, Scottish banking sought more and more a national basis. This it has now attained to, for there are no banks confining their operations within very limited areas. The only remaining provincial bank may be deemed a partial exception, but even they are fairly wide-spread. The banks have thus a strength and solidity such as is not general in other countries. In the United States, for instance, so-called national banks are to be found in every town, but their nationality consists in nothing more than the securing of their note-issues by a deposit of Government bonds. Every month a long list of new banks appears, and along with it a similar list of failures. These banks seem to be mere associations of small capitalists establishing themselves as single offices— a system of essential instability. Even in England until recently the number of small local banks was great, although they are now much lessened by the numerous amalgamations which have taken place during late years.

But if Scottish banking has now secured what, as regards its principles, may be considered an ideal condition, it has not done so without suffering in many severe struggles. The legislature wisely left it to itself— or rather the indifference of the Government allowed it to fight for its own existence ; but, if it suffered nothing from the attentions of the State, it had, on the other hand, to devise its own principles and form its own practice— operations of great difficulty and danger. It had to meet crises without proper knowledge of how they should be met, beyond that supplied by mother-wit. In consequence, there are many stumbles and many falls. But a sound bank, in the early days, was hardly any the worse for stopping payment. At one time, as we have seen, all the banks stopped payment, the only result being a temporary excitement on the part of the commonalty, arising from the inconvenience of not getting change for

£1 notes.　During another crisis, almost all the Edinburgh private banks were swept away ; but those who remained gained in credit and in experience.　These were the blows that moulded the system, and it is surprising that the total loss sustained by creditors from the failure of banks in Scotland is quite insignificant.

But, it may be said, the Scottish banks have, within the period of what may fairly be considered the matured system, supplied two instances of gross failure, the later of which is probably the most disgraceful which any thoroughly consolidated country has experienced.　It must be admitted that this is so, and that the three great banking disasters of Scotland—the Ayr Bank, the Western Bank, and the City of Glasgow Bank—show an appalling increase in ratio of calamity.　And it is not sufficient answer to say that these events were the result of departure from the general system.　They certainly were so—nay, it was the ignoring of the principles and practice which experience had established as the general rule that produced the ruin of these banks.　But they cannot be excluded from the general estimate of Scottish banking. Indeed, it may be said that in no other country than Scotland could such a case as that of the City of Glasgow Bank have happened.　The excellence of the banking system had commended itself to the Scottish public in a manner not elsewhere experienced in regard to private companies, and it was this blind trust that rendered the disaster possible.　The only answer to the accusation is, that men fail in their strongest point.

The lessons to be derived from these experiences are, however, of more moment than accounting for them. These have been preached, rightly and wrongly, to such an extent, and acted on so wholesomely, that it only requires vigilant interest on the part of proprietors, depositors, and the public, to avert such events in the future.　And in regard to such vigilance, nothing is of more importance than insisting on the continued observance of the principles and practice which have proved so successful, and resisting new departures such as, under the specious assertion of a necessity for extended facilities, have three times brought grievous disaster on the nation.

APPENDICES

APPENDIX A

EARLIEST SCOTTISH BANK NOTES

BANK OF SCOTLAND,
EDINBURGH, 13*th May* 1902.

ANDREW W. KERR, Esq.,
    Royal Bank of Scotland,
        Hope Street.

DEAR MR. KERR—I have only now been able to look into the interesting questions—as to the dates, etc., of the earliest bank notes in Scotland—raised in your letter of 9th ultimo.

In the first place, I would like to mention that, in the course of my examination of the records of the Bank, I have quite failed to find any confirmation of the particular statement made by the writer of the *Historical Account of the Bank of Scotland*, to which you refer, viz. that there was an issue of 20s. notes in 1699.

The facts about the issue of 20s. notes appear to be these :— Early in 1699 an overture to print 20s. notes was brought before the Directors of the Bank, and after some discussion it was referred to a General Meeting of the Adventurers (Proprietors), which was held on 24th March 1699. At this meeting the matter was put to the vote, but, the negatives preponderating, it was set aside. Next year (1700) a Committee of Directors met to consider certain proposals made by the founder of the Bank (John Holland, the London Merchant), " concerning the supplying the want of notes for sums below £5." Mr. Holland suggested two ways, viz. (1) by using brass coins, and (2) by using tallies of timber. After careful deliberation the Committee, while unanimously agreed as to the advantages which would accrue from an issue of small notes, set aside Mr. Holland's proposals on the ground that they were " inconsistent with the laws of the Kingdom, and very impracticable both to the Bank and the Nation."

The question of the issue of £1 notes does not appear to have come up again until the year 1704, when a " new overture for making twenty-shilling notes " was brought before the Bank. The matter was discussed at several meetings of the Directors, and finally referred to a General Meeting of the Adventurers, which was held on 10th March 1704. At this meeting a resolution was passed that " twenty-shilling sterling notes " should be made and " be ready to go abroad as soon as possible " ; and the necessary steps were accordingly taken to have this done. In a succeeding minute these twenty-shilling notes are referred to as " twelve-pound Scots notes." The first entry, therefore, in the Bank's ledger for £1 notes appears on *7th April* 1704. They are entered in the books as £1 *sterling*.

With regard to *Large Notes*, these were issued from the time the Bank commenced business in 1696, and were of the values of £100, £50, £20, £10, and £5 sterling. In a minute, dated 26th February 1700, there is an instruction that " the Treasurer and Accomptant at signing the notes subjoin to their ordinary subscription the sum of the Bill in *Scots Money*."

The fact of the notes being at that early date printed in London (under the supervision of the English trustees of the Bank resident there) may throw some light on the circumstance of so large denominations being issued in sterling.

I trust I have answered the various queries contained in your letter, but, should any point have been overlooked, I will be very pleased to endeavour to supply the omission on hearing from you.—Yours very truly,

(Signed)   J. S. BARBOUR.

APPENDIX C

AMALGAMATIONS AMONG THE SCOTTISH BANKS

I.—AMALGAMATIONS WITH THE EXISTING BANKS

1. BANK OF SCOTLAND.
    Central Bank of Scotland.
    Caledonian Banking Company.
2. ROYAL BANK OF SCOTLAND.
    Dundee Banking Company.
        Dundee New Bank.
            Dundee Commercial Banking Company (No. 1).
            (Business only taken over.)
3. BRITISH LINEN BANK.
    Paisley Banking Company (Business taken over).
4. COMMERCIAL BANK OF SCOTLAND.
    Caithness Banking Company (Business only taken over).
    Arbroath Banking Company.
5. NATIONAL BANK OF SCOTLAND.
    Commercial Banking Company of Aberdeen.
    Perth Union Bank.
6. UNION BANK OF SCOTLAND.
    Glasgow Union Banking Company.
        Thistle Bank Company.
        Sir Wm. Forbes, J. Hunter & Co.
        Paisley Union Bank Company.
    Hunters & Co., Ayr.
        Kilmarnock Banking Company.
    Glasgow and Ship Bank.
        Glasgow Bank Company.
        Ship Bank.
    Banking Company in Aberdeen.
    Perth Banking Company.
        Perth United Company.

7. NORTH OF SCOTLAND AND TOWN AND COUNTY BANK.
  Town and County Bank.
  North of Scotland Bank.
8. CLYDESDALE BANK.
  Greenock Union Bank.
  Edinburgh and Glasgow Bank.
   Edinburgh and Leith Bank.
    Southern Bank of Scotland.
   Glasgow Joint Stock Bank.
  Eastern Bank of Scotland.
   Dundee Commercial Bank (No. 2).

II.—AMALGAMATIONS WITH BANKS WHICH HAVE FAILED

1. DOUGLAS, HERON & CO., or AYR BANK.
  John Macadam & Co., Ayr.
  Alexander Johnston, Hugh Lawson & Co., Dumfries.
2. KINNEARS, SMITH & CO.
  Thomas Kinnear & Sons.
  Donald Smith & Co.
3. WESTERN BANK OF SCOTLAND.
  Greenock Banking Company.
  Dundee Union Bank.
   Montrose Bank.
  Paisley Commercial Bank.
  Ayrshire Banking Company.
  Glasgow Banking Company (No. 2).
4. CITY OF GLASGOW BANK.
  Bank of Mona.

APPENDIX D

NOTE-ISSUES OF THE SCOTTISH BANKS

BANKS ISSUING UNDER ACT OF 1845.	AUTHORISED ISSUES.		AVERAGE ISSUES.				
	1845.	1917.	1863–4.	1882–3.	1900–1.	1916.	Four Weeks to 11th Aug. 1917.
	£	£	£	£	£	£	£
Bank of Scotland	300,485	396,852	472,148	868,190	1,185,885	2,320,581	2,743,586
Royal	183,000	216,451	502,974	798,229	1,052,386	1,956,930	2,406,791
British Linen	438,024	438,024	491,703	656,305	929,251	1,686,980	2,032,105
Dundee	33,451	...	46,259	...	...	...	...
Perth	38,656	...	...	...	...	...	...
Aberdeen	88,467	...	...	...	...	...	...
Commercial	374,880	374,880	537,840	793,413	1,031,158	1,935,425	2,288,675
National	297,024	297,024	454,375	659,768	889,672	1,691,761	2,102,872
Town and County	70,133	...	135,446	212,443	337,296	...	...
Union	327,223	454,346	592,519	809,511	1,061,547	1,673,364	1,955,767
Ayrshire	53,656	...	...	...	...	...	...
Western	284,282	...	...	...	...	...	...
Central	42,933	...	59,450	...	...	...	...
North of Scotland	154,319	224,452	205,373	383,363	476,549	1,342,673	1,506,063
Clydesdale	104,028	274,321	368,850	573,171	834,229	1,520,263	1,793,359
Caledonian	53,434	...	72,169	100,172	139,119	...	...
Eastern	33,636	...	...	...	...	...	...
City of Glasgow	72,921	...	357,581	...	...	...	...
Edinburgh and Glasgow	136,657	...	...	...	...	...	...
Totals	3,087,209	2,676,350	4,296,687	5,854,565	7,937,092	14,127,977	16,829,218

APPENDIX E

NOTE FORGERIES NOT MENTIONED IN THE TEXT

Discovered.	Bank.	Denomination.			Date of Note.	Remarks.
1767	Thistle . . .	£1	0	0	..	Man hanged at Edinburgh.
1780	Bank of Scotland	1	1	0	..	Manchester merchant hanged in Edinburgh.
1783	Do.	1	1	0	Feb. 2, 1774	..
1787	Dundee . . .	1	0	0	Aug. 1, 1777	Man and woman arrested at Edinburgh.
1788	Bank of Scotland	1	1	0	Mar. 1, 1780	Very imperfect.
,,	Glasgow Merchant	1	0	0	Feb. 2, 1782	" Coarsely wrote."
1789	Bank of Scotland	1	1	0	..	Man transported for fourteen years, Dumfries.
1790	Paisley . . .	1	1	0	Oct. 3, 1785	Man hanged at Glasgow.
1797	Do. . . .	1	1	0	..	Man hanged at Edinburgh.
1800	Royal . . .		..		..	Verdict, " Not proven."
,,	Ship . . .		..		..	Man hanged (several crimes).
1813	Galloway . .		..		..	Man transported for life.
1817	Thistle . . .		..		..	Man transported for seven years.
,,	Greenock . .	1	1	0	..	Man hanged at Glasgow.
1820	Paisley . . .	5	0	0	..	Man hanged at Stirling.
,,	Bank of Scotland	1	0	0?	..	..
1823	Royal . . .	1	0	0?	..	Death sentence respited at Ayr.
,,	Ship . . .	1	0	0?	..	Death sentence on three men at Dumfries.
1824	Dundee Union .	1	0	0	..	Discovered in Dundee.
1908	Clydesdale . .	5	0	0	July 11, 1906	Pen written.
,,	British Linen .	5	0	0	..	Pen written.

APPENDIX F

BANKS DEFUNCT WHOSE NOTES ARE STILL RETIRED

Issuing Banks.	Retiring Banks, etc.
Aberdeen	Union.
Arbroath	Commercial.
Ayrshire	National.
Caledonian	Bank of Scotland.
Central	Do.
City of Glasgow	Assets Company, Ltd., Edinburgh.
Dundee	Royal.
Dundee Commercial	National.
Dundee Union	Do.
Eastern	Clydesdale.
Edinburgh and Glasgow	Do.
Edinburgh and Leith	Do.
Falkirk	British Linen.
Sir Wm. Forbes & Co.	Union.
Glasgow	Do.
Glasgow and Ship	Do.
Glasgow Joint Stock	Clydesdale.
Glasgow Union	Union.
Greenock	National.
Greenock Union	Clydesdale.
Hunters & Co., Ayr	Union.
Kilmarnock	Do.
Montrose	National.
Paisley	British Linen.
Paisley Commercial	National.
Paisley Union	Union.
Perth	Do.
Perth Union	National.
Perth United Company	Union.
Ship	Do.
Southern	Clydesdale.
Thistle, Glasgow	Union.
Town and County	North of Scotland and Town and County.
Western	National.

APPENDIX G

LEITH BANKING COMPANY

THERE is some dubiety as to the date of the close of the Leith Bank's career. Boase says it was sequestrated 7th May 1836, while all the other authorities state that it failed in 1842 (25th April, sequestrated 7th May). That the latter statement is correct may be considered proved by the contemporary record of Robert Allan in his stock-exchange circular of 2nd May 1842, that " The Renfrewshire and the Old Leith Banks—both private establishments—have suspended payment within the last month. They are expected ultimately to pay in full "—an anticipation that was not fulfilled. It is curious, however, that the Edinburgh Almanac ceases after 1836 to include the Leith Bank in its main list of Scottish banks, but includes it under the heading of Leith institutions (with three branches) until 1842, after which notice ceases. Perhaps the bank was in difficulties in the crisis 1836–7, but continued in a semi-active state until 1842. There cannot be any doubt, however, that in some shape or form it existed into 1842.

APPENDIX H

WESTERN BANK OF SCOTLAND

RETURNS TO OUTSTANDING SHAREHOLDERS

				Payable.
1st Return of	£25 per share of £50	.	1861 or 1862.
2nd	,,	10	,,	.	12th March 1862.
3rd	,,	5	,,	.	1st Oct. 1862.
4th	,,	5	,,	.	15th April 1863.
5th	,,	5	,,	.	18th Dec. 1863.
6th	,,	7 : 10s.	,,	.	1st Sept. 1865.
7th	,,	7 : 10s.	,,	.	2nd Sept. 1867.
8th	,,	3	,,	.	17th Sept. 1868.
9th	,,	4	,,	.	21st Aug. 1873.
10th	,,	0 : 15s.	,,	.	24th July 1877.

Total . . £72 : 15s. ,, = £145 : 10s. per cent.

APPENDIX I

BERTRAM, GARDNER & CO.

An interesting reminiscence of private banking in Edinburgh occurred after the foregoing pages were in the press. On October 29, 1917, a petition was presented to the Court asking authority to call a meeting of the creditors of Bertram, Gardner & Co., who failed in 1793 (see *ante*). The occasion was the discovery, by the representatives of a creditor, of a fund of £3750 accumulated from a dividend of £585 in a debtor's bankrupt estate. Lord Sands, in the Bill Chamber, gave warrant to hold the meeting. As the sum available would not, probably, provide a larger dividend than sixpence per pound, no considerable individual interest was involved in the transaction, but the incident is illustrative of the accumulative power of money placed at interest. Judging by the support given to the firm at the time of their failure, they seem to have enjoyed good credit in their circle. They did not issue notes themselves, but probably used those of the Royal Bank.

INDEX

THE END

Printed in Great Britain by R. & R. CLARK, LIMITED, *Edinburgh.*